**Cooperation Experiences
in Europe and Asia**

Cooperation Experiences in Europe and Asia

Edited by

Hoon Jaung and Yuichi Morii

Shinzansha Publisher, Tokyo

Shinzansha Publisher Co., Ltd.
6-2-9-102 Hongo, Bunkyo-ku Tokyo, Japan
Tel +81 (0)3-3818-1019   Fax +81 (0)3-3818-0344
henshu@shinzansha.co.jp
©2004, Hoon Jaung and Yuichi Morii et al.
printed in Japan ISBN4-7972-3330-3 C3331

All right reserved. No part of this publication may be reproduced, stored in a retrieval system, or transmitted, in any form or by any means, electronic, mechanical, photocopying, recording or otherwise, without the prior permission of Shinzansha Publisher Co., Ltd.

Whilst every effort has been made to ensure that the infomation contained in this book is correct neither the author nor Shinzansha International can accept any responsibility for any errors or omissions or for any consequences resulting therefrom.

Preface

The articles in this volume were originally presented at an international conference on "Learning from History: Comparing Cooperation Experiences in Europe and East Asia," held in Tokyo from November 8-10, 2003 sponsored by DESK (Deutschland- und Europastudien in Komaba / German and European Studies in Komaba) program of the University of Tokyo and the Japan Foundation. The conference was a part of multi-year joint research efforts among Japanese and Korean specialists on European politics. Yuichi Morii of the University of Tokyo and Hoon Jaung of Chung-Ang University initiated the collaborative research with the purpose of enhancing academic cooperation between Korean and Japanese students of European politics and the EU.

After a few mutual visits to Seoul and Tokyo, the two-nation team chose the theme of 'comparing regional cooperation in Europe and East Asia' as its first joint work. It was natural and timely that participants to this joint project were drawn to this topic given the coming age of East Asian regionalization. The researchers shared the notion that European experiences do not provide a model but offer lessons for East Asian regionalization. Thus, three specialists on East Asian regionalism from Hong Kong, Japan and Korea joined our study.

Then, revised papers from Tokyo conference were presented at the second major meeting in Fukuoka, held on December 19-20, 2003 at Kyushu University. The meeting, which was supported by the Research Center for Korean Studies at Kyushu University, Chung-Ang University and the Japan Foundation, brought together European specialists and Asian specialists. The one and half day meeting was filled with serious, enlightening and at times heated debate. For this meeting, Professor Young-Jak Kim of Kookmin University not just served as the moderator for a full day meeting tirelessly but also offered insightful comments on each paper.

Preface

The editors are grateful to all the contributors to this volume for their cheerful cooperation. We found that academic cooperation in East Asia will be as vibrant and crucial as in economic and other key spheres of regional cooperation. We also would like to acknowledge supports of several individuals and institutions for this joint effort: Mr. Osamu Honda of Japan Foundation Seoul Office, the DESK program at the University of Tokyo, the Research Center for Korean Studies at Kyushu University, and Chung-Ang University.

March 2004

Hoon Jaung, Seoul
Yuichi Morii, Tokyo

Summary Table of Contents

Preface

Authors

Introduction

Chapter *1*   Hoon JAUNG
Comparing Cooperation Experiences in Europe and East Asia: Challenges in Theory and Practice 3

Part I: Issues in the Development of the European Union

Chapter *2*   Kaoru KURUSU
Patterns of Regional Security Management: an Overview of Developments in Europe and East Asia 29

Chapter *3*   Ariyoshi OGAWA
Making Regionalism Legitimate?: European Integration and beyond 57

Part II: National Visions and Experiences of Cooperation in Europe and Asia

Chapter *4*   Jae-Seung LEE
France and Early European Integration: 1945-1957 83

Chapter 5   Yuichi MORII
Germany and European Integration: Consolidation of
the Political System and its Norms 111

Chapter 6   Won-Taek KANG
Britain and European Integration: Some Implications
for East Asian Countries 133

Chapter 7   Machiko HACHIYA
Overcoming History: Greece, Turkey, and the European
Union 155

Chapter 8   TING Wai
China: Visions for Regional Cooperation in East Asia 179

Chapter 9   Cheol-Hee PARK
The Development of Korea's Regional Strategy in
Northeast Asia 213

Chapter 10   Toshiya HOSHINO
Japan in an East Asian Community Building 241

Table of Contents

Preface

Authors

Introduction

Chapter *1*   Hoon JAUNG
    Comparing Cooperation Experiences in Europe and East
    Asia: Challenges in Theory and Practice 3

    1. Introduction (3)
    2. Revisiting European Theories of Regionalism: Functionalism, Intergovernmentalism, Realism, and Constructivism (6)
        2.1. Functionalist Paradigm (6)
        2.2. Intergovernmentalism (8)
        2.3 Realism (11)
        2.4 Constructivism (13)
    3. Analyze These!: Modes, Process, and Actors of Regionalism in East Asia and Europe (17)
    4. Conclusion: The Region's Future Lies in Its Past (22)

Part I: Issues in the Development of the European Union

Chapter *2*   Kaoru KURUSU
    Patterns of Regional Security Management: an Overview
    of Developments in Europe and East Asia 29

    1. Introduction (29)
    2. Regional Security Complex (30)
    3. Factors Conducive to Regional Security Governance (33)

      3.1 Power Structure: Structural-Realist Approach (33)
      3.2 (Non)Security Externalities: Rationalist-
          Neorealist Approaches (35)
      3.3 Identities and Norms: Constructivist Approach
          (37)
      3.4 Domestic Level Explanation (38)
  4. Typology of Regional Security Governance (39)
      4.1 Balance of Power/ Concert of Powers (39)
      4.2 Cooperative Security (40)
      4.3 Security Communities/ Integration (41)
  5. European and East Asian Experiences Revisited (45)
      5.1 Security Management in Europe (45)
      5.2 Security Management in East Asia (50)
  6. Conclusion (53)

Chapter *3*   Ariyoshi OGAWA
Making Regionalism Legitimate?: European Integration
and beyond... 57

  1. Introduction: The Debate over Post-National Legitimacy
     (57)
  2. Aspects of Constitutionalization of Europe (63)
  3. The Convention—A Deliberative Enterprise? (67)
  4. Beyond the European Context: NAFTA and APEC (71)
      4.1. NAFTA (71)
      4.2. APEC (73)
  5. Conclusion: Towards Theoretical Comparison of
     Regional Cooperation (75)

Part II: National Visions and Experiences of Cooperation in Europe and Asia

Chapter *4*   Jae-Seung LEE
France and Early European Integration: 1945-1957 83

  1. Introduction (83)
  2. The Creation of ECSC (85)
      2.1. Postwar European Cooperation (85)

2.2. Plan Monnet and Plan Schuman (87)
　　　2.3. French Choice of ECSC (90)
　3. Failed Attempt: EDC and EPC (93)
　　　3.1. The Idea of EDC (93)
　　　3.2. The Idea of EPC (95)
　　　3.3. French Rejection of EDC and EPC (96)
　4. From Messina to the Treaty of Rome: EEC and Euratom (99)
　　　4.1. Reviving the European Agenda (99)
　　　4.2. Negotiating the Economic Integration (100)
　　　4.3. The French Choice of the Treaty of Rome (104)
　5. Conclusion (106)

Chapter 5　　　　　　　　　　　　　　　　　　Yuichi MORII
Germany and European Integration: Consolidation of
the Political System and its Norms 111

　1. Introduction (111)
　2. The Desire to Restore Sovereignty and Territorial Unity (114)
　　　2.1. The Allies and the Occupation Policies (115)
　　　2.2. The Establishment of the Federal Republic (115)
　3. The Schuman Plan as a Decisive Turning Point (118)
　　　3.1. Domestic Constraints (119)
　　　3.2. International Constraints (120)
　　　3.3. The Schuman Plan and the German Rearmament Issue (121)
　4. The Consolidation of the "West" European Integration Policy in Germany (123)
　5. Germany between France and the Atlantic (126)
　6. Conclusion (129)

Chapter 6　　　　　　　　　　　　　　　　　Won-Taek KANG
Britain and European Integration: Some Implications
for East Asian Countries 133

　1. Introduction (133)
　2. Britain and European Integration: An Awkward Partner (135)
　　　2.1. "Exit options" of Britain: the Commonwealth (135)

      2.2. Challenges to Britain's Framework of Institutions (138)
      2.3. Britain and the United States: The Atlantic versus the Continent (141)
  3. Implications for East Asia (144)
      3.1. Sovereignty and Nationalism (144)
      3.2. Relationship with the United States: Something Special? (147)
      3.3. Possibilities of an "Exit" Option (150)
  4. Conclusion (152)

Chapter 7   Machiko HACHIYA
Overcoming History: Greece, Turkey, and the European Union 155

  1. Introduction (155)
  2. A History Overcome (156)
      2.1. Franco-German Rapprochement (156)
      2.2. Enabling Settings (158)
      2.3. Summary (162)
  3. A History to be Overcome (163)
      3.1. Overview of the Relationship between Greece and Turkey (163)
      3.2. Post-war Era (166)
      3.3. Search for Rapprochement (170)
      3.4. Summary (173)
  4. Implication of the European Experience (174)

Chapter 8   TING Wai
China: Visions for Regional Cooperation in East Asia 179

  1. Introduction (179)
  2. From Bilateralism to Multilateralism: China's Learning Process in her Formulation of Foreign and Security Policy (181)
  3. On Multilateralism and International Regimes (185)
  4. China and ASEAN: Towards a New Model in Regional Cooperation? (188)
  5. China and ASEAN Regional Forum (ARF) (195)
  6. Asia-Pacific Economic Cooperation (APEC) and Open Regionalism (197)

7. Shanghai Cooperation Organization under the "Leadership" of Beijing (200)
8. On the Relationship between China, Japan, and South Korea within the Framework of Regional Cooperation (204)
9. Conclusion (207)

Chapter 9   Cheol-Hee PARK
The Development of Korea's Regional Strategy in Northeast Asia 213

1. Korea's Place in the World (213)
2. Period One: Virtual Absence of Regional Strategy—from 1945 to the mid-1960s— (216)
3. Period Two: Trilateral Alliance under the Cold War Setup —from the mid-1960s to the late 1980s— (219)
    3.1. The First Phase: The Park Chung Hee Era (219)
    3.2. The Second Phase: The Chun Doo Hwan Era (225)
4. Period Three: Reaching Out to the Socialist Countries —from the late 1980s to the late 1990s— (228)
5. Period Four: Korea's Initiative to Build Northeast Asian Community—from the late 1990s to the present— (232)
    5.1. Phase One: The Kim Dae Jung Era (232)
    5.2. Phase Two: The Roh Moo Hyun Era (235)
6. Conclusion (236)

Chapter 10   Toshiya HOSHINO
Japan in an East Asian Community Building........................... 241

1. Introduction (241)
2. Japan's Diplomatic Approaches to East Asia (243)
    2.1 Background of "Three Principles of Japanese Diplomacy" (243)
    2.2 Scope of Discontinuity in Japan's Diplomatic Priorities (245)
3. Japan's Diplomacy in East Asia (248)
    3.1 Five Periods of Japan's East Asian Diplomacy (249)
    3.2 Japan's Place in East Asia in the post-Cold War Context (252)
4. Converging Balance with Community in East Asia (255)
    4.1 With the U.S. or Without the U.S.? (255)

4.2 Koizumi Initiative—Pursuing Balance of Power within a Community (257)

5. Conclusion (259)

Authors

Machiko HACHIYA is lecturer at the Faculty of Law, Kyushu University in Fukuoka, Japan since 2000. After having worked at the Delegation of the European Commission in Japan from 1986 to 1993, she studied the international politics and the European politics at the University of Tokyo, then at Kyushu University. She wrote articles and book chapters on the principle of subsidiarity, and on comitology. Her current research is on the EU-Turkey relation.

Toshiya HOSHINO is professor at the School of International Public Policy, Osaka University (OSIPP), Japan and a research fellow at Stanford Japan Center-Research, Stanford University. He previously worked at the Japan Institute of International Affairs, the Woodrow Wilson School at Princeton University, and the Embassy of Japan, Washington, DC. His current research interests include the Japan-US security alliance in the context of Asia-Pacific regional security cooperation as well as the US-United Nations relations in the field of international peace and security.

Hoon JAUNG (*editor*) is professor of political science at Chung-Ang University in Seoul, Korea. He has published many articles on comparative politics in both English and Korean. His works have appeared in Electoral Studies, the Journal of East Asian Studies, Asian Update, and other scholarly journals. His current research projects include the future of East Asian cooperation, dynamics of two presidency phenomenon in the US and Korean politics and others.

Won-Taek KANG is assistant professor at Department of Political Science, Soongsil University, Seoul, Korea. He has published in many journals including Electoral Studies and Journal of Theoretical Politics. He is currently interested in roles of party leaders in British elections.

Kaoru KURUSU is associate professor at the School of International Public Policy, Osaka University (OSIPP), Japan. She previously worked at Kyushu University and Kobe University. She has published a number of articles and book chapters on European security regimes, human security, and Japanese policy toward the United Nations. Her current research interests include the reconstruction process of the Balkans.

Jae-Seug LEE is assistant professor at Institute of Foreign Affairs and National Security, Ministry of Foreign Affairs and Trade, Korea. He received Ph.D. from Yale University and has taught at Yale University, Seoul National University, and many other institutes in Korea. He has published numbers of books and articles on French European monetary policy and European integration in diverse aspects. His current research also includes EU's foreign policy and East Asian regional cooperation.

Yuichi MORII (*editor*) is associate professor at the Graduate School of Arts and Sciences, the University of Tokyo, Japan. He previously worked at the University of the Ryukyus and at the Tsukuba University. His research areas include German foreign policy and politics in the European Union. He is a member of the Executive Committee of the German and European Studies Program (Deutschland- und Europastudien in Komaba: DESK) at the University of Tokyo.

Ariyoshi OGAWA is professor of European Politics at Rikkyo University. He is the editor of EU Shokoku [The EU and its Member States] (Tokyo: Jiyukokuminsha, 1999) and the author of numerous articles and books on Scandinavian and European Politics. Among them is Džemal Sokolović and Florian Bieber (eds.), Reconstructing Multiethnic Societies: The Case of Bosnia-Herzegovina (Aldershot: Ashgate, 2000).

Cheol-Hee PARK is assistant Professor at the Institute of Foreign Affairs and National Security (IFANS) under the Ministry of Foreign Affairs and Trade, Korea. He got Ph.D. in political science at Columbia University, USA, and worked at the National Graduate Institute for Policy Studies (GRIPS), Japan. His research areas include Japanese politics, Korea-Japan relations and Korean diplomacy in general. He has published a number of articles on Japanese politics and diplomacy as well as on international relations in East Asia.

Authors

TING Wai obtained his PhD in Political Science and International Relations from the University of Paris-X, France. Formerly Research Fellow at the Institute of Southeast Asian Studies, Singapore, he is now associate professor at the Hong Kong Baptist University. His research interests include Chinese domestic politics and foreign policies, and theories of international relations. He has published widely in Chinese, English and French on Chinese diplomacy, Sino-American relations, Indochina problems, China and Northeast Asia and South Asia, Mainland China-Hong Kong relations, and external relations and international status of Hong Kong.

Introduction

CHAPTER *1*

COMPARING COOPERATION EXPERIENCES IN EUROPE AND EAST ASIA : CHALLENGES IN THEORY AND PRACTICE

Hoon JAUNG

1. Introduction

It is a cliché to say that history repeats itself. Yet, history never takes the same developmental path across different points of space-time. After one century of emulating European political development, East Asians[1] now seem to be willing to follow European experience again: regional cooperation among nation-states. While the import of the nation-state concept from Europe has brought about tremendous achievement—and terrible pains—to East Asia, the peoples of the region are once again

---

[1] While the definition of East Asia is contentious, we delimit it to China, Japan, North and South Korea, and Taiwan in this chapter. The traditional meaning of East Asia has been confined to these four countries among Chinese, Japanese, and Koreans. From the 1960s, the boundary of East Asia became complicated with the rise of Southeast Asia that comprises Malaysia, Indonesia, Philippines, Singapore, Thailand, and others. The reason why I stick to the traditional concept of East Asia has to do with the fact that East Asia has been a historically constructed regional entity for a long period of time in Asia compared to the alternative conceptions.

turning their gaze toward Europe in order to forge a suitable regional cooperation framework of their own in the hopes of bringing stability and prosperity to the region. In this effort, both theorists and policymakers in East Asia view the European Union (EU) as the most sophisticated and institutionalized form of regional cooperation.

However, experience has, thus far, defied initial expectation toward regional cooperation among East Asians both in theory and practice. Despite some progress in recent years, particularly after the Asian financial crisis in 1997, policymakers in East Asia realize that regional cooperation faces more uncertainties than initially expected. They are not sure of whether there will be a coherent cultural and political identity in East Asia; whether East Asian regionalism will be cooperative and coexistent with the existing U.S. hegemony and the rise of China; and whether economic interdependencies will develop into cooperation in politics and other realms. The prospect is no less doubtful on the theoretical front. Students of East Asian regionalism have had difficulties building coherent theoretical framework to characterize the pattern and sources of (under)development in East Asian regional cooperation.

The poverty of theory is paradoxical, but explicable. Theorists have lamented that analysis of East Asian regional cooperation has been "under-theorized," lacking coherent concepts and theoretical arguments about causes and processes of regional cooperation.[2] Considering the abundant theoretical resources derived from European experiences, it is paradoxical that the study of East Asian regionalism has been notoriously underdeveloped. There are two main explanations for this. On the one hand, there has been a simple and context-blind application of extant theories based on the European experience. Equipped with various perspectives like neo-functionalism, intergovernmentalism, and constructivism, students have tried to explain movements toward regional cooperation in East Asia. Yet, such efforts have not yielded greater insight as there are abundant dissimilarities between European and East Asian regional cooperation. On the other hand, theorists have long been

---

[2] John Ikenberry and Michael Mastanduno, eds., *International Relations Theory and the Asia-Pacific* (New York: Columbia University Press, 2003), p. 2.

1. Comparing Cooperation Experiences in Europe and East Asia: Challenges in Theory and Practice

interested more in the underdevelopment rather than the development in East Asian regionalism. Concerned chiefly with the lack or absence of multilateral institutions in the region, they appear ill prepared to explain the sudden rise in regional cooperation.

Neither Eurocentrism nor an idiosyncratic approach fittingly characterizes or explains the movement toward regionalism in East Asia. What is required is a flexible application that utilizes theoretical resources from the European experience in the context of East Asian culture and history. Searching for an appropriate theory does not mean we reject the usefulness of extant theoretical framework as a whole, nor should we be locked into the cultural and historical idiosyncrasies in East Asia. Hence, this article aspires to aid in that search for a theory of East Asian regionalism by exploring a third way between Eurocentric and idiosyncratic approaches. The third way begins with a reexamination of the extant theories of regionalism, exploring how the context-blind application of extant frameworks is inappropriate for explaining East Asian movement toward regionalism. Such exploration will demonstrate both the usefulness and limitations of extant frameworks by unraveling East Asian regional cooperation. We then consider the divergence between European and East Asian regionalism. Only when we grasp the divergences and commonalities between the two regions will we be able to overcome context-blind applications and begin constructing a meaningful theory.

In the next section, we will reexamine major theoretical frameworks (in particular, functionalism, intergovernmentalism, realism, and constructivism) focusing on their insights and limitations in understanding East Asian regional movement. In the following section, we will investigate divergences between Europe and East Asian regionalism focusing on the concept, process, actors, modes and motivations of regional cooperation— in other words, the "region" and "regionness," and "regionalism" and "regionalization" of the two—as well as political integration and economic integration, and the U.S. role in both Europe and East Asia.

2. Revisiting European Theories of Regionalism: Functionalism, Intergovernmentalism, Realism, and Constructivism

2.1. Functionalist Paradigm

When one tries to import theories of regionalism to East Asia, functionalist paradigm should be at or near the top of the list. As a dominant theoretical paradigm for regionalism from the early phase of European integration in the 1950s, functionalist paradigm (e.g., functionalism, neofunctionalism, and transaction cost theories) has positive—if not naïve—perspective on the evolution of regionalism. Focusing on the demand side of regional cooperation, functionalism sees increasing economic interdependence as the prime source of the development of multilateral institutions within a region.[3] Simply put, those groups and individuals who are involved in trans-border economic activities in trade and finance see potent interest in developing multilateral institutions for enhanced economic exchanges while eliminating barriers. To enhance economic efficiency in terms of production and exchanges, transnational actors attempt to unravel tariff and non-tariff barriers and other regulations while constructing regional standard rules and institutions with regard to trade, investment, and finance. Functionalists also claim that such economic integration spills over into the political arena.

In Europe, functionalists have been criticized for not analytically explaining how and why economic interdependence leads to the rise of multilateral institutions. For instance, functionalist paradigm has not been able to provide a proper explanation for the "integration sclerosis" suffered by European nations despite the highly advanced economic interdependence in the 1970s, nor has it been able to elucidate the sudden integration "resurgence" in Europe since the late 1980s, despite the lack of

---

[3] Ernest Haas, *The Uniting of Europe: Political, Social, and Economic Forces, 1950-1957* (Stanford: Stanford University Press, 1958); David Mittrany, *A Working Peace System: An Argument for the Functional Development of International Organization* (London: Oxford University Press, 1943/4).

further economic interdependence.[4]

In a strikingly similar vein, functionalists in East Asia have difficulty explaining the paucity of multilateral institutions in a region that already boasts a high level of interdependence in trade and investment. In the early 1990s, East Asian nations sustained "functionalist demand" for regional institutions with a high level of intra-regional interdependence. Yet, such demand has not materialized into the form of multilateral institutions and political integration. Furthermore, the sudden upsurge of bilateral and some regional arrangements within this region since the late 1990s has not come from a concomitant rise of economic interdependence. By any measure, the level of interdependence has not changed remarkably since the 1990s.[5] Thus functionalism helps only to highlight the traditional underdevelopment of regionalism in East Asia but fails to explain the recent growth in regional movement.

Despite its limited explanatory power, functionalism offers valuable insights into the future of East Asian regionalism. The functional model has identified principal supranational agencies at work in the process of international change like supranational businesses, civic organizations, and the like.[6] Particularly notable is the role of civic organizations and supranational actors in cultivating intra-regional interactions. Though long been dominated by the state interactions, East Asia is now experiencing a rapid growth in NGOs and INGOs engaging in active intra-regional cooperation. These civic groups are active in transmitting international norms, working as coalition partners for governments, and functioning as "bridging" organizations that work outside diplomatic relations.[7] In this sense, functionalism is worth revisiting if we focus on the diversification

---

[4] Wayne Sandholtz, "Choosing Union: Monetary Politics and Maastricht," *International Organization*, vol. 47 (1993), pp. 1-40.

[5] John Ravenhill, "A Three World Bloc? The New East Asian Regionalism," *International Relations of Asia-Pacific*, vol. 2 (2002), p. 172.

[6] Michael O'Neill, *The Politics of European Integration: A Reader* (London: Routledge, 1996), p. 130.

[7] Susan Pharr, "Coming from Behind: The Rise of Global Civic Activism in East Asia," paper presented at an International Conference on "Peace, Development, and Regionalization in East Asia," Seoul, September 2-3, 2003.

of interactions and their impact on the move toward regionalism.

In a similar vein, the liberal paradigm has offered high expectations for regional cooperation with the advent of democratization and increasing web of international organizations in East Asia. Inspired by Immanuel Kant, liberal theorists posit that democratization in South Korea (ROK) and Taiwan would enhance convergence of political values and identities, bringing in momentum for close cooperation. They share with the advocates of the "democratic peace thesis" that democratic convergence would reduce uncertainties in the security order and trigger cooperation in the social and economic spheres.

2.2. Intergovernmentalism

As theorists have begun to realize that demand alone does not bring about regional cooperation, they have begun to look at the supply side dynamics of regionalism. Some theorists concentrate on the political leadership of hegemonic power that supplies public goods for regionalism (in particular, the role of U.S. leadership in regional cooperation), while some students have focused on the efforts of nation-states that have been searching for common interests and built up institutional networks within the region. These scholarly attempts have led to the rise of intergovernmentalism that combines various traditions of international relations theory to explain the evolution of the European Community and European Union. As we will discuss the role of U.S. hegemony in our revisit of realism, let us first concentrate on reexamining the insights and limitations of intergovernmentalism for East Asian regionalism.

While intergovernmentalism brings together various currents of international relations theory, the most significant implication comes from its notion of the centrality of the state and state sovereignty. Intergovernmentalism places the negotiation process and preference convergence among nation-states at the core of regional cooperation, while sharing neo-realism's conception of anarchic order of international relations and neo-liberal emphasis on institutions.[8] Advocates of

---

[8] Robert Keohane and Stanley Hoffmann, eds., *The New European Community: Decision-Making and Institutional Change* (Boulder, Colo.: Westview Press, 1991).

1. Comparing Cooperation Experiences in Europe and East Asia: Challenges in Theory and Practice

intergovernmentalism see the evolution of the European Community as the rational behavior of states trying to minimize costs and vulnerabilities in a world of global anarchy.

At a first glance, intergovernmentalism seems to shed new light on the direction and nature of East Asia regionalism, especially when one considers the centrality of nation-states in East Asia. States have without a doubt dominated domestic politics, economies, and international relations among East Asian countries. Despite vast differences in economic and political systems, Japan, South Korea, Taiwan, and China all reflect the prevailing role of the state in organizing market economy, sustaining political stability, and managing international relations.

Yet, when it comes to convergence of state preferences, intergovernmental perspectives seem to yield both opportunities as well as challenges toward regional cooperation. On the one hand, there is increasing room for preference convergence among East Asian nations as they share the need for reduced barriers for investment and trade and for enhanced arrangements to deal with the instability in financial markets. On the other hand, there are daunting constraints that thwart the process of preference convergences and institutional networks. The three key nations in East Asia reveal the vast diversity in the structure of economic and political systems. With regard to economic systems, although the Japanese developmental state inspired the model for rapid economic development in South Korea, Taiwan—and later China—differences abound in the ways each has organized its market economy.[9] The Chinese economic system in particular, with its dramatic transition from a socialist to market economy, demonstrates this divergence well.

Divergences among the political systems are even more profound. Japan has sustained liberal democracy for more than five decades even though it has often suffered from persistent political corruption and lack of vibrant political leadership. South Korea belongs to a class of developing democracies, touted as a successful case in the third wave of democratization in Asia. Once again, China shows a striking contrast

---

[9] Meredith Woo-Cumings, ed., *The Developmental State* (Ithaca: Cornell University Press, 1999).

between its political system and those of the previous two as it cautiously struggles to enhance the political participation of its citizens. In a nutshell, while East Asian states may develop some convergence of economic interests as manifested during and after the Asian financial crisis in 1997, they are finding it highly complex and difficult to translate such convergence into institutional networks given the variety of economic and political systems.

Another challenge for intergovernmentalism has to do with the notion of "pooling sovereignty." Keohane and others hold that European nation-states increasingly pooled their sovereignty into the European Union to maximize intergovernmental cooperation and benefits. Such reasoning, however, must face the cold reality that East Asian states uphold the concept of sovereignty as inseparable and nontransferable. Considering the traditional commitment to sovereignty among policymakers and citizens, there is only a slim chance for the region to develop any kind of sovereignty pooling in the foreseeable future.[10] Yet, as the historical institutional perspective convincingly emphasizes, there may be unintended consequences of increasing cooperation that eventually compromise sovereignty in the region.[11] In this sense, as historical institutionalism suggests, we need to reexamine the factors influencing the unintended pooling of sovereignty (e.g., the resistance of supranational actors, short-term perspective of policymakers, sunk and increasing costs of exiting regional cooperation, etc.).

---

[10] Recently, several liberal thinkers in this region fiercely criticized the predominance of the notion of nation-state and nationalism among East Asian people. They view them as major hindrances against East Asia's transition to a postmodern and globalized world. See Kozakai Toshiaki, *Nation as an Imagination* (Paris: Payot and Rivages, 2000) or the translated version by Bang Kwang-Sok, *Minjoken Obda* (Seoul: Puriwa Ipari, 2003).

[11] Paul Pierson, "The Path to European Integration: A Historical Institutionalist Analysis," *Comparative Political Studies*, vol. 29 (1996), pp. 123-63. Indeed, several liberal academics in East Asia recently advocate the need to "think and act" beyond the nation-state to further regional cooperation in the region. See Choi Won-Sik, *Balgyun Euirosoeui DongAsia* (*Revisiting East Asia*) (Seoul: Moonhakgwa Jiseongsa, 2000).

2.3 Realism

Theories of European regionalism have been developed in a skewed manner. Functionalism, neo-liberalism, and recently constructivism have virtually dominated theoretical discourse on European regionalism, whereas realists have been—relatively speaking—marginalized. Yet realism provides more promise than the others in explaining both underdevelopment of and prospects for East Asian regionalism. The appeal to realism stems from the fact that the state and its power relations still dominate international relations in East Asia.

With regard to the underdevelopment of East Asian regionalism, realists offer a convincing explanation that emphasizes power relations. At the heart of realist explanation is the role and strategy of the United States as the hegemonic power in the region. Realists trace the nature and strategy of American hegemony in postwar Europe and East Asia to unravel the disparate development of regionalism in the two regions. In Europe, realists argue that U.S. hegemony preferred to build multilateral institutional frameworks for reasons of security and economic community building.[12] Such U.S. preference formed on account of the interplay among the so-called German question, Russian threat, resistance of European state against U.S. hegemony, and the like. In stark contrast, the U.S. hegemony was in favor of relying on bilateral webs in managing postwar political, economic, and security order in East Asia due to the historical enmity and resistance to Japan's active role in the region.

Realists still concentrate on the role and status of U.S. hegemony in illuminating recent ups and downs of East Asian movement toward regional cooperation. It was American triumphalism in the milieu of the Asian financial crisis that triggered East Asian nations to come together to test the waters for constructing multilateral arrangements, like an Asian Monetary Fund, that excluded the United States.[13] Such abortive efforts

---

[12] Joseph Grieco, "Realism and Regionalism: American Power and German and Japanese Institutional Strategies During and After the Cold War," in Ethan Kapstein and Michael Mastanduno, eds., *Unipolar Politics: Realism and State Strategies after the Cold War* (New York: Columbia University Press, 1999).

[13] John Ravenhill, "A Three World Bloc? The New East Asian Regionalism,"

only reinforced the notion among East Asian nations that the U.S. attitude is a vital force in any substantial movement toward regional cooperation as long as the United States projects its hegemonic power into the region.

However, when it comes to the future direction of East Asian regionalism, realism seems to be as much at a loss as other theoretical frameworks derived from European experiences. The foremost difficulty for the realist paradigm is that power relations in East Asia remain so uncertain that they defy an easy and simple characterization. Nonetheless, realists have managed to delineate four possible scenarios: a continuance of U.S. hegemony, bipolar system with U.S. and Chinese power, multipolar balance of power, and pluralistic security community.[14] All realists can say now is that various domestic and international factors will decide which of these scenarios will emerge. In other words, if we stick to the centrality of the state and power relations in regional politics in East Asia, we can predict that grave uncertainties will remain and cause the states to hedge their bets. Despite ample uncertainties, we need to concentrate on a few key pillars of power to sustain our search for a theory of East Asian regionalism. Those pillars should include the Sino-U.S. relationship,[15] U.S.-Japan alliance, and U.S.-ROK alliance.[16]

In dealing with these pillars, realism still reveals its limitations. For instance, realists would expect more conflict than cooperation between the United States and Japan after the end of cold war. From a realist's point of view, as an economic giant, Japan may attempt to balance itself against the U.S. hegemony. However, historical memory and consciousness keep Japan from doing so. Its defeat in World War II by the United States and resultant reluctance against deep involvement with security affairs has led

---

International Relations of Asia-Pacific, vol. 2 (2002), p. 171.
[14] Ikenberry and Mastanduno, op.cit., pp. 423-30.
[15] Minxin Pei, "Coping with American Hegemony: The Evolution of China's Strategy for Stabilizing Sino-American Relations since the End of the Cold War," paper presented at an International Conference on "Peace, Development, and Regionalization in East Asia," Seoul, September 2-3, 2003.
[16] Daniel Okimoto, "KASA and JASA: Twin Pillars of Asia's Security Architecture," paper presented at an International Conference on "Peace, Development, and Regionalization in East Asia," Seoul, September 2-3, 2003.

Japan to keep a close alliance with the United States, even after the virtual disappearance of the Russian threat. Realists also have difficulties explaining the Sino-U.S. relationship.[17] In general, China tries her best to sustain a cooperative relationship with the United States on political and economic fronts to sustain China's recent rapid economic growth. However, at times Beijing dares to confront Washington on the issue of Taiwan, even at the risk of escalating conflict with the world's hegemon and tarnishing China's image within the international community. In a nutshell, whereas East Asian international order is still predominated by the centrality of the nation-state, the great power relations in this region are not as tense as (neo)realists sometimes tend to stress.

2.4 Constructivism

With the rise of constructivism as a major current in international relations theory, the ideational dimension has received renewed attention in theoretical debates on regionalism.[18] Constructivism rediscovered the significance of shared identity, social knowledge and consciousness in the developing process of regional arrangements. It emphasizes the role of regional identity among European policymakers and citizens amidst the rise of the European Union.[19]

In this sense, constructivism has often cited the absence or lack of coherent regional identity as a major source of underdevelopment of regionalism in East Asia. It has compared the coherent regional entity and identity in Europe with enmity and hatred in East Asia. Constructivists noted the enduring influence of the memories of World War II and insufficient political reconciliation among East Asian peoples. They posit

---

[17] Thomas Berger, "Power and Purpose in Pacific East Asia," in John Ikenberry and Michael Mastanduno, eds., *International Relations Theory and the Asia-Pacific* (New York: Columbia University Press, 2003).

[18] Alexander Wendt, *Social Theory of International Politics* (New York: Cambridge University Press, 1999).

[19] For instance, see Charles Kupchan, "Regionalizing Europe's Security: The Case for a New Mitteleuropa," in Edward Mansfield and Helen Milner, eds., *The Political Economy of Regionalism* (New York: Columbia University Press, 1997).

that such burden from the past has constrained the evolution of the sense of "we-ness" among East Asians.

Despite increasing appeals to many students of regionalism, constructivism cannot escape criticism. The drawback of constructivism comes from its ambiguous conceptualization of regional identity and incomplete empirical ground. On the one hand, while political leaders often mentioned "European vision" of integration from the initial stage of European integration in the 1950s, European identity among most European citizens was somewhat mixed. In fact, they have sustained, to a certain degree, a common notion about the territorial boundedness and shared myths of origin and historical memories about the region called "Europe." However, it is highly doubtful that Europeans shared a common bond of mass, standardized European culture.[20] Rather, there was more diversity across national cultures than convergence toward a European culture. Indeed, various opinion polls have shown that the majority of citizens in the European Union still refer to themselves as being either French, Italian, German, etc. (i.e., one's national identity) rather than having developed a European identity.

If regional identity has been a cornerstone of European regionalism, such identity was something that was vaguely shared among European citizens and was actively mobilized by policymakers from above. That is why Europeans are now gravely concerned with the deficiency of European identity among citizens even after the emergence of the EU. This has led to a heated debate about democratic deficit in the European Union, emphasizing the lack of people's participation and tepid loyalty toward the EU.[21]

In sum, we may say that European identity has been evolving in more economic and legal than cultural and ideational terms with the progress of multilateral economic and legal institutions in Europe. If we take into account this path of regional identity in Europe, the prospect for

---

[20] Anthony Smith, "National Identity and European Identity," in Peter Gowan and Perry Anderson, eds., *The Question of Europe* (London: Verson, 1997).

[21] Svein Andersen and Kjell Eliassen, *The European Union: How Democratic Is It?* (London: Sage Publications, 1996).

regional identity in East Asia is not so pessimistic as many constructivists envisage. It is likely that East Asians may develop regional identity along economic and legal lines when East Asian nations accumulate institutional webs facilitating regional economic interactions. In this vein, a positive trend exists. Despite vast cultural differences, East Asian nations have been witnessing a growing convergence of economic ideas. Seeing the need for regional policy coordination to cope with increasing instability, these nations seem to accept neo-liberal ideology as a guiding principle in the age of globalization.[22]

Constructivism provides both promises and pitfalls. If we keep lamenting the lack of regional awareness and cultural identity in East Asia, we will fall into pitfall of Eurocentrism. Yet, if we view the concept of regional identity from a developmental perspective, in particular, along the line of economic and legal identity, constructivism helps substantively survey the future of East Asian regionalism. On the one hand, as constructivists focus on an ideational source for the recent rise of cooperation in the region, they can shed light on the nature of East Asian regionalization. According to them, the logic of the developmental state, which has led the economic miracles of Japan and South Korea, is a major driving force for international economic cooperation. Instrumental considerations for national economic growth have pushed Chinese, Japanese, and Korean governments to put more time and effort toward regional cooperation. The concern with regional peace and prosperity are only secondary factors in these moves, a distinction from the experience of Europe. In this sense, there is a narrow ideational consensus among East Asian nations with regard to the goal of cooperation. Yet, if East Asian countries see regional cooperation as a means of international mercantilism, the future of regional cooperation will prove to be shaky and unpredictable.

On the other hand, constructive perspective provides useful insight into the constraining factors for regional cooperation. For instance, (neo)realists and (neo)liberalists have difficulties explaining the lukewarm

---

[22] S. Gill, "Globalization, Market Civilization and Disciplinary Neo-Liberalism," *Millennium*, vol. 24 (1995), pp. 399-424.

cooperation between Japan and South Korea, which could serve as the main engine for enhanced cooperation in the region. The two countries not only share security concerns and are closely allied with the United States, but they are also are interconnected through massive trade, investment, and technological cooperation. History, however, continues to get in the way. South Koreans still harbor resentment toward Japan on account of Korea's thirty-five-year occupation under Japanese colonialism (1910-1945). Japan looks rather aloof in regional cooperation given her close alliance with the United States and status of global economic giant. Both obstruct a closer relationship from developing. In this vein, it is noteworthy that constructivists call for the need to look into the content of regional consciousness among policymakers and their strategies to constrain historical enmity and translate shared economic ideas into multilateral institutions.

Revisiting extant theories of regionalism uncovers crucial clues that can assist our search for a theory to explain East Asian regionalism. Most of all, as the process of regional cooperation is multidimensional, non-linear, and heterogeneous, any one perspective alone neither can nor should provide analytical framework to grasp the structure and process of regional cooperation in East Asia. It does not mean that complexity and open-endedness in East Asian movement toward regionalism defy any coherent theoretical account. Rather, it suggests that we need live debate among various perspectives. As each perspective focuses on a certain dimension of regional movement, exchanges and mutual accommodation among diverse perspectives would yield framework(s) sensitive to the realities in East Asian regionalism.

Another lesson from revisiting theories is the need for clarifying the object and scope of analytical exploration. As developed in the context of Europe, regionalism theories tend to focus on key aspects of European integration. Theses are, however, certainly distinct from East Asian realities. For instance, the role of U.S. has been wrongly neglected by theories of European regionalism, while political integration in East Asia has not been as prominent as in Europe. Thus, vast differences between the two regions with regard to crucial forces, motivations, and mode of regional movement exist and must be taken into account.

1. Comparing Cooperation Experiences in Europe and East Asia: Challenges in Theory and Practice

3. Analyze These! : Modes, Process, and Actors of Regionalism in East Asia and Europe

In order to build a context-sensitive theory, distinctive forces, motivations, and mode of East Asian regionalism deserve our attention. This section compares regional cooperation in Europe and East Asia focusing on eight crucial factors (see table 1-1). Although the list may not be exhaustive, these eight factors shall be our focus.

Table 1-1 Features of Regional Cooperation in Europe and East Asia

	East Asia	Europe
Actors	A Few Member States	A Number of States
Leadership	Not Clear	Franco-German Axis
Level of Economic Development	Heterogeneous but Rapidly Growing	Homogeneous
Production Relations	Hierarchical	Horizontal
Regional Identity	Complex	Homogeneous
Institutional Formality	Low	High
Regional Slogan/Ideology	Vague	Ideology
U.S. Influence	Hegemonic	Strong

As indicated in table 1, there are several striking contrasts between regional cooperation in the two regions. East Asia comprises only a few member countries (China and Taiwan, Japan, and North and South Korea), but lacks political leadership that provides incentives, ideology, and political entrepreneurship toward institutionalized regional settlement. While Europe includes a number of member states (fifteen and several candidates), Franco-German co-leadership has provided political leadership for the last five decades.

In terms of economic structure, the two regions are also sharply distinct. Members of the EU sustain relatively homogeneous levels of economic development, while East Asian countries show a wide disparity (though it has diminished somewhat over the recent years). More

17

importantly, the production relationship is hierarchical in East Asia but horizontal in Europe. Unlike European countries, East Asian countries are connected to a hierarchical production chain commanded by the Japanese economy.

The two regions also show a stark contrast in terms of regional identity. European countries have shared a common ground for regional identity in terms of geographical limitations, goals of regional cooperation, political values toward democracy, and the like. Regional identity among East Asian countries is at best contestable: diversity looms large in terms of political values, memory of regional history, vision for regional cooperation, and so on.

Taken together, we can differentiate regional cooperation in Europe and East Asia as "regionalism" and "regionalization." Regionalism refers here to "regional intergovernmental cooperation to manage various regional problems, while regionalization means an ongoing process of economic integration deriving primary motive force from markets, trade and investment."[23] In other words, what we call East Asian regionalism is East Asian regionalization. It is an increasing economic integration characterized by weak institutionalization and driven mainly by market forces. As one Japanese observer even writes, the distinctive feature in East Asia is regionalization without regionalism.[24] In contrast, European regionalism involves a highly institutionalized intergovernmental cooperation across the realms of trade, investment, education, finances, technology, and defense. In a few words, East Asian cooperation is "open," "soft," and "diffused," while European cooperation is "closed," "institutionalized," and "deep."

This distinction is not intended to overemphasize the fact that East Asians are lagging behind in the race toward regionalism. Instead, it suggests looking at movements toward regionalism from a developmental

---

[23] Samuel Kim, "Regionalization and Regionalism in East Asia," paper presented at an International Conference on "Peace, Development, and Regionalization in East Asia," Seoul, September 2-3, 2003.

[24] Yoshinobu Yamamoto, ed., *Globalism, Regionalism and Nationalism: Asia in Search of Its Role in the 21st Century* (Malden, Mass.: Blackwell, 1999).

1. Comparing Cooperation Experiences in Europe and East Asia: Challenges in Theory and Practice

perspective. According to this, European regional integration is still on the road to regionalism, though it has achieved most sophisticated and advanced political and economic integration. In addition, the developmental perspective leads us to look more at the actors and processes in economic integration than other dimensions in East Asia. What appears is a demand for investigation into:

- "the degree to which the dynamic economic density . . . that had developed in the last two decades provide a positive context within which new discursive structures of regional economic and security cooperation might flourish";
- "the degree to which these enhanced economic interactions . . . strengthen the incentives of regional state policy-making elites to identify with one another in the interest of greater collective action and/or policy coordination"[25];
- and the way that enhanced economic integration helps form shared consciousness among policymakers and transnational middle classes in the region.[26]

Concentration on economic integration seems to hark back to functionalist theory. Yet focusing on economic integration does not necessarily mean importing the optimistic vision of regionalism and methodological naïveté of functionalism.

Also, we should distinguish the notion of "region" in Europe and East Asia. From the early phase of regional integration, Europeans have shared a relatively well-defined, delimited notion of the "European region." In contrast, the current notion of region in East Asia is at best fluid and still in the process of being constructed. If we consider "region" to be a socially, economically, and culturally (re)constructed entity, East

---

[25] Richard Higgott, "The International Political Economy of Regionalism: The Asia-Pacific and Europe Compared," in William Coleman and Geoffrey Underhill, eds., *Regionalism and Global Economic Integration* (London: Routledge, 1998), p. 55.

[26] Takeshi Shiraishi, "East Asian Regionalization and the Question of Identity," paper presented at International Conference on "Building an East Asian Community," Seoul, December 17, 2001.

Introduction

Asians are still in the embryonic stages of constructing the notion of "East Asian region."

Europeans had a stable and definitive notion of the European region in geographical, cultural, historical, and economic terms when the idea of regional integration began to build steam in the late 1940s and get under way in the early 1950s. While there was no natural, given region in Europe, most Europeans accepted the notion of "European region" by the geographical limit of the Urals and cultural and historical denominators. In comparison, the question of "What constitutes the East Asian region?" is widely open-ended. East Asia has defied a simple and straightforward definition due to cultural diversity, economic and political disparity, and geographical indefiniteness. It has been proved a naïve assertion that emphasizes the role of Asian values and East Asian Confucian tradition as a springboard for regional unity. Close examination undoubtedly has revealed the vast diversity of cultural identity among the peoples of East Asia.

The East Asian region is no less difficult to delimit in geographical terms. Traditional geographical concept includes China, Taiwan, Japan, and Korea, which is now often called Northeast Asia. The recent surge of political and economic weight of Indonesia, Malaysia, Singapore has likewise coined the geographical concept of Southeast Asia. The notion of East Asia including both Northeast and Southeast Asia has gained increasing currency among academics, policymakers, and business leaders. Yet, there is a wide gap between Northern and Southern parts of this region with regard to regional identity, geopolitical structure, and economic power. Furthermore, there are several alternative conceptions of geographical entity in this region, like "the Greater China region" and others. In a word, the concept of "East Asian region" is fluid. It means that we need to concentrate now on the formation process of the East Asian region rather than comparing the role of the notion of region in Europe and East Asia.

In addition, when we explore the characteristics and prospects of East Asian regionalism, we have to take into account the hegemonic role of the United States. Given that the United States does not exist within the region's geographical boundary but has been playing a crucial, hegemonic role in the economic, politico-military order of the region, it must be considered a nonresident member-state. Indeed, "East Asian region" virtually means East Asia plus the United States. The United States has been, undoubtedly, the hegemonic power shaping political, economic, and security structures. As the main architect of postwar settlement since 1945, the United States has constructed a regional order in East Asia that is basically distinctive from that of Europe. This U.S.-led regional order still largely persists while constraining and facilitating the prospect of regional cooperation. The East Asian economy has been more dependent on the U.S. market than the European economy. The Japanese and South Korean economic miracles through the 1960s and 1980s, respectively, were only possible because of their access to the U.S. market; reliance on such access persists. Now, the Chinese economy seems to be following suit as it continues to create a huge trade surplus with the United States. This economic structure largely constrains the development of regional cooperation in East Asia. As the East Asian economy is vulnerable to volatility in the U.S. market, inward-looking institutionalization to cope with common economic policy issues would seem to be a hard thing to achieve anytime soon.

Security and power structures show similar challenges for East Asian countries. Unlike the case of Europe, the United States has built a web of bilateral security alliances rather than a multilateral security regime in East Asia since the end of World War II. Historical enmity among East Asian countries and lack of restraining power on U.S. hegemony in the region has been responsible for the rise of this structure of bilateral security arrangements centering on the United States. As a result, East Asia has been devoid of a multilateral security community, a crucial pillar underpinning regional cooperation in Europe for more than five decades.

The immense uncertainty in the security order surely poses a great challenge for the future of East Asian regionalization. The United States still stands at the core of such order. On the one hand, it is a reassuring development that the United States and Japan have been enhancing their cooperative relationship on security issues since the end of the cold war. However, the regional security order confronts a major source of uncertainty: the unsettled Sino-U.S. relationship. The current relationship between the two countries oscillates between strategic partnership and strategic competition, with the long-term prospect unpredictable at best. The future of East Asian cooperation undoubtedly will be highly dependent upon how this great challenge is managed. The future direction of the U.S.-East Asian relationship also will be a major underpinning of East Asian regionalization. In this vein, not just realists but also any serious students of East Asian cooperation should closely monitor how the U.S. military, economic, and cultural power appeals to the political elite, economic sectors, and social strata in East Asia.

4. Conclusion: The Region's Future Lies in Its Past

As East Asian regionalization comes of age, the study of East Asian regionalism will surely be a booming industry across various disciplines in the years to come. Yet, the prospect of constructing a coherent theoretical framework will remain a daunting task. As we have reviewed above, analytical approaches to European regionalism have only limited explanatory power for East Asian regionalization due to vast differences between the two regions. Although East Asians share with Europeans normative aspirations toward intra-regional cooperation, we now know that the processes and dynamics of such development in the two regions diverge considerably.

Thus the challenge for those trying to develop a theory that attempts to explain East Asian regionalism is two-fold. On the one hand, the theory should sustain methodological rigor and conceptual clarity. For this purpose, importing theory on regionalism that is based on the European experience is critical, as such theory has been refined over the past five decades or so through fierce theoretical debate involving various perspectives. Liberal, realist, and structural perspectives have influenced one another, culminating in enhanced explanatory power and methodological rigor. In this vein, discursive competition among various approaches toward East Asian regionalization is essential.

On the other hand, theory on East Asian regionalism should be anchored in the cultural and historical context of the region. As we discussed above, theories of European regionalism have shown numerous limitations—and contributions—in exploring the characteristics and prospects of East Asian regional cooperation. For better understanding, functionalism, intergovernmentalism, constructivism, and realism should incorporate East Asian historical memory and cultural tradition: such as historical enmity among East Asian countries from the last century, nationalism, East Asian preference for informal arrangements rather than institutional settlements, tradition of hierarchical international order, and so on. These East Asian traditions not only facilitate but also constrain regional cooperation, leaving the shape of its future—at least in part—at the mercy of this duality.

Eventually, these conflicting factors bring about a convergence with and divergence from European experiences in East Asia. The combination of these will mold the mode, strength, and stability of East Asian regionalism. In this sense, Europe's past will not be the future of East Asia. On the contrary, East Asia's future will be based upon its past. All we know now is that East Asia is in much better shape in terms of economic vibrancy, social diversification, and political dynamics than it was one-and-a-half centuries ago, when the first wave of East Asian regionalization started its abortive experiment.

References

Andersen, Svein and Kjell Eliassen. *The European Union: How Democratic Is It?* London: Sage Publications, 1996.

Gill, S. "Globalization, Market Civilization and Disciplinary Neo-Liberalism," *Millennium*, vol. 24 (1995), pp. 399-424.

Grieco, Joseph. "Realism and Regionalism: American Power and German and Japanese Institutional Strategies During and after the Cold War," in Ethan Kapstein and Michael Mastanduno, eds., *Unipolar Politics: Realism and State Strategies after the Cold War*. New York: Columbia University Press, 1999.

Haas, Ernest. *The Uniting of Europe: Political, Social, and Economic Forces, 1950-1957*. Stanford: Stanford University Press, 1958.

Higgott, Richard. "The International Political Economy of Regionalism: The

Asia-Pacific and Europe Compared," in William Coleman and Geoffrey Underhill, eds., *Regionalism and Global Economic Integration*. London: Routledge, 1998.

Ikenberry, John and Michael Mastanduno, eds. *International Relations Theory and the Asia-Pacific*. New York: Columbia University Press, 2003.

Katzenstein, Peter, et al. *Asian Regionalism*. Ithaca: Cornell University East Asia Program, 2000.

Keohane, Robert and Stanley Hoffmann, eds. *The New European Community: Decision-Making and Institutional Change*. Boulder, Colo.: Westview Press, 1991.

Kim, Samuel. "Regionalization and Regionalism in East Asia." Paper presented at an International Conference on "Peace, Development, and Regionalization in East Asia," Seoul, September 2-3, 2003.

Kupchan, Charles. "Regionalizing Europe's Security: The Case for a New Mitteleuropa," in Edward Mansfield and Helen Milner, eds., *The Political Economy of Regionalism*. New York : Columbia University Press, 1997.

Mittrany, David. A. *Working Peace System: An Argument for the Functional Development of International Organization*. London: Oxford University Press, 1943/4.

Moravcsik, Andrew. *The Choice for Europe: Social Purpose and State Power from Messina to Maastricht*. Ithaca: Cornell University Press, 1998.

Okimoto, Daniel. "KASA and JASA: Twin Pillars of Asia's Security Architecture." Paper presented at an International Conference on "Peace, Development, and Regionalization in East Asia," Seoul, September 2-3, 2003.

O'Neill, Michael. *The Politics of European Integration: A Reader*. London: Routledge, 1996.

Pharr, Susan. "Coming from Behind: The Rise of Global Civic Activism in East Asia." Paper presented at an International Conference on "Peace, Development, and Regionalization in East Asia," Seoul, September 2-3, 2003.

Pei, Minxin. "Coping with American Hegemony: The Evolution of China's Strategy for Stabilizing Sino-American Relations since the End of the Cold War." Paper presented at an International Conference on "Peace, Development, and Regionalization in East Asia," Seoul, September 2-3, 2003.

Pierson, Paul. "The Path to European Integration: A Historical Institutionalist Analysis," *Comparative Political Studies*, vol. 29 (1996), pp. 123-63.

Ravenhill, John. *APEC and the Construction of Pacific Rim Regionalism*.

New York: Cambridge University Press, 2001.

_____. "A Three World Bloc? The New East Asian Regionalism," *International Relations of Asia-Pacific*, vol. 2 (2002), pp. 167-95.

Sandholtz, Wayne. "Choosing Union: Monetary Politics and Maastricht," *International Organization*, vol. 47 (1993), pp. 1-40.

Shiraishi, Takshi. "East Asian Regionalization and the Question of Identity." Paper presented at International Conference on "Building an East Asian Community," Seoul, December 17, 2001.

Smith, Anthony. "National Identity and European Identity," in Peter Gowan and Perry Anderson, eds., *The Question of Europe*. London: Verson, 1997.

Wendt, Alexander. *Social Theory of International Politics*. New York: Cambridge University Press, 1999.

Woo-Cumings, Meredith, ed. *The Developmental State*. Ithaca: Cornell University Press, 1999.

Yamamoto, Yoshinobu, ed. *Globalism, Regionalism and Nationalism: Asia in Search of Its Role in the 21st Century*. Malden, Mass.: Blackwell, 1999.

PART I

Issues in the Development of the European Union

PART II

CHAPTER 2

PATTERNS OF REGIONAL SECURITY MANAGEMENT: AN OVERVIEW OF DEVELOPMENTS IN EUROPE AND EAST ASIA

Kaoru KURUSU

1. Introduction

This chapter examines patterns of regional security management, which currently win renewed interest both empirically and theoretically. Over the past fifty years, scholars of security studies and international relations have conducted considerable number of research about security issues. However the dynamics of the Cold War has diverted scholars' attention from the very subject of regional security management. Why are states in given regions interested in collective management of security? How are regional patterns of governance shaped? This chapter will also observe the development of regional security governance in Europe and East Asia[1] with the aim to identify regional factors contributing to the formation of regionally specific patterns and frameworks for security management.

There have been rich literatures on regional integration in general, such as the works by Karl Deutsch and Ernst Haas in the 1950s, and those

---

[1] In this chapter, East Asia includes Southeast Asia and Northeast Asia.

with renewed interests in regional integration of the 1990s. However, there are only few focused and systematic studies on regional security. Barry Buzan's *People, States and Fear*[2] can be regarded as a precursor of recent efforts to theorize regional security. His book conceptualizes 'regional security complex,' and it has been used in recent scholarly efforts to grasp regional security structures comprehensively. Another strand of study on regional security has been the constructivist school, including the volume *Security Communities*, edited by Emmanuel Adler and Michael Barnett.[3] Yoshinobu Yamamoto's conceptual study on security regimes and cooperative security is also valid and insightful in considering a regional framework.[4] This chapter incorporates the contemporary insights into the analysis of regional security cooperation.

2. Regional Security Complex

The concept of 'regional security complex' (hereafter RSC) is defined as *a group of states whose primary security concerns are linked sufficiently closely that their national securities cannot realistically be considered apart from one another.*[5] It focuses on regional systems as the level of analysis between states and the international system.

Buzan argues that at its very foundation of a RSC operates a

---

[2] Barry Buzan, *People, States and Fear* (New York: Harvester Wheatsheaf, 1991).

[3] Imanuel Adler and Michael Barnett eds., *Security Communities* (Cambridge: Cambridge University Press, 1998).

[4] Yoshinobu Yamamoto, "reisen go no anzenhosho: kyocho teki anzenhosho to shinraijosei wo megutte" (Post-Cold War Security: Cooperative Security and Confidence-building), in Hiroshi Kimura ed., *Kokusai kiki gaku (Studies on International Crisis)* (Tokyo: Sekaishiso sha, 2002): 26-58; Yamamoto, "Kyocho teki anzenhosho no kanousei" (Possibilities of Cooperative Security), *Kokusai Mondai* (International Affairs) 425 (1995): 2-20.

[5] Buzan, *op. cit.,* 190; Barry Buzan, "The Post-Cold War Asia-Pacific Security Order: Conflict or Cooperation?" in Andrew Mack and John Ravenhill eds., *Pacific Cooperation: Building Economic and Security Regimes in the Asia-Pacific Region* (Boulder: Westview Press, 1995), 131.

2. Patterns of Regional Security Management: an Overview of Developments in Europe and East Asia

traditional sub-systemic idea of (1) *balance of power*.[6] More importantly the principal defining element in the formation of RCSs is (2) *patterns of enmity and amity*. Patterns of enmity include border disputes, interests of ethnically related populations, ideological alignment, or longstanding historical links.[7] Amity means other actors' expectation of support or protection. Moreover, high level of trust and friendship can also serve as a binding force.[8]

In defining the shape and structure of security complexes (3) *cultural and ethnological patterns* may well be an important contributing factor, though Buzan considers them second to the patterns of amity/enmity. Commonly shared culture by a group of states increases members' attention to one another and legitimizes mutual interventions in security affairs.[9]

In short, regional security complex emerges from *interdependence of rivalry* as well as that of *shared interests among states* with geographical proximity. Usually regional security complexes derive from geographical proximity, but an outside actor can also become a member of the RSC when its interest and presence is rooted in the region. American position in the Middle East is one example of extra-regional actor's strong influence.

The neorealist-rationalist David Lake, in an attempt to operationalize the concept of RSC, presents regional security interdependence in terms of *'externality'* or *'spillover.'*[10] RSC is then *a set of states affected by at least one trans-border but local externality that emanates from a particular geographical area*. Externalities can be negative as well as positive. This study's assumption is that RSCs are shaped not only by externalities objectively defined, but more significantly, by the perception of members of RSCs that their own security interests are interdependent.

---

[6] Buzan, *People, States and Fear*, 138.
[7] *Ibid*, 190.
[8] *Ibid*, 194.
[9] *Ibid*, 196.
[10] David Lake, "Regional Security Complexes: A Systems Approach," in David Lake and Patrick Morgan eds., *Regional Orders: Building Security in a New World* (University Park: Pennsylvania State University Press, 1997), 48.

Sources of regional externalities are not limited to inter-state relations. (4) *Transnational security threats* also enhance regional security awareness. Concerns over trans-border organized crimes, drug trafficking, and illegal trade of small weapons have created various forms of regional security cooperation. (5) Potential and actual externality emerging from *social disorder in a neighboring country* also plays a role in the formation of RSCs, though previous studies on regional security management have not always paid attention to it. This study, however, argues that the concept of RSC is also useful in considering how internal threats and dangers are managed.

From this perspective, real and potential disorder arising from internal conflicts contributes to the formation of regional security complexes. Wallensteen and Sollenberg's idea of regional conflict complex (hereafter RCC) is enlightening in this regard.[11] RCCs are *situations where neighboring countries experience internal or interstate conflicts, with significant links between the conflicts*. These links can be so substantial that changes in conflict dynamics or the resolution of one conflict may impact a neighboring country. One type of such linkage is trans-border incompatibility, for example, an ethnic group living across border areas. Another type is direct or indirect support (economic, military, territorial etc.) to a governmental or non-governmental group in a neighboring state. Dynamics of RCCs influence the formulation of a specific type and gravity of RSC.

Local security relations are often influenced by dynamics of wider security complexes and vice versa. For instance, the war in Bosnia was nested in complexity of West Balkan area. European countries' perception, that externalities from West Balkan RCC would influence wider European regional security complex, encouraged the European actors' involvement to control civil wars. Their intervention was not motivated only by their vested interests in the Balkans, but also by the perception that they are located in 'Europe' where no such 'uncivil' acts should take place. The US

---

[11] Peter Wallensteen and Margareta Sollenberg, "Armed Conflict and Regional Conflict Complexes," *Journal of Peace Research*, vol. 35, no. 5 (1998): 623-624.

considered a gradual retreat from the European regional security complex after the Cold War, but after all, concerns over NATO's credibility and domestic public opinion led the U.S. government to re-intervene in the region. In this way, destabilization of West Balkan RCC contributed to the transformation of European RSC in the first half of the 1990s.

3. Factors Conducive to Regional Security Governance

Regional security governance or patterns of conflict management generally emerge according to characteristics of RSCs, and also demands and perceptions of regional members. Based on three strands of IR scholarship, the following section briefly discusses causal relationship between regional governance and factors contributing to its creation. (i) The structural-realist school emphasizes regional *distribution of power*, and, more importantly, global distribution of power. (ii) The neorealist-rationalist school proposes the concept of *security externality* emanating not only from *enmity and amity* in inter-state relationship, but from *internal conflicts, domestic disorder, or transnational threats.* Non-security externalities also contribute to the formation of regional framework. This perspective is similar to the functionalist explanation that presupposes spillover effect and trans-border interdependence, although neo-realists argue that inter-state relationship is more competitive in nature. (iii) The third possible explanation is by the constructivist school, which focuses on *identities and norms*. Furthermore, relevance of other factors should be taken into consideration. (iv) At the domestic level state policies and coordination process among state elites is indispensable for the formation of regional governance framework for security issues. State policies may be designed through governmental leadership, or it may be understood as an outcome of domestic political process.

3.1 Power Structure: Structural-Realist Approach
Realists argue that regional security management is closely related to

regional power distribution and global systemic factors.[12] Consideration of power relationship should be located at the core of any analysis of security issues. Hypothetically, when regional structure is uni-polar, the region will be relatively autonomous from outside interference.[13] It is easier to manage negative security externalities. Western Hemisphere is an example of regional unipolarity, where the US is a preponderant power.

In a multi-polar region such as the Asia-Pacific and Middle East, competition among regional powers is severer. Though relatively autonomous from intervention of external powers, cooperation for conflict management will be problematic without a predominant hegemonic power. 'Concert of powers' may appear at best. On the other hand, a bi-polar regional system will also be relatively competitive. Because regional powers of both sides are prone to appeal to outside powers, the region will be less autonomous.

In comparison with the global system that is virtually closed, regional systems are more open and frequently subject to intervention by outside actors.[14] The more competitive the global system becomes, the more constraints will be posed on the region. As witnessed in the Cold War era, in a bi-polar global system, constraints on regional governance were most binding. A uni-polar global system will pose relatively small constraints on regional systems.

Global powers such as the US and former Soviet Union used to penetrate regional systems during the Cold War. Buzan describes this phenomenon as an 'overlay'. However, in the loose global system of the post-Cold War period, great powers are prone to intervene even without substantial interests, motivated by extra-regional interests or domestic political factors. The US intervention in Somalia is such an example. Moreover, global powers can be substantive members of regions. In the West Balkan security complex, the US maintains its troops in the region. According to realists, power distribution is a fundamental underlying factor constraining modes of regional security management. Nevertheless,

---

[12] Lake, *op.cit.*, 60.
[13] *Ibid*, 60.
[14] *Ibid*, 62; Buzan, *op.cit.*, 198.

structural-realist hypothesis fails to fully explain variations in modes of cooperation. It cannot predict, for instance, the emergence of different types of cooperative security regimes (be it OSCE or ARF) in Europe and Asia respectively.

3.2 (Non) Security Externalities: Rationalist-Neorealist Approaches
Perception of regional members about one or a combination of externalities within the given RSC is likely to lead to some kind of regional security governance. If regional security governance is regarded as the management of externalities in the region, conflict management then becomes a 'public good.' Consequently, the larger the externality, the more it will influence states' actions. And the more costly to eliminate negative spillover by one country, the less likely states successfully modify individual behavior.[15] Hence, demands for cooperation will increase. When ad hoc cooperation accompanies transaction costs, there will be support for a security regime to reduce such costs.

The extent to which externality in a given region affects actors will be diverse among actors and create different preferences among them. Specific forms of security cooperation have to be negotiated by regional actors based on their preferences.[16] Outcomes of coordination can be the re-stabilization of a regional balance of power by consultation; institutionalization of dialogue between regional powers; creation of confidence-building measures; or creation of regional security regimes.

Concern over domestic instability and social disorder also becomes a reason for members to form some type of regional framework. The ASEAN and GCC states constructed their own regional arrangements because of their concern over regime's stability and desirability to coordinate their policies against domestic insecurity.[17] Non-security

---

[15] Lake, *op.cit.*, 50.
[16] Lake, *op.cit.*, 53-55.
[17] Rosemary Foot, "Pacific Asia: The Development of Regional Dialogue," in Louise Fawcett and Andrew Hurrell eds., *Regionalism in World Politics: Regional Organization and International Order* (Oxford: Oxford University Press, 1997), 95; Imanuel Adler and Michael Barnett, "Studying Security Communities in Theory,

externalities such as transaction costs in promoting economic interests might trigger security cooperation in order to create a more stable environment. For instance, foreign direct investments rely heavily on expectations that recipient countries are free from social and political risks.

In turn, domestic conflicts often have 'externalities' at a regional level (and in rare cases at a global level). Regional actors became interested in controlling internal conflicts, partly because they desire to control externalities originating from internal conflicts that would subsequently affect themselves. Increasing perception of externalities create regional interests in the management of internal conflict.

Traditionally internal turmoil or disorder is a matter to be controlled by a sovereign state. Russia intervened in Chechen conflict regarding it as a domestic issue. Governments of ASEAN countries are in agreement to treating internal conflict as matter of exclusive domestic jurisdiction. However, if we observe a relatively dominant current trend, various regional organizations and regimes have addressed their willingness and readiness to control internal conflicts in their respective regions. OSCE and NATO in Europe and ECOWAS in West Africa are such examples. At the global level, since the late 1980s, one of the most important tasks for the UN has become the resolution of ethnic and internal conflicts. This was clearly expressed in Boutros-Ghali's *Agenda for Peace* and other UN reports. Due to UN's financial and physical constraints, UN member states occasionally prefer to leave substantial management of internal conflict to the regions. Thus, regional perspective is relevant for analysis of internal conflicts, especially in view of changing situations after the Cold War.

Hypothetically it is assumed that, for management of internal conflicts, existing frameworks or mechanisms (if there is any) for controlling inter-state conflicts are employed. But internal conflicts or other externalities emanating from regional conflict complex (RCC) can strengthen or transform tasks and the nature of such regional establishments. Conceptual redefinition of meaning(s) of 'security' in the

---

Comparison, and History," in Adler and Barnett, *Security Communities*, 415.

2. Patterns of Regional Security Management: an Overview of Developments in Europe and East Asia

1990s such as the renewed focus on internal conflicts and transnational threats in Europe led to the transformation and reorganization of regional security institutions. This includes transformation of NATO from an alliance against the Soviet bloc to the one characterized by more comprehensive and cooperative nature. Other examples are EU activism in civilian aspect of crisis management and new peacekeeping tasks.

3.3 Identities and Norms: Constructivist Approach
Material factors alone do not shape regional governance patterns. The constructivist approach introduces concepts of identity and norm to the study of regional security. It examines how regional identity and interests are socially constructed in order to see how regions are inter-subjectively defined. Such explanation includes hypothesis about how regional 'we-feeling' is shaped, states' interests are transformed, and subsequently how such shared identity contributes to the creation of regional security communities. An increase in social communication and social learning is emphasized in the process of identity creation.[18] Some studies of this strand emphasize how national elites are publicly and informally engaged in the process of creating a cognitive region.

Constructivist approach and rationalists alike emphasize the institutional aspects. For the latter, institutions reduce transaction costs pertaining to the establishment of ad hoc mechanism for conflict management. For constructivists, institutions play a role in engaging social actors and states in imagining themselves as sharing common norms and identity. Furthermore institutions become a place for identity formation, which produces additionally shared identity and interests.

Constructivist institutions cannot be separated from power considerations. Occasionally major systemic changes in power configulation lead to reformulation of identities, and in such cases institutions become a site where politics of recognition and legitimization take place. The end of the Cold War, the collapse of the Soviet Empire, and the demise of Yugoslavia precipitated reconsiderations of identities in

---

[18] *Ibid*, 415.

Europe and political and security arrangements such as the NATO and EC/EU.

A constructivist study suggests, on the other hand, that a flow of negative externalities (such as illegal drugs) from neighbors decreases the degree of mutual trust, and lead to prospective decline in security communities.[19] In this case, the rationalist approach may be more appropriate in explaining emergence of policy coordination to eliminate such threats. Furthermore, security communities might not emerge between two asymmetrical powers such as in the relationship between US and Mexico.[20] It will raise a sense of vulnerability associated with proximity on the part of the weak and help maintain a low level of trust. As such example demonstrates, there is a need to examine interest and power factors again even when identity formation is the central concern for scholars.

Another strand of sociological and cognitive explanation focuses on 'isomorphism,' in other words, how agents in international system (states and other actors) replicate internationally dominant trends, norms and modalities. For instance, the OSCE's practice and rules developed in the last two decades, such as preventive diplomacy and confidence-building, inspired other regional organizations. Nonetheless, regional 'cultural' and 'historical' contexts undoubtedly influence specific modalities of (non) cooperation. Uniqueness of the so-called "ASEAN-Way," collegial consensus-building style and informal nature of political process also affected modalities of cooperative security regime of ARF. Sociological institutionalists emphasize diffusion of western culture and norms, but established patterns or regimes are rather 'embedded' in specific regional contexts.

3.4 Domestic Level Explanation

Political scientists have also tried to explain regional modes of security

---

[19] Imanuel Adler and Michael Barnett, "Security Communities in Theoretical Perspective," in Adler and Barnett, *Security Communities*, 22.

[20] Guadalupe Gonzalez and Stephan Haggard, "The United States and Mexico: A Pluralistic Security Communities," in Adler and Barnett, *Security Communities*, 325.

management from a domestic perspective. Some paid attention to regional security cooperation in terms of state-promoted policies, to explain why states have to claim regionalist policies. As already mentioned, such policies are pursued to secure national stability against perceived externalities, or they might be driven by strongly shared regional identity. Today, state leaders in democratic countries are increasingly subject to pressures by political parties, interest groups and the public opinion. Hence, regionalist policies are often shaped by political leadership and through a complex domestic political process.

4. Typology of Regional Security Governance

Regional security management may entail the coordination of actions on ad hoc basis without institutionalization, the institutionalization of regular meetings, or the creation of formal institutions. Such management styles will include 1) balance of power, 2) concert of powers, 3) regional cooperative security, 4) regional collective security, 5) (pluralistic) security community, and 6) integration.[21]

4.1 Balance of Power/ Concert of Powers
Regional balance of power is constrained by power distribution at the global level. Furthermore regionally unique patterns emerge as a consequence of regional power distribution as well as patterns of enmity/amity between regional members. If there is no perception about enmity, there will be no need for balance of power. Balance of power becomes observable, when there is no reliable collective security mechanism to protect regional states from physical threats.
Alliance is a concept closely related to balance of power. Under the

---

[21] This typology is based on Morgan's study. Patrick Morgan, "Regional Security Complexes and Regional Orders," in Lake and Morgan eds., *Regional Orders*, 32-33. Morgan dose not include regional cooperative security in his classification, but considering increasing importance of management of non-conventional conflicts, the concept of cooperative security is incorporated into this typology.

bipolar system of the Cold War, relatively stable alliance system emerged in European continent between the NATO and Warsaw Pact. Asian experience after the WWII showed a more diverse picture, and the region was marked not only by global bipolar competition but also by rivalry among China, the Soviet Union and the US.

Concert of powers is a governance system similar to balance of power. But it presupposes some kind of coordinated behavior based on shared rules among regional powers, such as seen in the 19th century Europe. They are not formal rules, but regional powers expect other members to obey certain codes of conduct, and when necessary they might arrange consultations. Even today, operation of concert system can be observed. For instance in the management of Bosnia, formal decision-making body was the ICFY (established by the EU and UN in 1992), but an ad hoc Contact Group (US, Russia, Germany, France and Britain) made the actual and more significant decisions.

4.2 Cooperative Security

Cooperative security is defined as a framework in which potential sources of diffuse and unclear threats exist within. Based on the comprehensive approach, measures employed against such threats or dangers are usually non-military. The main function of cooperative security system is the provision for dialogue among members and prevention of conflicts. Yamamoto clarified different stages of "cooperative security" that may be incorporated into the above definition.[22] Methods taken by cooperative security regimes range from 1) trust-building through dialogues, 2) preventive diplomacy, 3) conflict resolution, to 4) confidence-building and security measures/ arms control.

Characteristics of regional cooperative security framework differ according to the degree of commitment by regional members and institutionalization. They range from trust-building through dialogues such as seen in the practice of the ARF since 1994, to the military confidence and security-building measures and preventive diplomacy or conflict

---

[22] Yamamoto, "Reisen go no anzenhosho," 26-38.

management developed in the OSCE area after the end of the Cold War. In the last decade the OSCE's practice is increasingly targeting internal conflicts and trans-border dangers. Albeit with some limitation, in 1995, the ARF also introduced the concept of preventive diplomacy, though this excludes border disputes among members and human rights issues.

If regional members agree to collective employment of military measures such as peace-keeping and peace-enforcement, the framework could be regarded as a regional collective security system. In case of Europe, the CSCE's Helsinki II Document of 1992 refers to peace-keeping under the CSCE, though it has not been realized. Though at an early stage, the new collective security concept has begun to incorporate military management of internal conflicts and trans-border dangers, in addition to traditional inter-state wars as the founding fathers of UN initially assumed.

Global power distribution constrains the possibility of cooperative or collective security. When constraints (over-lay) posed by the competitive global system are too tight, as they were during the Cold War period, governance systems for regional security, other than the balance of power, are not easily established. The current uni-polar system has created a more permissive environment for bourgeoning multi-lateral regional security frameworks. Finally, the main factors encouraging the creation and accelerate the growth of cooperative security frameworks are the perception of externalities within the region, and regional actors' acceptance of common norms.

4.3 Security Communities/ Integration
Rationalist explanation asserts that cooperative security frameworks emerge as a consequence of the existence of potential threats, and of the framework's members' perception of externalities arising from those threats within the system. On the contrary, constructivist explanation emphasizes the psychological and identity aspects in the development of security communities, and how the process of communication contributes to the socialization of norms among member states.

A (pluralistic) security community is defined as a region where sovereign states exist but no organized violence occurs between them, because people in the region share dependable expectations of peaceful change in resolving disputes.[23] North America and West Europe are undoubtedly security communities in this regard. The European approach to security, in a sense, has been to promote integration, exemplified by the creation of the EC/EU. ASEAN and OSCE regions may be on the long way towards the formulation of security communities as well.

As already seen, some functions of cooperative security are specifically intended for building regional security communities. Various policies and practices are invented to promote dialogues and to support the internalization and institutionalization of norms (such as human rights and rule of law in certain European cases). In the previous decade, the Council of Europe, EU and OSCE have introduced schemes to enhance the socialization of such norms into new member states.

The concept of a security community could be extended to the relationships among social actors as well. Concepts such as social communication and common identity formation, which are used in analyzing pluralistic security communities, could be similarly employed for inter-ethnic or inter-group relations. The importance of sub-regional confidence-building approach to resolving internal conflicts is clear. When countries with a potential risk of internal conflict have existed in the periphery, European countries extended preventive measures to outside areas by effecting a complicated combination of policies such as economic and/or legal arrangements, and consolidation into a common European identity. For example, regional members' awareness about the special characteristics of West Balkan RCC has engendered a 'sub-regional approach.' The West Balkan RCC is now treated as a sub-regional system in post-conflict peace-building process in the framework of the Stability Pact for Southeast Europe. This approach encourages not only confidence-building between countries that were previously engaged in conflict, but is also prospective of formal or informal integration of those peripheral countries into the European region.

Figure 2-1 shows a summary of modes of regional security

---

[23] Imanuel Adler and Michael Barnett, "A Framework for the Study of Security Communities," in Adler and Barnett eds., *Security Communities*, 30.

2. Patterns of Regional Security Management: an Overview of Developments in Europe and East Asia

Figure 2-1 Characteristics of RSC and subsequent Regional Governance

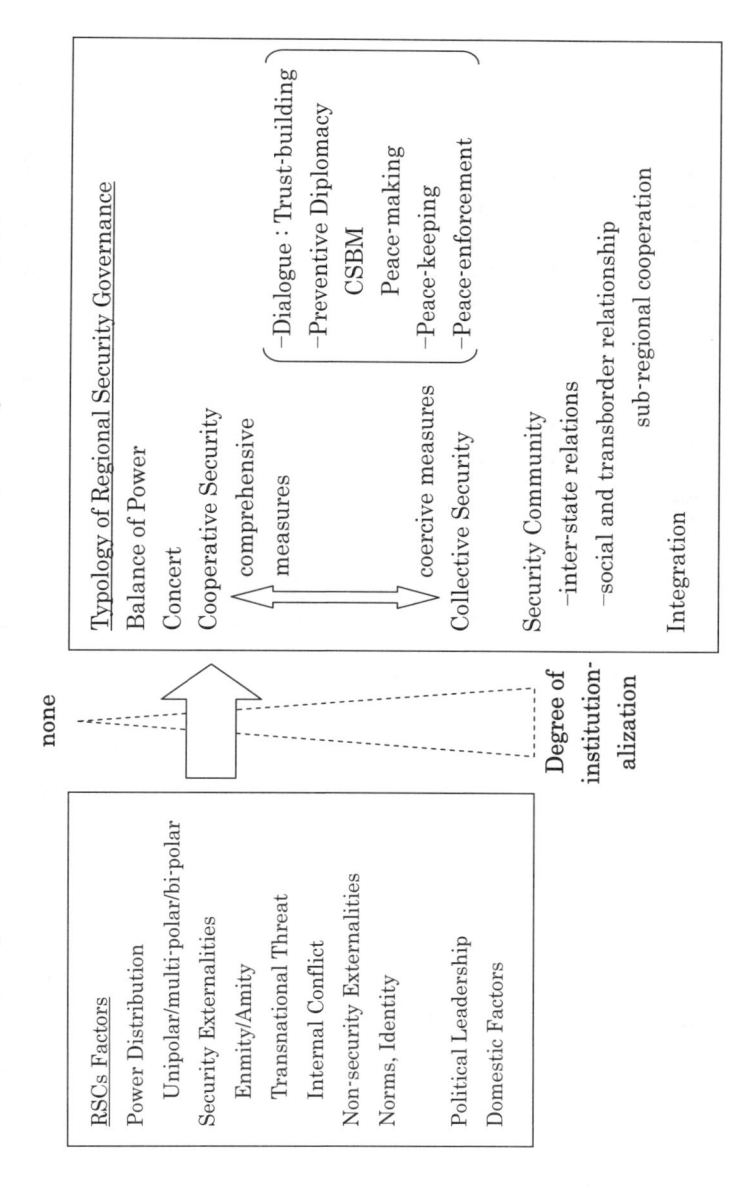

Typology of Regional Security Governance
- Balance of Power
- Concert
- Cooperative Security
  - comprehensive measures ⟷ coercive measures
    - Dialogue : Trust-building
    - Preventive Diplomacy
    - CSBM
    - Peace-making
    - Peace-keeping
    - Peace-enforcement
- Collective Security
- Security Community
  - inter-state relations
  - social and transborder relationship
  - sub-regional cooperation
- Integration

Degree of institutionalization: none →

RSCs Factors
- Power Distribution
  - Unipolar/multi-polar/bi-polar
- Security Externalities
  - Enmity/Amity
  - Transnational Threat
  - Internal Conflict
- Non-security Externalities
  - Norms, Identity
- Political Leadership
- Domestic Factors

Part I: Issues in the Development of the European Union

Figure 2-2 Factors Conducive to balance of power

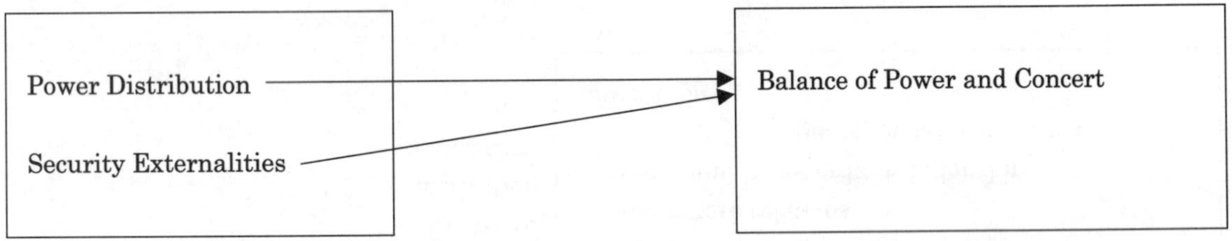

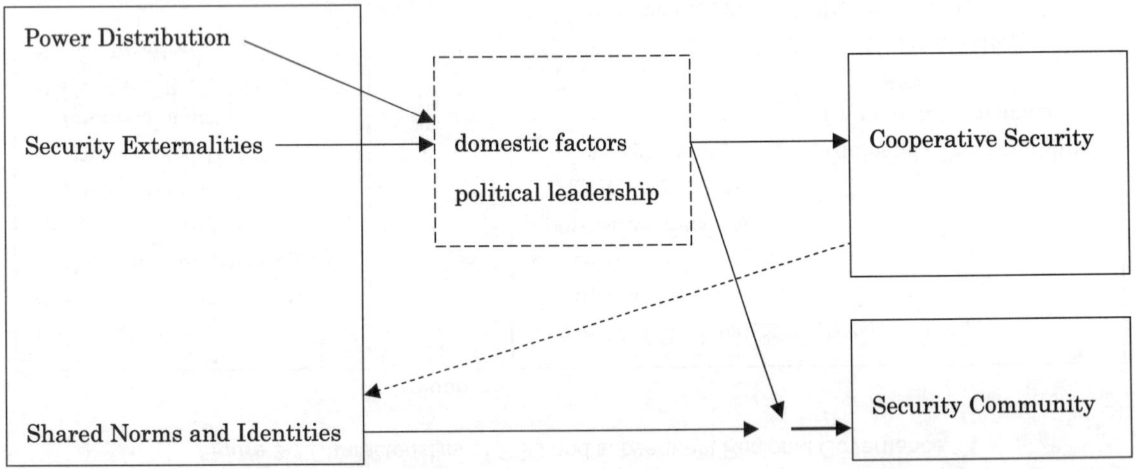

Figure 2-3 Factors Conducive to Cooperative Security and Security Community

management and contributing factors. As Figure 2-2 demonstrates, the realist model is located at the upper scale. Figure 2-3 suggests that for the creation of a cooperative security framework, security externalities are relevant factors and are often intervened in by domestic political factors of the member states. Social communication and shared norms are important factors in explaining the formation of security communities. Though it is meaningful to single out particular factor(s) that foster a specific pattern of regional cooperation, normally several factors contribute to the formation of cooperation. For instance the creation of cooperative security regimes and security communities are not free from the constraints of the international and regional power configuration. In the following section, patterns of regional security management in Europe and Asia will be outlined based on perspectives previously argued.

5. European and East Asian Experiences Revisited

5.1 Security Management in Europe
After the Second World War, the Cold War brought about a provisional stability on European continent. The US-Soviet confrontation at the global level worked as an 'overlay' that stymied the reemergence of indigenous patterns of security relations in Europe. It effectively contained the resurgence of regional hegemony by Germany and deterred instabilities that might have risen from Southeastern Europe. This global 'overlay' influenced the modalities of European security cooperation.

European integration was an important component of US policy, intending to strengthen its allies' capacity to defend against the Soviet threat. The provisions of the Marshall Plan, the set-up of the Organization for European Economic Cooperation (OEEC), and West Germany's rearmament within the framework of NATO were initiated under American pressure. West European integration was sub-regional within a wider trans-Atlantic security community. At the same time, West European integration was structured around the security dilemmas of France and West Germany. The establishment of the European Coal and Steel Community was designed to put old rivalries behind them and launch into greater economic cooperation in Western Europe to overcome (non)security externalities. Despite failing to agree on the European Defense Community, forty years of effort to transform economic and social relations in West Europe was able to ease national antagonism that existed between major powers in the region. Commonality of culture and history also worked favorably in creating a sense of community.

European détente in the first half of the 1970s developed under the structural constraints of the US-Soviet relationship. However, the origins of détente stemmed from a separate movement in European countries dissatisfied with the long-lasting division of the region and the astringent confrontation between the two blocks. Non-aligned and neutral countries initiated active movements in searching for common ground between the East and West. Then West German chancellor Willy Brandt introduced a new Ostpolitik, which accepted the Eastern boundaries in the hope of long-term transformation and liberalization within communist regimes.[24]

The Conference on Security and Cooperation in Europe represented the loosening of bipolarity. Perceptions about security externalities arising from the division of Europe were articulated in agendas for the prospective Conference in Europe. These security externalities were not necessarily symmetrically perceived. For West European governments, externalities had to include such issues as reunification of family members. For the Soviets, consolidation and legitimization of their sphere of influence was the major priority stemming from their vulnerability. Although the Soviets were merely paying lip service in agreeing to the Helsinki norms, as well as tactically linking stipulations to their own benefits, a new process of communication and consultation was gradually institutionalized in the follow-up meetings through the 1970s and 80s.

The end of Cold War meant the removal of global 'overlay.' The effect was the biggest where the Cold War imposed itself most strongly.[25] The theory of regional security complex suggests that, after the release of the Cold War 'overlay,' distinct regional security dynamics would emerge.

---

[24] Helga Haftendorn, *Sicherheit und Entspannung* (Baden-Baden: Nomos Verlags Gesellschaft, 1983).

[25] Buzan, "The Post-Cold War Asia-Pacific Security Order," 140.

2. Patterns of Regional Security Management: an Overview of Developments in Europe and East Asia

It argues that the local patterns of amity/enmity and balance of power will be reactivated. As William Wallace assumes, however, it would be "easier to build and maintain regional order within a stable global order" and it would be more unproblematic "to build a regional order under the impetus of external pressures and external leadership than through agreement among the major regional powers," let alone "pressure by a potentially hegemonic regional power."[26] Though the demise of the Cold War caused a short-lived euphoria about the future of European order, it became gradually clear that removal of the global 'overlay' invigorated underlying indigenous security relations and regional balance of power considerations. On the other hand, former communist states desired the extension of the West European 'security community' to the Northeast and Southeast. They identified themselves culturally and historically as a part of 'Europe' and laid claims for accession to the European Community and NATO. The prospective new members' desire and self-image that they should be regarded as a part of 'Europe' was an important and accelerating factor in the process.

In the Paris Charter of 1990, members of the OSCE announced the release of Europe from the Cold War 'overlay.' Structural changes during this period might have caused the dissolution of regional security arrangements developed during the Cold War. However, the end of the division of Europe was followed by developments such as collapse of the Soviet Union and Yugoslavia. These events triggered internal civil conflicts in Southeastern Europe and former Soviet republics, in areas geographically close to Western European countries, which, in turn, became concerned about increased risks of instability in transitional areas. Since then, the perception among European states of potential and actual externalities from unstable transitional societies has played a significant role in the transformation and the redefinition of European security organizations.

European security institutions are now tasked with extending the

---

[26] William Wallace, "Regionalism in Europe: Model or Exception?" in Fawcett and Hurrell eds., *Regionalism in World Politics*, 227.

security community beyond its current borders, towards the Northeast and Southeast. Soon it became clear that Russia's earlier maneuver to place the OSCE as central organization of European security failed. During the 1990s security organizations in Europe began to shape 'layers' of security arrangements with NATO as its pillar. Security in Europe became more dependent on the NATO's new cooperative arrangements stretched to the non-member states. Such supplementary arrangements include the Euro-Atlantic Partnership Council and the Partnership for Peace, and later, the expansion of NATO eastwards.

New tasks were assigned for other European security arrangements. The European Union, the OSCE and the Council of Europe were set to work complementarily to the peace assured by NATO. In the early 1990s, West European countries were heading towards higher integration and launched the Common Foreign and Security Policy in 1992, though they have not been yet accustomed to reconciling their differences. The CFSP was also intended at binding a united Germany more closely to its western neighbors.[27] Partly due to uncertainty about the continuity of US military involvement, especially in view of similar conflicts such as in Bosnia and Kosovo, European countries, headed by Germany and France, had to develop European defense identity and prepare combined joint task forces. The expectations about EU's role in the field of conflict management in European peripheries have only increased rapidly.

Some regarded the OSCE as a practical cooperative security organization better suited to cope with non-traditional threats. European governments equipped the OSCE with new institutions such as an early warning mechanism, including the HCNM (High Commissioner for National Minorities) and Conflict Prevention Center. The OSCE's characteristics could be termed 'seminar diplomacy' which integrates academic experiences and diplomatic discourse. Constructivist theory emphasizes the importance of such a process as the socialization and internalization of norms. For constructivists, the main method for transnational dialogue, a key mechanism for transmitting or 'teaching'

---

[27] Wallace, *op.cit.*, 221.

2. Patterns of Regional Security Management: an Overview of Developments in Europe and East Asia

norms and practices of cooperative security, is to allow elites and civil societies to identify with each other and construct common understandings.[28]

However, it has become clear that pan-European norms have not yet been fully shared among member states, especially at a sub-national level. In this sense, it is too early to label the OSCE area as a security community. Civil wars and inhumane practices in the former Yugoslavia were shocking examples. After the Bosnian conflict and the Kosovo war, it became increasingly recognized that norm sharing must be also targeted at sub-national level, local communities as well as trans-border areas. Regional organizations such as the EU, OSCE and Council of Europe are now targeting local communities and civil societies by introducing democratic norms. The EU began to stress the importance of sub-regional cooperation originally for East European candidates, and after the Kosovo war, for Southeast European states as well. This practice was aimed at helping them satisfy the conditions for EU membership and at promoting confidence-building at the micro level. This reemphasizes the importance of security community-building from the societal level, as Deutsch affirmed.

To summarize, European experiences from 1945 were largely constrained by global 'overlay.' Emergent patterns were the bipolar alliance systems of NATO and Warsaw Pact. At the same time, West European countries carried on with the integration of the European Community not only for economic reasons, but also in order to steer long-existing hostile relations toward a more stable security community and to consolidate their position against threats by Communist countries. Removal of the global 'overlay' triggered a revival of regional security patterns as well as increased uncertainties about the US commitment in the region. NATO formulated a New Strategic Concept in response to the changing international structure. The reorganization of regional security arrangements was observed. Governments have been faced with exigent task of effectively utilizing several regional organizations, based on

---

[28] Adler and Barnett, "Security Communities in Theoretical Perspective," 18.

division of labor, with a purpose of stretching the West European security community to the transitional societies in new Europe.

5.2 Security Management in East Asia

Experiences of regional cooperation have been very limited in Southeast Asia, and especially so in the case of Northeast Asia. Balance of power continues to be the central mechanism of regional security management. After liberation from European and Japanese colonial domination, East Asia had become a site of global strategic competition between the United States and Soviet Union. Superpower 'overlay' to some degree prevented the emergence of strong indigenous security relations among the states of the region.[29]

In the long run, communist states in the region did not show internal cohesiveness. By 1960 China emerged as an independent great power in the region. It strategically changed its allegiance with the Soviets in the 1950s to anti-Soviet alignment with the US in the 1970s. Regional order was centered on bilateral military alliances with the United States or the Soviet Union (and later China), whereas there was little horizontal linkage among countries that allied with the same superpower.

After the demise of the Cold War, it was expected that the removal of the constraints imposed by US-Soviet rivalry would release the indigenous diversity in Asia. The Soviet power ceased to be a major actor and would no longer pose threats and could no longer promise support to its ex-allies. In the Southeast Asia, changes took place, such as the improvement of ASEAN's relationship with Vietnam and Cambodia. It was, however, unclear how long the US commitment to regional security would continue in the future. China's emerging influence, with its military build-up and rapid economic growth, bred uncertainty. Unlike the situation in Europe, traditional military threats and nuclear proliferation still remained a major source of externalities. Most of the bilateral alliances would continue to exist, though they were subjected to a redefinition of roles, such as Japan's acceptance of more 'responsibility' in neighboring seas.

---

[29] Buzan, "The Post-Cold War Asia-Pacific Security Order," 136.

2. Patterns of Regional Security Management: an Overview of Developments in Europe and East Asia

Removal of the superpower 'overlay' means that each region will probably have to deal with indigenous insecurities by itself. There has been, however, no clear historical record of experiences to help manage such regional discrepancies. Nor has there been a common threat perception in the region since 1945.[30] In Southeast Asia, external threats emanated largely from the communist expansion of China and Vietnam, but the perception of that threat did not converge among regional members. The importance of domestic concerns in ASEAN countries has been rather noteworthy.[31] Concerns over domestic vulnerabilities in each state, especially concerning communist insurgency at home and the stability of their regimes, were more commonly shared in the region.

In Northeast Asia, Chinese and Korean distrust of Japan has been a considerable obstacle in establishing cooperative framework, let alone in deepening a 'we-feeling' toward a 'cognitive region.' Unlike Europe, no regional security framework has been built after 1945 that would render Japan more acceptable in the region. This stands in stark contrast with Europe, where multilateral arrangements such as NATO and EC/EU incorporated former enemy states into West European security community. Japan was locked into a bilateral alliance with the United States, and no security ties with South Korea and other neighbors were developed. In Northeast Asia, until recently there had been a limited number of elements binding its states and societies together.

In responding to uncertainties caused by global structural change in the late 1980s, several ideas about a multilateral security framework were proposed. Proponents of such comprehensive multilateral framework were, then-Soviet President Michael Gorbachev, Australian Foreign Minister, Gareth Evans, and Canadian State Secretary for External Affairs, Joe Clark. They assumed that a cooperative security regime should be built in Asia that would mirror a European model. However, their earlier proposals were vigorously attacked by the United States, because at that

---

[30] Foot, *op.cit.*, 230.
[31] Adler and Barnett, "Security Communities in Theoretical Perspective," 19; Amitav Achara, "Collective Identity and Conflict Management in South-East Asia," in Adler and Barnett, *Security Communities*, 198-227.

time, the Bush administration still believed bilateral alliances should be the only reliable measure to secure regional stability in Asia.[32] Several East Asian leaders also criticized the idea, since they believed European model would be inappropriate in the distinct context of Asia. Asian skeptics asserted that formal multilateral framework would not be appropriate for Asia, and that cultural, economic, and political diversity in the region would not allow a common framework to emerge.

ASEAN members desired that the US continue to be engaged in some form in the region and that potential regional powers such as China and Japan were locked into a dialogue. The ASEAN Post Ministerial Conference of July 1991 became an important starting point for multilateral security dialogue. By 1993 the Clinton administration came to support the idea of regional dialogue, as long as the US could fully participate. In July 1993, ASEAN announced the establishment of the ARF including the seven dialogue partners plus China and Russia and observers Vietnam, Laos and Papua New Guinea. The dialogue framework that emerged from ASEAN came to encompass states of the larger Pacific Asia. In 1993, the Council for Security and Cooperation in Asia Pacific (CSCAP) was established to foster future-oriented discussion on regional security. It incorporates the so-called 'track two' dialogue process involving academics and officials acting in a private capacity. Such arrangements have been a non-formalistic mechanism of dialogue and consultation among regional members, what Robert Scalapino called a 'soft regionalism.' Member states of ARF as well as 'track two' specialists of CSCAP have established mechanism of dialogue in order to build a "community" among them. It can be regarded as a highly self-conscious region-building to promote socialization of elites and to manage conflict. However, it should be still located at a very early stage of cooperative security, and much too early to call it a security community.

In Northeast Asia, the current regional security complex consists of Russia, the US, China, Japan, ROK, DPRK, Mongolia, and Taiwan, and it

---

[32] Paul Kerr, Andrew Mack and Paul Evans, "The Evolving Security Discourse," in Andrew Mack and John Ravenhill eds., *Pacific Cooperation: Building Economic and Security Regimes in the Asia-Pacific Region* (Boulder: Westview Press, 1995), 236.

is roughly multi-polar (with US as the global power, and Russia, China and Japan as regionally influential powers.) Management of security issues is basically based on the balance of power between China and the US. After the WW II, this system's major objectives had been balancing out China and containing Japanese military expansion. The collapse of the Cold War structure challenged bilateral alliances with the United States, but lasting uncertainties in the region did not easily allow alliances to dissolve. In the mid-1990s, Japan and the US reconfirmed their bilateral alliance and prolongation of US involvement in the area, although Japan now has to take more responsibility for its own security and regional stability.

In the past decade, the externality from North Korean issues increasingly became significant among regional states, and this perception of common interests has led to greater concert among major powers, such as the six nations consultation framework for North Korea. Realists commonly view that the post-Cold War Asia will witness militarily and economically strong China. This observation stresses the relevance of the balance of power concept as analytical tool as well as actual government policy. Nevertheless a possibility that cooperative security measures might complement (though it seldom replaces) policies of balance of power should not be discounted. ASEAN members have not resorted to military measures since its establishment. Though it cannot be regarded as full security community, it has discernible foundations for a security community. There have been slow but gradual developments in East Asia in terms of the multilateralism and institutionalization of security management.

6. Conclusion

Current regional security in East Asia is governed mainly by balance of power, but an early stage of cooperative security is also emerging. US bilateral alliances with the Philippines, Korea and Japan remain the key to the stability of the region. This mainly owes itself to a severe power configuration and historical patterns of enmity/amity. Even under such severe circumstances, the process for a gradual development of a cooperative security framework, through ARF and CSCAP's dialogue and political confidence-building efforts, have become relatively tenable. This is mainly due to perceived externalities and political will, especially on the part of ASEAN members and other regional powers.

The West European pattern has characteristically belonged to categories between that of a security community and integration. To the East and South, various kinds of cooperative security measures have been offered to states that desire to become part of European security community. Perception about (non)security externalities, especially those originating from an uncertain environment, contributed to consolidation and revitalization of security arrangements, most importantly, NATO and EU.

Balance of power remains a persistent reality of international politics in both regions. However, combined with stability projected by military alliances, cooperative security regimes are also expected to improve regional environment by alleviating a security dilemma arising from balance of power policies. In the European case, a security community was built as result of the expansion of regional interdependence, regional social communication, and the existence of a common threat. However, the environment that enabled this security community was just as much a result of policies of national governments as it was a product of international power structure after 1945. Since both cases in Europe and East Asia are embedded in their specific regional contexts, it is not realistic to simply apply the European model to East Asia. Asia and its sub-regions should design security mechanisms suited to their particular environment. Now we must assume that it will require a gradual, long-term process before a security community would be built in East Asia.

References

Adler, Imanuel and Michael Barnett eds. *Security Communities.* Cambridge: Cambridge University Press, 1998.

Buzan, Barry. *People, States and Fear.* New York: Harvester Wheatsheaf, 1991.
Fawcett, Louise and Andrew Hurrell eds. *Regionalism in World Politics: Regional Organization and International Order.* Oxford: Oxford University Press, 1997.
Haftendorn, Helga. *Sicherheit und Entspannung.* Baden-Baden: Nomos Verlags Gesellschaft, 1983.
Hagman, Hans-Christian. *European Crisis Management and Defense: The Search for Capabilities* (Adelphi Paper 353). The International Institute for Strategic Studies, 2002.
Lake, David and Patrick Morgan eds. *Regional Orders: Building Security in a New World.* University Park: Pennsylvania State University Press, 1997.
Mack, Andrew and John Ravenhill eds. *Pacific Cooperation: Building Economic and Security Regimes in the Asia-Pacific Region.* Boulder: Westview Press, 1995.
Wallensteen, Peter and Margareta Sollenberg. "Armed Conflict and Regional Conflict Complexes." *Journal of Peace Research*, vol. 35, no. 5, 1998, 623-624.
Yamamoto, Yoshinobu. "Kyocho teki anzenhosho no kanousei" (Possibilities of Cooperative Security), *Kokusai Mondai* (International Affairs), no. 425, 1995, 2-20.
Yamamoto, Yoshinobu. "Reisen go no anzenhosho: kyocho teki anzenhosho to shinraijosei wo megutte" (Post-Cold War Security: Cooperative Security and Confidence-Building). In Kimura, Hiroshi ed. *Kokusai kiki gaku (Studies on International Crisis),* Tokyo: Sekaishiso sha, 2002, 26-58.

CHAPTER 3

MAKING REGIONALISM LEGITIMATE?: EUROPEAN INTEGRATION AND BEYOND

Ariyoshi OGAWA

1. Introduction: The Debate over Post-National Legitimacy

Does it make sense to ponder the legitimacy of international, supranational, or transnational organizations? True, democracy and legitimacy have been advocated as not only the banner of Euro-skeptic and antiglobalization arguments, but also one of the major official concerns about the institutional reform of the European Union (EU).[1] However, conventional knowledge of democracy seems no longer valid in discussing European or regional democracy. For, neither "demos" nor "sovereignty" can be identified or located, even if the post-national polities in the making are positively characterized as multi-level or cosmopolitan modes of governance.

There are at least three different ways of evaluating the state of democracy in the era of Europeanization:

    1. The critical evaluation in reference to national-democracy;

---

[1] Dublin European Council, Presidency Conclusions, Section IV, December 13 & 14, 1996.

2. The confirmative evaluation that refutes normative criticism by analogy;
3. The multivalent evaluation which views post-national legitimization as complex, fragmented or incompatible.

The first group of arguments is apprehensive about asymmetry between the kratos and the demos at the regional level. The kratos, that is the capabilities of international/regional institutions such as the Councils of Ministers, the European Commission (EC), or the European Court of Justice (ECJ), have grown substantially, while the peoples of Europe haves not created a demos with corresponding common identity and political representation. The European Parliament, which has acquired greater power since the Single European Act in 1986 and through the subsequent treaties, still cannot be ranked as a European legislature by national standards. The "European parties" and the European elections—with ever sliding turnouts—are perceived by voters as no more than sub-arenas of national party politics.[2]

Some scholars focus on socioeconomic and sociocultural prerequisites as well as on politico-institutional ones. Claus Offe argues that the cognitive framework as being "European" is not generally shared beyond a narrow segment of elites. The limited integration for economy of scale has left behind European-wide social and employment policy regimes. There is a tendency for social fragmentation, rather than for more innocent optimism of "subsidiarity," such as the "Padanian" secession movements in North Italy or the proposal for regional differentiation of the social security system in Germany (even if the same symbol of "subsidiarity" is used there).[3]

The second group of arguments, such as Giandomenico Majone's "regulatory state" theory, demarcates systems of specified competences,

---

[2] In the 1999 European Parliament election, the voter turnout dropped below 50 percent for the first time.

[3] Claus Offe, "The Democratic Welfare State in an Integrating Europe" in Michael Greven and Louis W. Pauly, eds., *Democracy beyond the State?: The European Dilemma and the Emerging Global Order* (Lanham: Rowman & Littlefield, 2000), pp. 82-84.

including the EU, from the national system. If one properly understands the European Community as the "regulatory model," i.e. a system that is not endowed with comprehensive legal or material competences but with specific functions and advantages to contributes to credible policy commitments. What is relevant is superior efficiency and accountability, rather than legitimization through electoral and majoritarian representation.[4]

In line with Majone, Andrew Moravscik dismisses the "democratic deficit" argument that suspects the European Union as a "superstate" (or bureaucratic despotism) in the making, which reveals illegitimate biases to a serious degree. The first basis of his counterargument is that the EU is an exceptionally weak federation without the full-fledged capacities of advanced industrial states—such as coercive force, budgetary power, extensive bureaucracy, and social and cultural policy. His second basis of argument is that, even if the Councils are far more influential than the European Parliament, the former is represented by the national governments directly elected by the citizens. So, there is no one-sided deprivation of democratic legitimacy. The third basis of his argument is that no modern liberal democracy is governed only by electoral and parliamentary activities but also by increasing delegation of power to nonparticipatory, nonmajoritarian institutions and experts: judges, expert officials, central bankers, and so on. Otherwise, contemporary democratic system with technical, political, and logistical complexity quickly becomes ungovernable. "The European constitutional order, like any other constitutional order, inhabits the world of the second-best."[5]

The multivalent evaluation of post-national legitimacy seems to have broader but intricate outlook over the discussion. Fritz Scharpf made an issue of incapacity of "positive integration" in the European integration

---

[4] Giandomenico Majone, "Europe's 'Democratic Deficit': The Question of Standards," *European Law Journal*, No. 4 (1998), pp. 5-28.

[5] Andrew Moravcsik, "Federalism in the European Union: Rhetoric and Reality," in Kalypso Nicolaidis and Robert Howse, eds., *The Federal Vision: Legitimacy and Levels of Governance in the United States and the European Union* (Oxford: Oxford University Press, 2001), pp. 179-87.

that has been constrained by supremacy of "negative integration" and the joint-decision trap.[6] In his following works, he is concerned about the gap between input-oriented and output-oriented dimensions of legitimacy, the latter of which is more and more sought through international problem-solution, often to the sacrifice of the former.[7]

Also presented is a picture of "fragmented legitimacy" that characterizes the state of Europeanized politics. What is observable is that there is no one "legitimacy," but only multiple legitimacies fraught by different actors, institutions, and reasons—such as technocratic, representative, judicial, and last but not least, social legitimacy claimed by various social movements/organizations.[8] The transnational social movement organizations at the European or Brussels level are, however, in a few cases directly representative of grassroots or the masses. Moreover, there are disparities of resources, knowledge, and thus of influence over policymaking among different social or public interest groups. For instance, the European Women's Lobby was successful in promoting the gender agenda before the Amsterdam IGC on the one hand, but the European advocacy groups for immigrants and refugees still remain subject to lack of influence and segmentation of national/ethnic groups.[9]

It is nearly a mission impossible to judge the post-national legitimacy

---

[6] Fritz W. Scharpf, "Negative and Positive Integration in the Political Economy of European Welfare States," in Gary Marks, Fritz W. Scharpf, Philippe C. Schmitter, and Wolfgang Streeck, *Governance in the European Union* (London: Sage, 1996), pp. 15-39.

[7] Fritz W. Scharpf, "Interdependence and Democratic Legitimation," in Susan J. Pharr and Robert D. Putnam, eds., *Disaffected Democracies: What's Troubling the Trilateral Countries?* (Princeton: Princeton University Press, 2000), pp. 101-20; Fritz W. Scharpf, *Governing in Europe: Effective and Democratic?* (Oxford: Oxford University Press, 1999).

[8] Ariyoshi Ogawa, "Yoroppaka to Seijiteki Seitosei" [Europeanization and Political Legitimacy], in Japan Association for Comparative Politics, ed., *EU no nakano Kokumin Kokka—Demokurashi no Henyo* [*Nation-States in the EU: Transformation of Democracy*] (Tokyo: Waseda University Press, 2003).

[9] Doug Imig and Sidney Tarrow, *Contentious Europeans: Protest and Politics in an Emerging Polity* (Lanham: Rowman and Littelfield, 2001).

3. Making Regionalism Legitimate?: European Integration and beyond

by a yardstick that satisfies all of the substantial standard (Majone), institutional standard (Dahl's polyarchy criteria), and radical/cosmopolitan democrat standard. At this point, it may be worth revisiting the definition of legitimacy.[10]

In his classical article on democratic political systems and their efficiency, effectiveness and legitimacy, Seymour Martin Lipset writes:

> [T]he stability of a given democratic system depends not only on the system's efficiency in modernization, but also upon the effectiveness and legitimacy of the political system. . . . By effectiveness is meant the actual performance of government as defined by the expectations of most members of a society, and the expectations of powerful groups within it which might threaten the system. . . . Legitimacy involves the capacity of a political system to engender and maintain the belief that existing political institutions are the most appropriate or proper ones for the society.[11]

Lipset's consideration on legitimacy goes beyond the stable democratic system, and suggests that "Legitimacy may be associated with many forms of political organization including oppressive one" and that a "crisis of legitimacy is a crisis of change."[12]

These points are relevant to our analysis on the legitimacy of European integration and that of other forms of regional cooperation. In this chapter, I will examine the prospects of emerging regional polities, by a very loose definition of legitimacy that purports to a long-term intersubjective belief that maintains the development of the integration

---

[10] See Offe's ironical but precise remark: "Everywhere, one reads the same thing: the European Union is a political construct sui generis—no (longer) a confederation not (yet) a federal state, but a 'would be polity'." It is an accurate but not very useful observation." Offe, op.cit., p. 63.

[11] Seymour Martin Lipset, "Some Social Requisites of Democracy: Economic Development and Political Legitimacy," *American Political Science Review*, No. 53 (1959), p. 86.

[12] Ibid., p. 87.

process.

Lipset stresses that a crisis of legitimacy is likely to occur, in a transitional system, if (a) the major groups do not secure "entry into politics" or, if (b) the status of major conservative institutions is threatened.

Point (a) should not be left out of consideration simply as "regulatory state" theory argues, and also should be located in broader frameworks than solely in the majoritarian one. Figure 3-1 is a revised conceptual framework derived from Michael Zürn's article, which suggest the democracy beyond the nation-state consists of a mixture of all these dimensions (deliberative/aggregative, individuals/organizations). I simplified the original figure and added the right side column (national representatives), for while both Zürn and I focus on the function of deliberative process, I put more emphasis on the deliberation by national representatives rather than that by sectoral representatives as Zürn, who brings together territorial and sectoral organizations in his original figure, and especially Joerges and his colleagues, who allege 'comitology' as deliberative process.[13]

Figure 3-1 Components of a Democratic Process beyond the Nation-state

Procedures	ACTORS		
	Individuals	Organizations	National Representative
Deliberative	Direct deliberative democracy	Expertocracy	Deliberative Convention
Aggregative	Majoritarian democracy	Bargaining Eurocracy	Intergovermentalism

Note: Original figure in Zürn 2000, Table 5.1, p.102.

In the context of national-democratic modernization, the monarchical institutions are regarded as the conservative institutions referred in point

---

[13] Christian Joerges, "'Good Governance' through Comitology?" in Christian Joerges and Ellen Vos, eds., *EU Committees: Social Regulation, Law and Politics* (Oxford: Hart Publishing, 1999).

(b), while in the context of European integration, they may correspond to "nation-states." These points will lead us to an analysis on the equilibrium between law and politics, or narrowing "Exit" and "Voice," as considered in the next section.

2. Aspects of Constitutionalization of Europe

Some scholars do not hesitate to declare the victory of supranationalism in reference to the development of rule-of-law in the European Community. Stone Sweet and his colleague present a three-factor hypothesis of supranational constitutionalization.[14]

The first factor is "contracts," or codified rules to enable dyadic exchange relationship between actors. The second factor is effective triadic dispute resolution to lower transaction costs and to enhance credibility of the contractants. This function is primarily provided by a judicial system, which hereby also performs a political function to consolidate and maintain the regime. The third factor is legislating (i.e., to elaborate legal rules or to generate new ones where none existed). Although both legislators and judges contribute to legislating, the latter may legislate before the former do, for the political process is likely to be less institutionalized and subject to collective action problems than the judicial process.

The ECJ has legitimized itself, either implicitly or explicitly, as the supreme interpreter of this constitution in its decisions since 1960s. Today, the ECJ refers to the founding treaties as the "constitution of the Community." With this view, Article 177 of the Rome treaty provided one of the most important terms of reference. According to this article, the judges in a national court are allowed or supposed to turn to the ECJ for an authoritative interpretation of the EC law that seems relevant in deciding

---

[14] Alec Stone Sweet and Thomas L. Brunell, "Constructing a Supranational Constitution: Dispute Resolution and Governance in the European Union," *American Political Science Review*, No. 92 (1998), pp. 63-81; Martin Shapiro and Alec Stone Sweet, *On Law, Politics, and Judicialization* (Oxford: Oxford University Press, 2002).

on the dispute.

The constitutionalization of the European Community in this legal sense is empirically confirmed by the steadily increasing references to the ECJ by national courts as is indicated in figure 3-2. The national judges were not equally ready for supranational legal supremacy, but the national supreme court of each "Member State" formally accepted the doctrine by the end of 1980s.[15]

Figure 3-2 Annual Number of Article 177 of the Rome Treaty Reference to the European Court of Justice

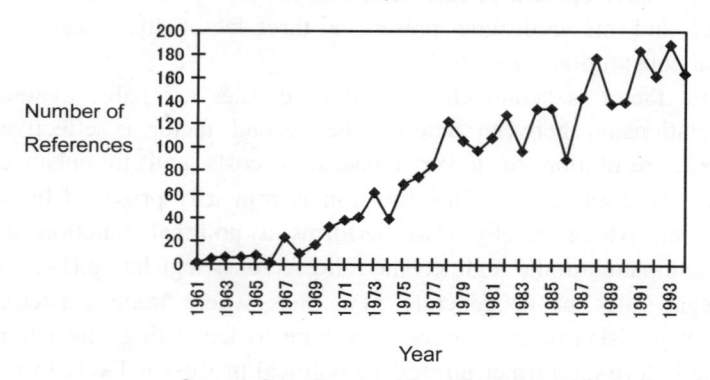

Sources: Stone Sweet and Brunell 1998, p. 67, Figure 1.

However, integration of legal and judicial order does not necessarily secure the political legitimacy. In the eyes of lawyers, the foundational process of the European Community would appear as an unprecedented development of supranational norms. This is regarded as "constitutionalization" from the legal point of view. Yet, the same historical phase was in turn observed by political scientists as resilient or having even strengthened intergovernmentalism, contrary to the expected supranational political integration.

Intriguingly, this gap of interpretation of European integration between lawyers and political scientists is not so much a paradox as sine

---

[15] Stone Sweet and Brunell, op. cit.

3. Making Regionalism Legitimate?: European Integration and beyond

qua non in the consolidation of the Community. We will look to Joseph Weiler's two-dimensional accounts on this point:

> Historically (and structurally) an equilibrium was established. On the one hand stood a strong constitutional process that, in radical mutation of treaty, linked the legal order of the Community with that of the Member States in a federal-like relationship. This was balanced by a relentless and equally strong process, also deviating radically from the Treaty that transferred political and decision-making power into a confederal procedure controlled by the Member States acting jointly and severally.[16]

Weiler bases the significance of such equilibrium mechanism on Albert O. Hirschman's classical thesis on "Exit," "Voice" and "Loyalty."[17] The Community obligations, once adopted, would foreclose the Exit of Member States, which occurred during the foundational period of the EC. Correspondingly, the Member States took control over Community decision making, in other words, assuring the Voice. The Commission has formally an exclusive power of proposal, but has been dependent on negotiations with COREPER, or the national experts and officials. The Luxembourg Accord in 1966 contained the decision making under the shadow of national veto. Representatives of the Member States also gained hand in regulation or management of the implementation stage.[18]

The Single European Act and constitutional transformation after 1992 engendered a major transformation of this equilibrium between the Exit and the Voice, or, between law and politics as I reformulate. In this phase of European integration, the qualified majority voting (QMV) regained generality. That accelerated some tendency of noncompliance by "opt-outs" or selective Exit (inter alia, Denmark and the United Kingdom),

---

[16] J.H.H. Weiler, *The Constitution of Europe: "Do the New Clothes Have an Emperor" and Other Essays on European Integration* (Cambridge: Cambridge University Press, 1999), pp. 35-36.

[17] Albert O. Hirschmann, *Exit, Voice and Loyalty: Response to Decline in Firms, Organizations and States* (Cambridge: Harvard University Press, 1970).

[18] Weiler, op.cit., pp. 30-31.

which made room for the variable geometry or multispeed tactics. Alternatively, Weiler also wondered if there is a general tendency toward loyalty. "[O]ne could look for evidence that the sustained period of equilibrium between Voice and Exit helped foster a loyalty to the new emergent polity in which Voice achieved through the normal channels of Community decision-making would be considered adequate."[19] But how would that possibly create "loyalty" beyond the "hard-core" Member States?

The concern for political restructuring from within the European Commission, in terms of efficiency, transparency, and legitimacy, was displayed by the White Paper on European governance, which contrived some "good governance" prescription such as the "open-method of coordination" or a more participatory approach with "civil society."[20]

But it was the speech at Humboldt University by the German Foreign Minister, Joschka Fischer in May 2000 that paved the way for the constitutional dialogue among the European leaders. In his speech, Fischer argued that the gradual process of mainly economic integration after 1950s with no blueprint for the "finality"—where the so-called "Monnet method" dominated—made only limited contribution to the political integration and democratization of Europe. In turn, he underlined the search for "Finalität" or the finality of European Union, which was originally a major public discourse to go back to the Schuman-Monnet plan.[21]

Fischer's proposal made a distinct constitutional—not governance—approach: 1) the European Parliament of two chambers—the first chamber elected out of national parliamentary representatives, and the second chamber constituted like either the American Senate model, or the German Bundesrat model of state representatives; and 2) the European government

---

[19] Ibid., pp.76, 99.
[20] Commission of the European Communities, COM (2001) 428 final, *European Governance: A White Paper* (Brussels, 2001).
[21] Joschka Fischer: "Vom Staatenverbund zur Föderation—Gedanken über die Finalität der europäischen Integration," Paper presented at Humboldt-Universität, Berlin, May 12, 2000.

or executive, the shape of which can be ranging between the two alternative poles—developing from the European Council which presently represent each national government, or developing from the European Commission with a new, directly-elected president.

Fischer's statement, though dependent on the preconceived structure of the existing national federal republics and devoid of the ideas of "realizing the pouvoir constituant," was challenging enough for Chirac, Jospin, and Blair to follow suit in remarking on the future of Europe.

Not surprisingly, Weiler took a very skeptical stand on the mind-set of Fischer's proposal. He argued that

> The advocacy for a European constitution is not what it purports to be. It is not a call for 'a' constitution. It is a call for a different form of European from the constitutional architecture we already have. And yet the current constitutional architecture, which of course can be improved in many of its specifics, encapsulates one of Europe's most important constitutional innovations, the Principle of Constitutional Tolerance.

Formal constitutionalization at the European level is, thus, likely to devastate the "Principle of Constitutional Tolerance," which is a non one-way concept and implies constitutional transactions at the Member State level, at the Union level, and among the Member States, too.[22]

3. The Convention—A Deliberative Enterprise?

Nevertheless, a more optimistic interpretation finds great interest in "how the majority of the conventioneers have institutionalized a 'deliberative setting' in order to counter-balance the logic of bargaining."[23]

---

[22] J.H.H. Weiler, "In defence of the status quo: Europe's Constitutional Sonderweg," in J.H.H. Weiler and Marlene Wind, *European Constitutionalism beyond the State* (Cambridge: Cambridge University Press, 2003), pp. 18-21.

[23] Paul Magnette, "Coping with Constitutional Incompatibilities: Bargains and Rhetoric in the Convention on the Future of Europe," *Jean Monet Working Paper*,

The Nice summit of the EU in 2000 set up this agenda in response to the European leaders' new agenda. The year after, it was agreed at the Laeken summit to set up a "Convention" to decide on the question whether the task of simplification and reorganization of the European Union might lead to the adoption of a formal constitutional text. The Belgian presidency next year made serious efforts for the Laeken mandate, but the methods the Belgian prime minister adopted were so flexible and diffuse as to contact each head of governments, to spark wider debates in civil society organizations and national arenas, or to stress that the Convention would remain a "preparatory body" before the inter-governmental decision to disarm suspicion of the most skeptic governments.

But there was a bid so that the Convention would not end up as just a large "wise men's" forum or a conventional intergovernmental bargaining. The Chairman of the Convention, Valéry Giscard d'Estaing, the former French resident, asserted a series of initial settings on his own authority, which played a key roll to direct the long-running sessions.

First, Giscard called for a "broad consensus on a single proposal" which would open the way towards a constitution for Europe, or a text that should be legally binding. The Laeken Declaration, as mentioned above, had not stepped in this point.

Second, he affirmed that the assemblies should not vote, while stressing that "consensus does not mean unanimity." The Member States rejecting a full-fledge constitution would be able to exercise their veto in the subsequent IGC, but they found difficulty denying the Convention yielding its own "consensus."[24]

In January 2004, the Franco-German proposal drove a wedge in the institutional debate. It was also meant to commemorate the Elysée treaty concluded between de Gaulle and Adenauer forty years ago. Agreed to by Chirac and Schröder, this joint paper proposed a president for the European Council, elected for five years or two-and-a-half years by the

---

March 14, 2003.
[24] Magnette, op.cit., pp. 7-9.

3. Making Regionalism Legitimate?: European Integration and beyond

Council's QMV, and a European foreign minister to integrate the rolls of the existing two high officials representing the Union's external position.[25] The Franco-German paper emphasized greater clarity, legitimacy and efficiency, and advocated a greater capacity for the Commission, especially in economic policy, and greater clout for the national parliaments as well. Nevertheless, the great powers' joint proposal immediately provoked a backlash among the smaller Member States that were concerned about great powers' dominance and preferred the continuity of the Commission methods.

In the course of something like a "consensus" being brewed, the British statements aroused disappointment and anger. But the British representative, Peter Hain, suggested that the United Kingdom would not make common cause with any group to wreck the Convention [271] and was positive for the Convention to forge out a single text.[26]

In the session July 9-10, 2003, Giscard declared the successful closing of the Convention before the Conventionells: "Son résultat est de proposer la première constitution, la constitution de l'an 03, pour l'Europe, et vous en êtes les auteurs! C'est une œuvre collective, le produit de seize mois de réflexion et de débats, et aussi d'intense travail," then, "You have proved that the Convention method works. You have ensured, by our success, that the Convention method lasts" and finally, "Coming from different backgrounds, countries, institutions, we have come to understand each other, to narrow areas of disagreement, to identify solutions acceptable to all."[27]

Was the Convention, which produced the draft Constitutional treaty of the Union, a first major experience of deliberative politics, the method of which is promised to last in the future?

We know that the process ran into rough water in the latter half of 2003. The Brussels European Council in December 2003 could not reach

---

[25] Peter Norman, *The Accidental Constitution: The Story of the European Convention* (Brussels: EuroComment, 2004), pp. 174-77.
[26] Ibid., p. 271.
[27] La Convention Européene, *Eléments d'intervention du Président Giscard d'Estaing en fin de séance.*

an agreement of constitutional restructuring not least because Spain and Poland vetoed the new voting system, which might give them less influence than was agreed in the Nice treaty in 2000. Poland had strong Eurosceptic pressure and Catholic voters who preferred a reference to God in the constitutional text. In addition, the divide between the U.S.-UK side and the Franco-German side over the war against Iraq, the referendum by the Swedes that rejected to join the euro zone, the breaking of the euro growth and stability pact, and other situations more or less cast dark clouds over the launched constitutional integration of Europe.

And written in the bottom line was a problem of (in)equality between the bigger and the smaller Member States, which can be simply solved neither by the supranational federalism nor liberal-intergovernmentalism. The Polish foreign minister legitimated his government's intransigent position against the Constitutional treaty as a defense of the European ideal for the smaller countries.

Antje Wiener takes up this problem not just as the Bigs vs. the Smalls conflict but also as a crisis of norm resonance between norm-setters and norm-followers. The East-Central European countries, in the compliance process before their accession, have to deal with the double standards or the transition rules to delay full lifting of borders, in such areas as minority rights and free movement for workers. Wiener points to the pitfall of a "snap-shot approach to constitutional bargaining." The validity of supranational norms is gained to the extent that both norm-setters and norm-followers establish interactive processes, where the "possibility of contestation" in each context and stage of the compliance process is crucial.[28]

Did the Convention prove to be a failure as a "method" to reconstruct the enlarging Union, with a view to enhance its political legitimacy as well as efficiency? Before coming to any conclusion, we will reach out for a broader perspective by briefly examining the development of the North

---

[28] Antje Wiener, "Finality vs. Enlargement: Constitutive Practices and Opposing Rationales in the Reconstruction of Europe" in J.H.H. Weiler and Marlene Wind, eds., *European Constitutionalism beyond the State* (Cambridge: Cambridge University Press, 2003), pp. 192-95.

American Free Trade Agreement (NAFTA) and Asia-Pacific Economic Cooperation (APEC) in the next section.

4. Beyond the European Context: NAFTA and APEC

The EU is not the only model of regional cooperation. The North America and Asia-Pacific regions have provided models of regional cooperation distinguished from the theoretically dominant European integration model.

4.1. NAFTA

In 1989, the Canada-United States Free Trade Agreement (CUFTA) was concluded. Five years later, Mexico, a state long dominated by the Partido Revolcionario Istitucional (PRI), decided to join the regime, which formed a deepened framework, the North American Free Trade Agreement.

I will not examine here the material performance of NAFTA in comparison with the EU, but the consequence upon the political legitimacy and democracy in each NAFTA member country.[29]

The democratic accounts of the three countries with the impact of NAFTA are diverse, that is, a democratic deficit in the case of Canada, a democratic surplus in the United States, and a democratic uncertainty in Mexico.[30]

NAFTA has been established as an explicit rule-based system. But both strong private sectors and governmental officials of the United States can often keep the rules from being neutrally enforced. Canada's soft lumber export and Mexico's tomatoes and brooms export were treated often according to the political pressure inside the United States, rather than to the agreement-based rules. In general, NAFTA remains a minor issue in the American politics. But the Mexican currency crisis of 1994 posed a threat close enough for the U.S. monetary authority to adopt a

---

[29] Stephen Clarkson, "Do Deficits Imply Surpluses?" in Greven and Pauly, op. cit., pp. 150-54.

[30] Ibid., p. 161; Carol Wise, ed., *The Post-NAFTA Political Economy: Mexico and the Western Hemisphere* (University Park: Pennsylvania State University Press, 1998).

solidarity policy—that is, to support the peso.[31]

In Canada, the peaceful and open exchange with the giant neighbor had a long history, and more harmonization was regarded unnecessary if it would jeopardize the smaller country's democratic sovereignty. What was expected of CUFTA was expansion of economic prosperity, which would also enhance the country's political footing. In practice, the Canadian governments, both national and subnational, came with difficulty in keeping arm's length relationship with Washington, especially in such areas as domestic industrial and microeconomic policies or social policy standards. The American pharmaceutical industry that claimed full protection of intellectual property rights is an illustration of the influential lobbies in NAFTA.[32]

The Mexican case is different from that of Canada, in that the impact of regional economic liberation was not cast on a democratic society but on a long-standing authoritarian regime. The potential effects of NAFTA might imply effective checks on transparency and corruption, the government's abidance by rules and judicial procedures, the empowerment of domestic social groups following the actions of foreign firms and labor organizations, and more autonomy of subregions benefiting from cross-border exchanges.

Toward the end of the 1990s, the political hegemony of the PRI eroded, first at the subnational level, then at the national level. The Chiapas uprising was seen and heard by an empathetic world audience as the country's groaning for democracy and minority rights. Yet the Chiapas insurgents were most hostile to the government's neo-liberal policy and NAFTA as a devastating blow to their communal agriculture. The regional trade liberation thus has had complex and even paradoxical effects on democratization in Mexico.

4.2. APEC

As exemplified by the ASEAN (the Association of South-East Asian

---

[31] Ibid., pp. 150-51.
[32] Ibid.,151-52.

Nations) and APEC, the Asia-Pacific region has opted—out of preference and necessity—for a much more simple and flexible framework.

APEC was formed in 1989, with the six ASEAN countries, South Korea, New Zealand, Canada, Japan, and the United States as the original members, and was expected to be the first viable and large regional framework for economic cooperation, with new important members added such as Hong Kong, China, Chinese-Taipei, Mexico, and Chili. APEC's most important characteristics are its open-regionalism and its principle of flexibility or voluntarism. These defining features are considered to be contributing to cooperation in a region with social and political diversity, different degrees of economic development, and market-driven economic cooperation.[33]

"Open-regionalism" had been agreed to since the beginning of APEC, the term was elaborated and emphasized by the Eminent Persons' Group (EPG) in its 1994-1995 report, and consists of 1) the maximum possible extent of unilateral liberalization, 2) a commitment to continue reducing its barriers to nonmember counties while it liberalizes internally on an MFN basis, 3) a willingness to extend its regional liberalization to non members on a mutually reciprocal basis, and 4) recognition that any individual APEC member can unilaterally extend its APEC liberalization to nonmembers on a conditional or unconditional basis. Thus, this principle was meant not to discriminate against nonmembers and to clear the "free-rider" or control problem.

In the late 1990s, the ambitious proposal for the EVSL (Early Voluntary Sectoral Liberalization) to move up partially the 2010/2020 liberation goal was launched. But it proved an unequivocal failure, which Fred Bergsten who had chaired the EPG deplored as the "death of the APEC." Even though its necrology seems too early, the APEC showed outward signs of systemic drawbacks.

The conflicts between national interests were apparently the major

---

[33] Akiko Yanai, "APEC ni okeru Jiyuka no Tokucho: WTO tono Soi" [Characteristic of APEC Trade Liberalization: Comparative Analysis with the WTO], in Jiro Okamoto, ed., *APEC Soki Jiyuka Kyogi no Seiji Katei: Kyoyu Sarenakatta Konsensasu* (Chiba: Institute of Developing Economies, 2001), p. 19.

cause of imbroglio during the negotiations in 1997-1999. However, attentive researchers detect the cognitive framework problem around "consensus that wasn't shared" alongside with the direct conflicts between national interests.[34] The United States perceived the emphases on voluntaristic or "consensual" principles as façades of reluctance to economic liberation, rather than as resilient varieties of politics and economies in Asia. Japan, on the other hand, would never interpret the voluntaristic principle as more than the unilateral right to cooperate à la carte. The United States, in coalition with Canada, Australia and New Zealand, launched the idea of "packaging" the EVSL, while condemning the attitude of Japan as protectionist. In fact, Japan, at a certain point, was ready to include the controversial fishing and forestry products in the framework of the EVSL. Yet Japan stood against the "package" strategy claiming that it would conflict with the general APEC principle of voluntarism.[35] Japan's position was originally isolated but effective enough to alienate the middle-positioned members such as China, Indonesia, Thailand, Malaysia, and the Philippines from joining the package-regime. Thus, APEC failed to provide a framework that would enable an evolutionary equilibrium between more binding regional norms—to any degree—and corresponding development of "Voice" and "Loyalty."

The aftermath was leaving the matter in the hands of the World Trade Organization, and then surging competition for bilateral FTAs in defense of national interests.

---

[34] Jiro Okamoto, "Shusho: Kyoyu sarenakatta Konsensasu" [Conclusion: Consensus that Was Not Shared], in Jiro Okamoto, ed., *APEC Soki Jiyuka Kyogi no Seiji Katei: Kyoyu Sarenakatta Konsensasu* (Chiba: Institute of Developing Economies, 2001), pp. 343-45; Woo Yuen Pau, "APEC after 10 Years: What's left of 'Open Regionalism'?" Paper presented at APEC Study Centre Consortium Conference, Auckland, New Zealand, May 30-June 2, 1999.

[35] Ibid., pp. 181, 335.

5. Conclusion: Towards Theoretical Comparison of Regional Cooperation

There are not many works that enable comparison of different regional cooperation on the grounds of incommensurable historical, cultural, political, and economic premises. Walter Mattli's exceptional work locates the plausibility of various regional integration projects in a wide-ranging analytical framework (figure 3-3). In his classification, the most plausible cases include the EU, Zollverein in nineteenth-century Germany, NAFTA, as well as EFTA before the UK's withdrawal, with both high potential market gains and a dominant regional leadership.[36]

Figure 3-3 Mattli's Classification of the Outcomes of Integration Schemes

(Potential) market gains from integration	(Uncontested) regional leadership YES	(Uncontested) regional leadership NO
Relatively significant	3 European Union NAFTA Zollverein EFTA (until 1973)	2 EFTA (after 1973) Asia Pacific Economic Cooperation Forum (APEC) MERCOSUR
Relatively insignificant	2 Central American Common Market (until 1969)	1 Bavaria-Wurttemberg Customs Union Middle German Commercial Union Central American Common Market (after 1969) ASEAN Economic Community of West African States LAFTA Andean Pact Caribbean Community Arab Common Market

Success rate : 3 = highest
1 = lowest

Source: Mattli 1999, Figure 3.3, p. 66.

However, Mattli's theory adheres to hegemonic power in regional

---

[36] Walter Mattli, *The Logic of Regional Integration: Europe and Beyond* (Cambridge: Cambridge University Press, 1999).

integration, with Prussia in the case of Zollverein taken as the prototype of successful regional leadership. In the NAFTA case, the United States may well be functioning as the regional (let alone global) hegemon, yet in the case of the European Union, it does not seem reasonable to see Germany as the single hegemon, even with its dominant economic power. The regionalization of economic rules has developed, with asymmetrical power of the United States in the NAFTA case, where regional democratic legitimacy is not addressed on any purpose. On the contrary, the APEC and the EU has non-hegmonic structure, even though the distribution of influence is not even among "Member States." The level of regional norm is high in the EU (low Exit), while it is very low in APEC (high Exit) (see figure 3-4).

Europe's new (and last?) resort to maintain the high regional norm and non-hegemonic (and enlarged) form of political process is *deliberative* political process at the expert and national representative levels. This strategy is still impaired by the big and small or norm-setter and norm-follower distrust, and lack of deliberation at the citizen level. Nevertheless, it may be regarded as a framework with an open possibility on the European Sonderweg to integration.

Figure 3-4 The Level of Regionalization of Norm and Regional Political Structure

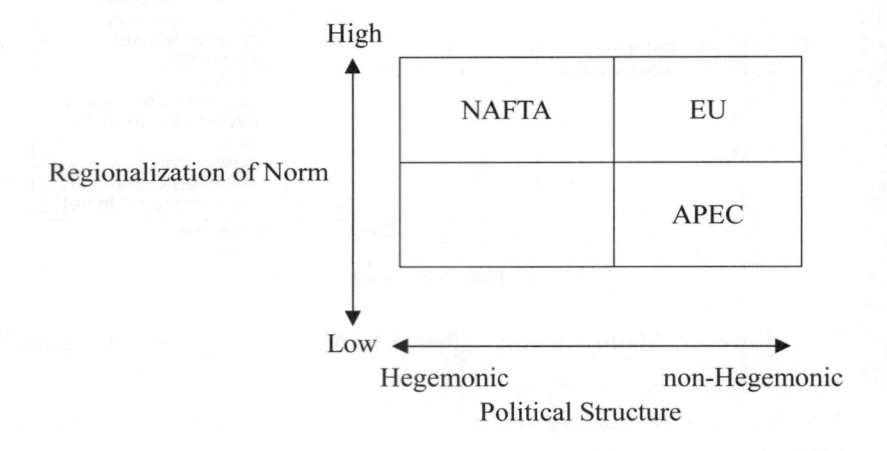

	Hegemonic	non-Hegemonic
High	NAFTA	EU
Low		APEC

Regionalization of Norm (vertical axis, High to Low)
Political Structure (horizontal axis, Hegemonic to non-Hegemonic)

References

Commission of the European Communities, COM (2001) 428 final. *European Governance: A White Paper* (Brussels, 2001).
Clarkson, Stephen. "Do Deficits Imply Surpluses?" in Michael Greven and Louis W. Pauly, eds., *Democracy beyond the State?: The European Dilemma and the Emerging Global Order*. Lanham: Rowman & Littlefield, 2000.
Fischer, Joschka. "Vom Staatenverbund zur Föderation—Gedanken über die Finalität der europäischen Integration." Paper presented at Humboldt-Universität, Berlin, May 12, 2000.
Hirschman, Albert O. *Exit, Voice and Loyalty: Response to Decline in Firms, Organizations and States*. Cambridge: Harvard University Press, 1970.
Imig, Doug and Sidney Tarrow. *Contentious Europeans: Protest and Politics in an Emerging Polity*. Lanham: Rowman and Littlefield, 2001.
Joerges, Christian. "'Good Governance' through Comitology?" in Christian Joerges and Ellen Vos, eds., *EU Committees: Social Regulation, Law and Politics*. Oxford: Hart Publishing, 1999.
Lipset, Seymour Martin. "Some Social Requisites of Democracy: Economic Development and Political Legitimacy," *American Political Science Review*, No. 53 (1959), pp. 69-105.
Magnette, Paul. "Coping with Constitutional Incompatibilities: Bargains and Rhetoric in the Convention on the Future of Europe," *Jean Monet Working Paper*, March 14, 2003.
Majone, Giandomenico. "Europe's 'Democratic Deficit': The Question of Standards," *European Law Journal*, No. 4 (1998), pp. 5-28.
Mattli, Walter. *The Logic of Regional Integration: Europe and Beyond*. Cambridge: Cambridge University Press, 1999.
Moravcsik, Andrew. "Federalism in the European Union: Rhetoric and Reality," in Kalypso Nicolaidis and Robert Howse, eds., *The Federal Vision: Legitimacy and Levels of Governance in the United States and the European Union*. Oxford: Oxford University Press, 2001.
Norman, Peter. *The Accidental Constitution: The Story of the European Convention*. Brussels: EuroComment, 2004.
Offe, Claus. "The Democratic Welfare State in an Integrating Europe" in Michael Greven and Louis W. Pauly, eds., *Democracy beyond the State?: The European Dilemma and the Emerging Global Order*. Lanham:

Rowman & Littlefield, 2000.

Ogawa, Ariyoshi. "Yoroppaka to Seijiteki Seitosei" (Europeanization and Political Legitimacy), in Japan Association for Comparative Politics, ed., *EU no nakano Kokumin Kokka-Demokurashi no Henyo* (*Nation-States in the EU: Transformation of Democracy*). Tokyo: Waseda University Press, 2003.

Okamoto, Jiro. "Shusho: Kyoyu sarenakatta Konsensasu" (Conclusion: Consensus that Was Not Shared)," in Jiro Okamoto, ed., *APEC Soki Jiyuka Kyogi no Seiji Katei: Kyoyu Sarenakatta Konsensasu*. Chiba: Institute of Developing Economies, 2001.

Scharpf, Fritz W. "Negative and Positive Integration in the Political Economy of European Welfare States," in Gary Marks, Fritz W. Scharpf, Philippe C. Schmitter, and Wolfgang Streeck, eds., *Governance in the European Union*. London: Sage, 1996.

——. *Governing in Europe: Effective and Democratic?* Oxford: Oxford University Press, 1999.

——. "Interdependence and Democratic Legitimation," in Susan J. Pharr and Robert D. Putnam, eds., *Disaffected Democracies: What's Troubling the Trilateral Countries?* Princeton: Princeton University Press, 2000.

Shapiro, Martin and Alec Stone Sweet. *On Law, Politics, and Judicialization*. Oxford: Oxford University Press, 2002.

Stone Sweet, Alec and Thomas L. Brunell. "Constructing a Supranational Constitution: Dispute Resolution and Governance in the European Union," *American Political Science Review*, No. 92 (1998), pp. 63-81.

Weiler, J.H.H. *The Constitution of Europe: "Do the New Clothes Have an Emperor" and Other Essays on European Integration*. Cambridge: Cambridge University Press, 1999.

——. "In Defense of the Status Quo: Europe's Constitutional Sonderweg," in J.H.H. Weiler and Marlene Wind, eds., *European Constitutionalism beyond the State*. Cambridge: Cambridge University Press, 2003.

Wiener, Antje. "Finality vs. Enlargement: Constitutive Practices and Opposing Rationales in the Reconstruction of Europe," in J.H.H. Weiler and Marlene Wind, eds., *European Constitutionalism beyond the State*. Cambridge: Cambridge University Press, 2003.

Wise, Carol, ed. *The Post-NAFTA Political Economy: Mexico and the Western Hemisphere*. University Park: Pennsylvania State University Press, 1998.

Woo, Yuen Pau. "APEC after 10 Years: What's left of 'Open Regionalism'?" Paper presented at APEC Study Centre Consortium Conference, Auckland, New Zealand, May 30-June 2, 1999.

3. Making Regionalism Legitimate?: European Integration and beyond

Yanai, Akiko. "APEC ni okeru Jiyuka no Tokucho: WTO tono Soi" (Characteristic of APEC Trade Liberalization: Comparative Analysis with the WTO), in Jiro Okamoto, ed., *APEC Soki Jiyuka Kyogi no Seiji Katei: Kyoyu Sarenakatta Konsensasu*. Chiba: Institute of Developing Economies, 2001.

Zürn, Michael. "Democratic Governance beyond the Nation State," in Michael Greven and Louis W. Pauly, eds., *Democracy beyond the State?: The European Dilemma and the Emerging Global Order*. Lanham: Rowman & Littlefield, 2000.

Part II

National Visions and Experiences of Cooperation in Europe and Asia

CHAPTER 4

FRANCE AND EARLY EUROPEAN INTEGRATION: 1945-1957

Jae-Seung LEE

Europe will be attained by concrete achievements generating an active community of interest.
                                                    Jean Monnet

1. Introduction

France has been known as the most ardent proponent of European integration. The Schuman Plan, initiated by Jean Monnet's idea, led to the creation of the European Coal and Steel Community (ECSC), which became a touchstone of European integration. In establishing the European Economic Community (EEC) and Euratom, France had been regarded as an active participant in promoting supranational components in European institutions.

However, contrary to the conventional wisdom that *Plan Monnet* and the Schuman Plan were the outcomes of French supranational initiatives, the French road to the European Community was a process of maximizing national interests—both economic and political in the context of domestic political competition. The creation of the ECSC and EEC was, to a large degree, a reluctant acceptance of France to guarantee her national interest in a changing European political and economic environment.

Part II: National Visions and Experiences of Cooperation in Europe and Asia

Integrated Europe did not emerge out of the humanitarian impulses of idealistic founders such as Jean Monnet, Robert Schuman, and Konrad Adenauer, but rather out of the selfish realization on the part of the participants that they could best achieve their national interests in concert rather than by themselves. France pursued integration in Europe in so far as it assured French economic and security interests. The contributions made by successive governments of France during the early period of European integration have reflected both domestic and external stimuli and constraints, which were carefully considered in terms of national interest.

This chapter explores the process in which France pursued early European integration, which led to the Treaty of Rome in 1957. In explaining the French position in major institutional developments during the early years of European integration—ECSC (1951), EDC/EPC (1954), and EEC/Euratom (1957)—following parameters will be used in this chapter:

- Political Interest: Geopolitical motivation comprises an important part of the political interest of France in this period. The German problem was at the center of French concerns throughout the early integration period. The maintenance of France as a great power was another key element in comprising French political interest in European integration.
- Economic Interest: Postwar reconstruction and the modernization of French industry was also at the core of French people's minds. French economic interest was also related to France's economic influence in Europe vis-à-vis Germany and Britain.
- European Ideology: Pro-European ideology of political leaders and policymakers was essential to pursue European integration. The idea of European integration and supranational institutions thus become an important parameter in explaining the French position.
- Political Context: Political instability of the Fourth Republic continued until 1958. Between 1946 and 1958, there were twenty-five governments, of which only one lasted more than a year. French ratification of the Treaty of Paris (1951) and Treaty of Rome (1957) was made in the context of complicated party coalition. Therefore, it

is essential to understand the dynamics of party politics and their position in explaining the French position in European integration.[1]

Part two, three and four of this chapter reviews the French position on major institutional development from the ECSC to the creation of the EEC in 1957. The concluding section summarizes the interplay of ideas, interests, and political context in French European policy during the early years of European integration.

2. The Creation of ECSC

2.1. Postwar European Cooperation
After the Second World War (WW II), Europeans became aware of their own weakness and were convinced that confrontation among European states should be avoided at all costs. The recognition of this reality evinced the necessity of European integration. Thus a number of cooperative mechanisms were introduced in the postwar years.

In 1948 the Organization for European Economic Cooperation (OEEC) was created at the initiative of the United States. The OEEC intended to liberalize trade among the member states and enhance monetary and economic cooperation among them.[2] In the same year, the Benelux countries introduced a common external tariff.

On March 17, 1948 representatives of France, the United Kingdom, and the Benelux countries signed the Brussels Treaty leading to a common defense aimed at preventing German rearmament and military cooperation

---

[1] Alain Guyomarch, Howard Machin and Ella Ritchie, *France in the European Union* (New York: St. Martin's Press, 1998), p. 6.

[2] The OEEC undertook responsibility for eliminating quantitative restrictions as part of its trade liberalization program. Established by the Marshall Plan as a mechanism to distribute aid money, the OEEC took no account of European cooperation or "integration" as an objective. The OEEC was godfather to the European Payments Union (EPU), which served as a temporal and functional link between the Marshall Plan on one side and the EEC and the EFTA on the other. John Gillingham, *European Integration: 1950-2003* (Cambridge: Cambridge University Press, 2003), p. 38.

in a crisis situation (Article 4).³ It also aimed at strengthening their economic and cultural ties.

In January 1949, the foreign ministers of the five Brussels Treaty countries agreed to the establishment of a Council of Europe based on the intergovernmental model. The Council of Europe was set up in May 1949 to facilitate political cooperation among European countries. ⁴ The Council was given very wide functions but no real power, given the unanimity rule. It stipulated that national defense matters do not fall within the scope of the Council of Europe (Article 1).⁵

The United States started intervening economically in Europe with the delivery of the massive economic help as outlined in the Marshall Plan. The United States also began to see the economic recovery of Germany and later its military contribution to Western defense as vital to Europe. In April 1949, the United States and ten European states signed the North Atlantic Treaty Agreement, which was the advent of the North Atlantic Treaty Organization (NATO), the great Western military alliance that would confront the Soviet Union.

European cooperation was actively being discussed at the moment the idea of ECSC was hatched. The European Payments Union was one successful measure, while OEEC did not record performance as expected. Criticizing that existing organization—OEEC, Brussels Treaty, Council of Europe—were making no real progress,⁶ Monnet proposed to abandon

---

³ "The Treaty of Economic, Social and Cultural Collaboration and Collective Self-Defence," Brussels, March 1948. The Brussels Treaty was replaced by Paris Treaty in 1954, in which "the cooperation to cope with Germany's aggression" was revised to "promote the unity and to encourage the progressive integration of Europe." "Protocol Modifying and Completing the Brussels Treaty," Paris, October 1954.

⁴ However, its statues did not claim to be the union, nor the federation of States, without mentioning the transfer of sovereignty. Their main function, therefore, has been to reinforce the democratic system and the human rights in the member states.

⁵ "Statute of the Council of Europe" London, May 1949.

⁶ During late 1948 and early 1949 the OEEC had tried to harmonize the national recovery programs of its member countries but it was not successful due to its complexity and the unwillingness of countries. William Diebold Jr., *The Schuman Plan: A Study in Economic Cooperation, 1950-1959* (New York: Praeger, 1959), p. 15.

past form and embark upon a transformation by establishing new authorities.[7]

However, political leaders in European countries were divided on the method for constructing Europe. In the immediate postwar period, a cautious "bottom up" approach was taken with intergovernmental cooperation.[8] An alternative method was that of sectoral integration that would lead eventually to a supranational organization. In the sectoral approach, integration was conceived as a dynamic process that involved bringing more policy sectors into structures for joint decision-making and policy implementation. This method was adopted partly in reaction to disappointment over the poor performance of the early attempts of Council of Europe and OEEC.[9]

2.2. Plan Monnet and Plan Schuman

One of the major concerns of postwar France was the relative underdevelopment of its economy in comparison to those of Germany and the UK. In 1944, over 25 percent of the labor force was still involved in agriculture, and often in inefficient peasant farming. The manufacturing and service sectors were both small-scale and nondynamic, and much capital and infrastructure had been destroyed during the occupation. Most political leaders were convinced that recovering from the wartime destruction required not only reconstruction but also modernization.[10]

The coal-steel conflict had been especially severe in the immediate postwar years. Sufficient coal and steel was essential for the industrial modernization of France. The capacity of the steel industry was rising

---

[7] Ibid.

[8] In the economic domain, the Ramadier government accepted Marshall Aid and membership of the loose, cooperative intergovernmental body, the OEEC. For defense, the Dunkirk Treaty with Britain in 1947, the 1948 Brussels Treaty (extending the Dunkirk arrangements to the Benelux states) and the 1949 Washington Treaty establishing NATO were all intergovernmental, including the Council of Europe. Guyomarch, op. cit., p. 22.

[9] Guyomarch, op. cit., p. 22.

[10] Guyomarch, op. cit., p. 5.

rapidly and searched for expansion through export.[11] The underlying problem had been that France had plenty of steel but not enough coal. German coal, especially from the Ruhr area, was crucial for French postwar reconstruction and industrialization.

The French *Plan de Mondernisation et d'Équippement*, so called the "Monnet Plan" was designed to offset the lack of wartime investment and to achieve European steel supremacy.[12] Monnet's policy was to decartelize coal and steel production and to break up a potential concentration of monopoly. He wanted to hogtie the Germans until they could be trusted or until France had gotten mean enough to handle them.[13] Restrictions had to be placed on German steel production even if it meant delaying Germany's recovery. A specially created International Ruhr Authority had the task of squeezing out as much coal as possible for exportation.[14]

The French national plan in January 1946 took into account French control of Saar industry and of the restrictions that France wanted to maintain on the industrial power of the Ruhr. France did not want to have a new, economically strong and rearmed Germany as its neighbor. France wanted a fragmented Germany, a country of "regions." The French had hoped that the International Ruhr Authority would continue to guarantee them access to German coal but German independence and the rise in Ruhr steel production were putting pressure on the supply.[15] The Authority, once regarded as a means to continue control, seemed to lose its initial influence.[16] France's attempts to have the Ruhr neutralized or otherwise controlled faced Anglo-American resistance. The Germans resented the controls imposed upon them and were upset by what appeared

---

[11] While France's steel output was rising above prewar levels, that of West Germany was lagging.

[12] The coal and steel industries absorbed about 30 percent of the funds disbursed by the Monnet Plan for modernization.

[13] Gillingham, op. cit., p. 25.

[14] Ibid., p. 24.

[15] Diebold, op. cit., p. 18.

[16] Ibid., p. 10.

4. France and Early European Integration: 1945-1957

to be French attempts to detach the Saar permanently from Germany.[17]

The option the French government had chosen was to find a new approach to the German problem. Monnet pointed out that the German situation was becoming increasingly more dangerous and France had no other choice but to seek to settle the German problem, which could not be settled with what France had in hand. France had to change what she had by transforming it.[18] Franco-German cooperation in the coal and steel industry became inevitable for the modernization of France. Monnet's plan was elaborated and visualized by France's Foreign Minister Robert Schuman.

Both international context and French domestic motivation affected the Schuman Plan.[19] Germany was moving toward increased independence, strength, and eventually rearmament. The French government had gone along reluctantly with American and British measures that relaxed controls on Germany.[20] Germany wanted to restore her full sovereignty and industrial potential, which was under the authority of the Occupation. Previous institutions for supervision would be dismissed or turned into international institution in which Germany could participate.[21] Schuman noted, "We shall deal directly with the Germans

---

[17] On the same day of ECSC signature, German Chancellor Konrad Adenauer wrote a letter to Robert Schuman confirming the French disposition regarding the issue of the Saar. Germany was still doubtful of what the ECSC would do for the fate of Germany. "Lettre de Konrad Adenauer à Robert Schuman, 18 avril 1951." Archives du ministère des Affaires étrangères, Paris, Coopération économique, vol. 520, f. 42.

[18] Jean Monnet, "Memorandum to Robert Schuman and Georges Bidault," May 1950.

[19] "Le Plan Shuman: Une nouvelle architecture pour l'Europe? 1950/2000," Colloque organize par l'Institut Historique Allemand et le Centre d'Information et de recherche sur l'Allemagne contemporaine (CIRAC) avec le soutien de la Fondation Robert Bosch (Stuttgart), Paris, les 28 et 29 avril 2000, AHF-Information No. 20, Volume 21, 2001.3.21.

[20] Diebold, op. cit., p. 10.

[21] "Note à propos de la participation de l'Allemagne à l'Autorité internationale de la Ruhr, annotée de la main de Robert Schuman, 3 décembre 1949." Archives du ministère des Affaires étrangères, Paris, Cabinet du ministre Robert Schuman, vol. 68, ff. 61-62.

and offer them equal status in return for mutual safeguards, not on paper but in the mines and factories of the Ruhr and Lorraine."[22]

The Schuman Plan was expected to enable the stabilization of the coal supply, fair competition, low consumer price, and industrial concentration of the Ruhr.[23] This proposal put together the two major sectors of heavy industry—coal and steel—under the international and also the supranational control of a new European institution, the so-called High Authority.

After eleven months of hard negotiations, the Foreign Ministers of France, Germany, Italy, Belgium, Netherlands, and Luxembourg—the original "Six"—signed the Treaty of Paris in April 1951, establishing the European Coal and Steel Community (ECSC). The common High Authority was presided by Jean Monnet.

2.3. French Choice of ECSC

Initially, the French government settled for a vague form of international control of the Ruhr. However, it had to find a different strategy when the Anglo-Americans, without consulting them, gave the Germans *carte blanche* to decide how and by whom the mines would be owned. When France realized that their initial position could not be maintained, France found the second best way to control the Ruhr in a supranational body.

French political leaders disagreed about the appropriate dimensions for the new Europe. Monnet and many Christian Democrats took an integrationist position. Supporters of the Schuman Plan included *Mouvement Républicain Polulaire* (MRP), Socialists (including Radical), and some Independents. Opponents were the Gaullists, the Communists, and some Independents. General de Gaulle and his supporters in the RRF (the Gaullist Party) advocated "*l'Europe des Etats*" instead of supranational European institution.[24]

---

[22] Diebold, op. cit., p. 11.

[23] "Note du Commissariat au Plan relative aux effets du plan Schuman sur les industries du charbon et de l'acier en France, 8 février 1951." Archives du ministère des Affaires étrangères, Paris, Secrétariat général, vol. 60, ff. 147-77.

[24] But party line-up was not a religious attachment. There were a certain degree of

4. France and Early European Integration: 1945-1957

At first, the ECSC was not wholeheartedly welcomed by the French people. Labor union and steel producers expressed their discontent. Some of them contended that Monnet had manipulated many technocrats and politicians.[25] The official voice of organized industry spoke against the Schuman Plan or pressed for amendments. The steel industry fervently raised objections. They were concerned with competitive disadvantage compared with those companies that operated in the Ruhr, as well as control of their industrial activity by an international bureaucracy.[26] The coal and steel community would have, in their minds, a more negative than positive impact on France.

The proponents of the ECSC Treaty argued that France would have to take economic risks in order to attain larger political gains. They claimed that France could get positive economic benefits from the pool and that without it France would still face many of the problems and risks. Under the ECSC, French and German buyers would have equal access to the coal from the Ruhr and the elimination of monopoly would contribute to the stabilization of supply in the long run. Increased competitiveness would increase the efficiency of the French steel industry.[27] Without the ECSC, France would have no safeguard when the German economy eventually liberalized.

There had been a general consensus that a unity of Europe was necessary and to support the Treaty was to support European unification. Opponents, including the Gaullists, asked for a stronger France in the new scheme but did not openly confront the European integration itself. The

---

disbarments within each party.

[25] "Lettre de protestation du Comité central d'Entreprise de l'Union sidérurgique du Nord de la France (USINOR) contre le plan Schuman à Marcel Plaisant," président de la Commission des Affaires Etrangères du Conseil de la République, 28 novembre 1951. Archives du ministère des Affaires étrangères, Paris, Papiers d'agents—Papiers Plaisant, vol. 144, f. 411-14; "Le plan Schuman à l'Assemblée nationale," dans la brochure B.E.D.E.S., Bureau d'étude et de documentation économique et sociale, 27 décembre 1951. Archives du ministère des Affaires étrangères, Paris, Cabinet du Ministre - Robert Schuman, vol. 144, f. 622-24.

[26] Diebold, op. cit., pp. 85-88.

[27] Ibid., pp. 91-92.

favorable vote in the Foreign Affairs Committee in the Assemblée Nationale was a victory for the proponents (26-18).[28]

The success of ECSC was also due to Monnet's vision and deft combination of showmanship and backstage hard dealing.[29] The "lock" of Konrad Adenauer, a Francophile German counterpart, on the chancellorship was also an important contribution.[30] Adenauer championed the Schuman Plan as an expedient means of bringing the occupation to an end.[31] He was willing to sacrifice the interests of the Ruhr to the greater good of reconciliation with France.

The coal-steel pool set in motion a process, led by West Germany, involving the delegation of sovereign powers to a transnational authority at the European level. Yet the High Authority of the ECSC did not effectively regulate the heavy industry of Western Europe and had no broader economic impacts as expected. The ECSC worked to the satisfaction of no one, yet its accomplishments as a learning process for further integration were substantial.[32] The ECSC cannot take much credit for preventing war in Europe but it has since served as the steppingstone toward European integration.

---

[28] Committee on Finance (3-8), Industrial production (21-17), Labor (21-20). The military affairs committee opposed the Treaty (21-15) and the committee on economic affairs asked for postponement (24-15). Ibid., p. 84.

[29] The main source of Jean Monnet's postwar power came from his special role as flow regulator along the American aid pipeline. Monnet could be the Frenchman that Washington trusted most. Gillingham, op. cit., p. 21.

[30] Gillingham, ibid., p. 22.

[31] The Federal Republic's economic strength would assure West European respect for its national interest. Political dwarfism and economic gigantism are the basis for the semi-sovereign status that has made Germany a model for the other great nations of Europe. Simon Petermann, "The ECSC, the EDC and the Messina Conference: Realities and Hopes," online at www.edc.spb.ru/conf2001/Petermann.html.

[32] Ibid.

3. Failed Attempt: EDC and EPC

3.1. The Idea of EDC

In France, the preoccupation of political leaders with the unresolved problem of territorial security still lingered during the early European integration process.[33] The war in Indochina and instability in North Africa pushed the French government into a difficult situation. In addition, the French economy suffered from inflation, chronic deficit in foreign accounts, and protectionism. Even though many Frenchmen recommended measures of fuller economic union, there existed a certain degree of mismatch between discourse and practice. Furthermore, a negative opinion about the inclusion of Germany in the Community prevailed.

France found itself in an awkward predicament. On the one hand, it was concerned about the rise of Communism, but on the other hand it looked askance at a possible re-emergence of Germany. Paris feared that the German army would develop into an independent institution, functioning outside of the control of the allies.[34] In order to cope with this predicament, the French government decided to utilize the Schuman Plan concept and apply it to military matters.

France had become alarmed at a U.S. proposal in the summer of 1950 to rearm the Germans in an Atlantic context, which was prompted by the outbreak of the Korean War. Faced with U.S. demands for German rearmament, French Prime Minister Pleven announced in October 1950 a plan for German remilitarization under the aegis of the EDC.[35] The

---

[33] A survey conducted in May 1953 showed the French fear of Germany. About 57 percent of the French people believed that the existence of German military troops would create a danger to France. Jarkko Tuominen, "The European Defence Community 1950-1954 : The second uneasy step towards the United States of Europe," online at www.valt.helsinki.fi/kvtok/1997/3181.htm.

[34] Jan Van der Harst, "The European Defence Community: A Failure in High Politics Integration," Jean Monnet lecture, University of Manchester, March 7, 2003.

[35] The suggestion is directly inspired by the recommendation adopted on August 11, 1950 by the assembly of the Council of Europe, demanding the immediate creation of a unified European army destined to cooperate with the American and Canadian Forces

Pleven plan provided for a European Army under the Atlantic umbrella run by a European Minister of Defense and the Council of Ministers, with a joint commander, common budget, and common arms procurement. A commissariat was to have oversight power over the multinational armed forces like that of the High Authority of the ECSC. The allocation of authority within the organization was keyed into the size of military budgets. The "top down" model, constitutional federalism, based on the idea that a major constitutional change was required to establish a "United State of Europe," was adopted in Pleven's EDC.[36] The army of a united Europe, composed of men coming from different European countries, would achieve a complete fusion of the human and material elements under a single European political and military authority.[37] By making German army units a part of integrated European divisions, a revival of a German *Wehrmacht* could be avoided. The projected creation of the European Army would also facilitate the implementation of the Atlantic programs.

France had the largest armed force on the continent, and Britain predictably refused to participate in the scheme. French officers were thus to be placed in command of a force composed largely of German troops.[38] Besides, the French could keep national forces apart from the European Army for colonial and other purposes. Only the Germans would have a European duty but no national option. It was a proposition to rearm the Germans without re-establishing a German army.[39]

The EDC was a policy conceived in the French national interest, dressed up in European language, and from a military standpoint having little other than symbolic significance. It concerned a French initiative to make German rearmament feasible within the controllable framework of a

---

in the defense of peace.

[36] Guyomarch, op. cit., p. 29.

[37] The main elements of the EDC treaty include: Division of different nationalities and the elevation to the level of national division; Common budget: Common armament program.

[38] Gillingham, op. cit., p. 29.

[39] Tuominen, op. cit.

European army.

Monnet was the architect of this idea, too.[40] Faced with possible German recalcitrance in the coal and steel talks, Monnet pressed Pleven to pursue the parallel idea of a supranational organization for European defense. Monnet seized the problem of rearming Germany and stressed the links between the Schuman Plan and a common defense policy. He insisted that France must regain the initiative because the Germans, with the aid of the United States, were going to rearm anyway and if they did it nationally, then whole process of integration and especially the Schuman Plan would be in jeopardy. The EDC emerged, to a large degree, as the French means of salvaging the Schuman Plan. Monnet cleverly simplified his "European idea" to this idea of only defending France's interests, which was easier for French political leaders to accept.[41]

Negotiations to form the EDC began in February 1951. Although Monnet was not directly involved in the EDC talks, he again used his influence behind the scenes to win powerful U.S. support for the Pleven Plan.

The "Six" countries signed the EDC treaty on May 27, 1952, in Paris. Article 38 of the Paris Treaty called for the establishment of a supranational political authority to direct the EDC. Ratification debates were successfully concluded in Germany (spring 1953), Netherlands (July 1953), Belgium (November 1953) and Luxembourg (April 1954).[42]

3.2. The Idea of EPC

Discussion on a European army and defense community required more discussions on foreign policy and a political community. At the insistence

---

[40] In the background of the Pleven Plan, the renewed Jean Monnet and his team (including Van Helmont, Hirsh and Alphand) played an important part in the conceptualization of the plan. Ibid.

[41] Tuominen, op. cit.

[42] For more discussion on the EDC, see Jan Van Der Harst, *The Atlantic Priority: Dutch Defence Policy at the Time of the European Defence Community* (UK: European Press Academic Publishing, 2003); Kevin Ruane, *The Rise and Fall of the European Defence Community: Anglo-American Relations and the Crisis of European Defence, 1950-55* (Houndsmill, UK: Palgrave Macmillan, 2000).

of French socialists that a political control mechanism be established to oversee the EDC, a new round of negotiations for a European Political Community (EPC) began soon thereafter. In September 1952 the foreign ministers of the Six acted on a resolution to entrust a parliamentary body with the task of implementing Article 38 by drafting the statute for the supranational European Political Community. The EPC would not only encompass the EDC and ECSC but also embrace foreign, economic, and monetary policy coordination. A proposal for the EPC came as a complement to the EDC but did not reached the treaty stage.

A special ECSC assembly accepted the draft for the EPC in March 1953. The EPC was to be the beginning of a comprehensive federation to which the ECSC and EDC would be subordinated. The institutional similarity between the ECSC and EDC was misleading, since the EDC and the projected EPC represented a first stage in a plan to build a federal Europe while the ECSC was based more on intergovernmental cooperation. Article 82 bore importance in that it became a starting point for the conclusion of the treaty establishing the European Economic Community.[43]

3.3. French Rejection of EDC and EPC

The Pleven Plan and European Defence Community broadly followed the ECSC model but they ran into a series of objections at the beginning. The immediate challenge came from the nationalist campaign in France against the European Army. Many doubted whether an allied command structure would be efficient and many French were doubtful about the ultimate subordination to NATO, and thus America. Moreover, there was a strong reluctance to relinquish governmental control over the state's armed forces.

---

[43] "The Community, while upholding the principles defined in Articles 2, 3 and 4 of the treaty instituting the European Coal and Steel Community, shall establish progressively a common market of goods, capital, and persons. "In order to achieve the aim mentioned in the preceding paragraph, the Community shall foster the coordination of the policy of the member States in monetary, credit and financial matters." "Draft Treaty Embodying the Statute of the European Community Adopted by the Ad Hoc Assembly," March 11, 1953.

4. France and Early European Integration: 1945-1957

At root there remained a deep unhappiness about rearming Germany.[44] Even the French military was not wholeheartedly supporting the proposal.

Initial reactions from other countries were also lukewarm. The United States preferred NATO, which had just been created in 1949. The United Kingdom (UK) was against such a supranational scheme. German Chancellor Adenauer was for the establishment of the EDC but there was considerable opposition within Germany, especially from the opposition Social Democrat Party. The Germans protested that the French proposal discriminated against them since a number of severe restrictions had been applied to Germany. The new British Foreign Secretary, Anthony Eden, firmly announced that Britain would not become a member of the EDC.[45]

During the first half of 1951, however, the United States changed its European policy. It had been disappointed with the achievement of the OEEC. Instead, the Shuman Plan seemed to be a step in the right direction and the Pleven Plan would be the next step. In addition, the United States felt a large-scale deployment overseas more and more burdensome. Truman and Acheson began to support the Pleven Plan and the idea of the EDC. Because of the intensification of the Cold War, it started to seem that the German rearmament would be real in the near future with or without the EDC. The United States pressed hard for the ratification of the EDC Treaty. Eisenhower had come to see the EDC as an end in itself. The campaign on behalf of the EDC culminated in the new Secretary of Secretary of State, John Foster Dulles's "agonizing reappraisal" speech of December 1953, in which he threatened to cutback military aid to Europe if the treaty were rejected.

The EDC problem was never easy for the political leaders of France. The French Fourth Republic was very unstable and governments merely tended to delay controversial issue like the EDC to be dealt with at a later date. The reluctance to sacrifice sovereignty increased. Delegation of power from the national level to European level was unbearable for the Gaullists, especially when the French army was involved. It was feared

---

[44] Trevor Salmon, *Building European Union: A Documentary History and Analysis* (Manchester: Manchester University Press, 1997), pp. 49-50.
[45] Ibid.

that the EDC would dilute French ability to fight elsewhere for their overseas territories.

In addition to the French uneasiness about German preponderance and rearmament, external situations made the ratification of the EDC treaty even more difficult. France, increasingly preoccupied with events in Indochina, suffered a decisive defeat at *Dien Bien Phu* in May 1954. After the signing the peace treaty on Indo-China, French dependence on the United States reduced considerably. After the defeat at *Dien Bien Phu* and the decision to abandon French colonial rule in Indo-China the French cabinet was finally in a position to risk the U.S. aid cutback.[46] From early 1953, the French seemed to look for ways to get rid of the treaty.[47]

Domestic political context was not favorable for ratification, either. Until late 1952, the pro-European MRP played a major role in French politics. But the election in late 1952 brought the Gaullist and Eurosceptic RPF considerable support. New government had to depend on the Gaullist support for its political survival. In the changed political situation, Schuman was replaced by George Bidault (MRP), a man who was much less convinced of the need to pursue an EDC. The influence of Monnet declined as well.

All these issues, coupled with implacable Communist opposition to German rearmament, resulted in the defeat of the EDC treaty in the French National Assembly in August 1954.[48] All the Communists voted against the EDC, as did all but two of the Gaullists. Only the MRP voted solidly for it. Other parties were about equally divided.[49] Even Monnet could not prevent the EDC from failing and the lukewarm stance of Mendès-France had doomed the EDC.[50]

---

[46] Gillingham, op. cit., p. 31.

[47] A large part of French politics preferred to reject the EDC right away but it could not do so because of its dependence on the U.S. in its colonial struggle in Indo-China. However, after securing the solution of the Indochina issue, the rejection of the EDC treaty had become predictable. Van der Harst, op. cit.

[48] The result of vote was 319 against, 264 for, and 43 abstentions.

[49] Petermann, op. cit.

[50] Dumulin described the failure of EDC as a "collective murder." Michel Dumoulin, ed., *The European Defence Community: Lessons for the Future?* (Brussels: Peter Lang

The damage done to the European integration was severe. Only the ECSC could survive in European integration. Instead of EDC, Great Britain, France, and the United States had agreed to shift to the NATO alternative for German rearmament. A loose intergovernmental defense organization to supervise the new German armed forces came from the British Conservative government led by Anthony Eden. The government of Mendès-France rapidly accepted this proposal, and in October 1954, the six members of the ECSC and Britain signed a treaty creating the Western European Union (WEU).[51]

4. From Messina to the Treaty of Rome : EEC and Euratom

4.1. Reviving the European Agenda
The initiative of re-launching Europe was taken by the Benelux countries in the form of a general common market. Dutch Foreign Minister Willem Beyen saw the EDC as a useful intermediate station on the road to further European integration, especially integration in economic matters. Within the framework of the EPC discussions, Beyen had launched his own Beyen plan for trade liberalization. Beyen recommended that a customs union be formed to advance European integration to the next stage. Beyen's proposal was developed as the core of the "Benelux memorandum," which served as the basic text for discussions at Messina. A customs union became the central feature of the communiqué issued after the Messina meeting. The proposal for a European customs union emerged from within the conceptual framework of ECSC institutions.[52]

At a meeting in Messina, Italy, in June 1955, ECSC foreign ministers discussed the future of European integration. Spaak had prepared a memorandum suggesting further integration along the lines of Monnet's idea for an atomic energy community and for a common market. The final report, presented at a meeting in Venice in May 1956, proposed that the

---

Publishing, 2000).
[51] Guyomarch, op. cit., p. 23.
[52] Gillingham, op. cit., p. 33.

two objectives of sectoral (atomic energy) integration and wider economic integration (a common market) should be realized in separate organizations with separate treaties.[53]

The Six were of the opinion that the objective of European construction should be achieved first of all in economic sphere. They believed that the establishment of a united Europe could be achieved through the development of common institutions, progressive fusion of national economies, creation of a common market, and gradual harmonization of their social policies. The goal of economic policy included the constitution of a European Common Market free of internal duties and all quantitative restrictions. It was recommended that these measures be made in stages.[54]

On March 25, 1957, the Six signed the Treaty of Rome, establishing the European Economic Community (EEC) and the European Atomic Energy Community (Euratom). The EEC was born based on a series of institutions: the European Commission, the European Assembly (later changed to the European Parliament) the Court of Justice, and the Economic and Social Committee. The other essential agreement included in the treaty was the adoption of a Common Agriculture Policy (CAP). The CAP enacted a free market of agricultural products inside the EEC and established protectionist policies that guaranteed to European farmers sufficient revenues, avoiding third countries products competition by means of granting agricultural prices. In addition to special provisions protecting agriculture and the French Union, the Treaty of Rome would contain numerous carefully drafted escape and safeguard clauses. The French could once again play a leading role in the integration process.[55]

---

[53] Petermann, op. cit.

[54] Major agreements at the Messina Declaration were: The joint development of the main channels of communication; cooperation on energy production and consumption; and peaceful development of atomic energy. "Resolution Adopted by the Ministers of Foreign Affairs of the Member States of the ECSC," Messina, June 1955.

[55] Gillingham, op. cit., p. 36.

4. France and Early European Integration: 1945-1957

4.2. Negotiating the Economic Integration

The idea of a common market accompanied heated debate at home. Fear had seized French business, bureaucrats, and the French public who had been accustomed to rely on protectionism.[56] The idea of a customs union was strongly opposed at first by some ministerial officials, as well as specific disadvantaged economic sectors. The *Quai d'Orsay* had argued that more time was needed to observe the effects of the ECSC and it would add a burden to EDC and EPC discussion. The *Quai d'Orsay* was skeptical of either the economic or political benefits of a customs union.[57] There was a concern, too, that the customs union would be a vehicle for restoring German political and economic hegemony in Europe. Furthermore, the external tariff set by the Benelux countries seemed too low and would be detrimental to France's external trade. France would have to choose between the French Union and European Union. On the other hand, the Finance Ministry was supportive on the idea of further economic integration. France had noticed the improvement in the French payments position in the EPU since 1954 and it gave confidence that the French economy could survive in a common market.[58]

Support for liberalization was led mainly by exporters and bankers. French industry was modernizing and French exports to Europe between 1953 and 1957 were almost doubled.[59] Large-scale business began to feel the necessity of closer commercial cooperation with other European countries, which led to a slow increase of support for trade liberalization. Big business was favorable to integration while small- and medium-sized firms were still reluctant. The Conseil National du Patronat Français (CNPF), the French Patron's Association, began to move toward support

---

[56] Gillingham, op. cit., p. 44.
[57] Frances M. B. Lynch, *France and the International Economy: From Vichy to the Treaty of Rome* (London and New York: Routledge, 1997), pp. 169-70.
[58] Ibid., p. 172.
[59] World trade increase about threefold in the 1950s. Intra-European exports and imports quadrupled while West Germany's exports and imports nearly quintupled during this decade. During these years the European economy was being internationalized and Europeanized. Gillingham, op. cit., p. 37.

for the customs union. The spread of the idea that economic modernization would be possible only through trade liberalization and concerns about economic isolation that other countries were moving toward trade liberalization.[60]

Compared to the cautious and conditional support from business, the position of agriculture was more positive. In the late 1940s and the early 1950s, French farmers had actively promoted integration. Farmers had consistently pressed for European cooperation since well before the Schuman Plan in the 1950s. Agriculture accounted for a higher share of employment (25 percent) in France, which was the second highest among the Six. However, the bulk of French production was in less competitive, land-intensive agricultural commodities. Subsidy, in the form of price supports, was necessary to farmers' prosperity. What France actually wanted was a Community-wide subsidy scheme.[61]

Before the EEC could be launched, France had to deal with the free-trade proposal designed by the British and officially sponsored by the OEEC. To the British, a free-trade area was in the end only a way to weaken the Six as the core of a new continental power. For France, closer relations with Britain were desirable but a FTA was just not in France's economic interest. The French government proposed to consider the FTA if only agriculture was included. Guy Mollet once considered an Anglo-French economic union to keep France out of the Common Market but he did not receive warm support from the British government.[62] Construction of a customs union that was compatible with the General Agreement on Tariffs and Trade (GATT) was opposed by French agricultural interests and would have done little to provide new investment and trading opportunities for present and foreign colonies. The French government concluded that the French Union could be maintained only through

---

[60] Andrew Moravcsik, *The Choice for Europe: Social Purpose and State Power from Messina to Maastricht* (Ithaca: Cornell University Press, 1998), p. 115.

[61] The treaty provided for a common organization of agricultural markets but offered few specifics. Gillingham, op. cit., p. 47; Moravcsik, op. cit.

[62] Mollet traveled to London but he was rebuffed because the British were reluctant to deal with French agriculture.

European financial assistance, investment, and market opportunities.

In this confronted situation, atomic energy and consequent discussion on the Euratom became a new breakthrough.[63] Euratom was accepted as "the lesser evil" than the customs union. The French government adopted a strategy to focus on the Euratom at first since there was considerable opposition to the Common Market Treaty within France. The Mollet government hoped that the very success of Euratom would, subsequently, make it easier to ratify the Common Market Treaty.

The French plan for Euratom received very positive endorsement domestically. However, the German government was adamant to link the two treaties and had the full agreement of Belgium and the Netherlands.[64] In this situation, Maurice Faure warned that France's partners would delay progress on the Euratom Treaty unless the French government took a decision in favor of a common market. The debate turned on the cost of non-acceptance. There had been concerns that France would be driven into isolation in both economic and foreign policy. The failure of the EDC and EPC added a burden for non-acceptance of the treaty. The French government loosened its emphasis on Euratom, which had been strongly pushed by Monnet, and replaced it with the common market.

The French government proposed several conditions to be met before moving from the first stage to the second and third stages of the common market. At the Foreign Ministers' Meeting in Venice in May 1956, the French Foreign Minister Pineau agreed to the Spaak Report on the condition that the length of time needed to proceed to the second stage of tariff reductions should depend on the progress made in harmonizing legislation and that the overseas territories should be included in the common market.[65] France also argued for the harmonization of social legislation from the stage one.

In the end, there was a compromise with general energy and technology sharing to make Euratom acceptable to Germany and the

---

[63] Monnet thought that the idea of economic community was too broad, especially after the failure of EDC and EPC. Instead he supported to initiate Euratom first.
[64] Lynch, op. cit., p. 173.
[65] Lynch, op. cit., p. 177.

inclusion of agriculture and protection of overseas territories into EEC to make it acceptable to the French.[66]

4.3. The French Choice of the Treaty of Rome

The January 1955 replacement of the anti-European French Prime Minister Pierre Mendès-France by Edgar Faure, a pragmatic European, was a turning point that re-launched the European integration. His successor, Guy Mollet,[67] was well disposed to advancing integration. Since 1956, France showed strong support for a customs union.

In January 1956, the French legislative elections led to a new center-left government. The number of Communist had increased from 100 to 150 while the Poujadist party won forty-two seats. Radicals led by Mendès-France opposed the idea of a common market. However, the number of Gaullists had fallen from eight to twenty. Even though the rest of the government, led by Mollet, was sympathetic to the idea of a common market, it feared a repetition of the EDC fiasco. The composition itself did not guarantee a successful ratification of the project.

Unlike the EDC ratification when unified opposition of the Gaullists and split among proponents (SFIO, Radicals, Conservatives), Gaullists were split whereas SFIO was reunited in the EEC votes. The vote united the Socialists, who had split over the EDC on geopolitical grounds. SFIO leaders stressed that the customs union and export-led growth were economic imperatives.[68] The treaty won over Conservatives and Radicals largely for economic reasons. The vote split the Gaullists because there was no agreement that any geopolitical issues were at stake.[69] Unlike previous antipathy to the EDC, de Gaulle himself remained silent in the EEC from Messina through ratification. De Gaulle's silence and the

---

[66] Inclusion of agriculture was initially acceptable and both Belgium and the Netherlands also had overseas territories at that point.

[67] Mollet was a minister for Europe, 1950-1951, president of the Council of Europe, 1954-56, a member of Monnet's Action Committee for Europe.

[68] The turning point was the singing of the London Accords, resolving the German situation. Moravcsik, op. cit., p. 121.

[69] Ibid., p. 116.

4. France and Early European Integration: 1945-1957

absence of compelling geopolitical arguments permitted a majority to support the treaty on essentially economic grounds.[70]

In January 1957, the French government secured almost all its conditions for the common market at the National Assembly. Then on July 10, 1957, the French National Assembly ratified the Treaty of Rome.[71]

Like the ECSC, the EEC was a means to tie Germany into Europe and render a future European war impossible. Geopolitical ideas and interests were still important; yet the German problem was less salient in the negotiation of the EEC than that of the EDC and ECSC. Coexistence with Germany has now become a given condition. A few sensitive issues on the German rearmament have been solved. Economic integration followed the resolution of outstanding geopolitical issues, such as the formation of NATO and the WEU, the disposition of the Saar and Moselle issues, and the launching of the French nuclear program.[72]

The problem of the colonies and France's great power status were also at the center of French concern during these years. Ties with French colonies began to weaken. The French empire was a network of bilateral treaties binding the colonies and dependencies to France, which provided for reciprocal protection. The preference zone called EURAFRICA was born. However, military and financial costs of the empire were unsustainable. The French government could no longer cope with the burden of financing investment in the overseas territories and was failing to mobilize sufficient private investment.[73] The European partners would have to donate to the development of the colonies in order to create

---

[70] Ibid., p. 117.

[71] The vote was 342 in favor and 239 against, including sixteen out of twenty-one (Gaullists).

[72] Lynch argues that the French government's decision to sign the Treaty of Rome was not its preferred foreign policy option. Even though the government justified it to the National Assembly in foreign policy terms, it was the strength of economic case, which ensured its success. After the Britain's rejection of Mollet's proposal for an Anglo-French Union, the French government had no foreign policy alternative left. Lynch, op. cit., p. 183; Moravcsik, op. cit., p. 118.

[73] Gillingham, op. cit., p. 48.

markets for French exports. Economic cooperation with continental European countries was the only remaining way to maintain close relations with the present and former colonies. The Suez crisis of November 1956 was another shock to the French people.[74] France realized that an alliance with Britain was little help and it shifted the focus of the French government to Germany and other continental countries.

The rise of German power, the prospect of decolonization, and the failure of the EDC engendered in the French a fear of diplomatic isolation. EEC provided an opportunity to repair the damage to their own prestige and position caused by their rejection of the EDC.

5. Conclusion

The path to the European Community was a strategic outcome to maximize France's national interest. Policymakers and political leaders considered constantly the two pillars of national interest—politics and economics.

The Fourth Republic constantly sought to control the economic power and diplomatic strength of Germany. Germany would eventually be restored to a position of equality in Europe, but at the price of merging a crucial component of its economy, its coal and steel productive capacity, with those of its neighbors, allowing France a way to keep some measure of control over the development of the German economy. More importantly, German rearmament would be controlled as Germany became integrated into Western Europe.[75] French ambition to maintain great power status, together with its management of its colonies, was another political interest for which European integration contributed toward.

A consensus about the need for economic recovery had been at the center of French strategy, as shown in the Monnet Plan. French postwar

---

[74] However, direct evidence for the widespread claim that the Suez crisis fundamentally altered French preferences is sparse.

[75] William Hitchcock, *France Restored: Cold War Diplomacy and the Quest for Leadership in France, 1944-1954* (USA: University of North Carolina Press, 1998).

economic policy had two objectives: industrial expansion and the liberalization of domestic markets within the EC.[76] Economic interest became more salient after the rejection of the EDC. As compared to the debacle of the EDC rejection in 1954, it was commercial interests that permitted rapid negotiation and ratification. The EEC negotiation deliberately avoided the confrontation with sensitive political issues. In fact, the concern of German rearmament under the transatlantic alliance became a reality by the beginning of EEC negotiations.

The idea of a supranational Europe was important but the idea alone could not drive integration strategy. Pro-European ideology was shared by a limited pool of political elites. Fear and doubt prevailed among the public and bureaucrats. In this uncertain political situation, the idea could play the role of a focal point, especially in establishing the ECSC. Jean Monnet was at the center of spreading the European idea during this period. However, the idea could only survive and only became effective when it combined with certain types of interests: the containment of Germany, economic modernization, France's *grandeur* in Europe and the world, etc.

In the political context, both inter- and intra-party alliances influenced the articulation of a particular type of interest and ultimately decided the stop-and-go results. Political support for supranational European institutions was rather pragmatic and interest-based and less ideological. The European federalist movement in France was modest and faced vehement opposition. Only the small Christian Democrats and MRP showed unquestioned support for supranational institutions and federal schemes. Deliberate political maneuvering had been crucial to advance integration strategy. In the end, the Fourth Republic succeeded in forging a coherent strategy for French economic and diplomatic recovery in Europe despite its legendary constitutional weakness and political squabbling.

The governments of both Edgar Faure and Guy Mollet, which directed policy making during the re-launch, championed the Monnet proposal as the preferred approach to integration because it provided not only a convenient "smokescreen" behind which France could protect its

---

[76] Moravcsik, op. cit., p. 193.

interests but also a bargaining chip that could be traded for economic concessions needed to make French entrance into a future customs union politically acceptable.

French stance on European integration was a need-based one. France was desperate to suggest the supranational institution of ECSC at the last moment to guarantee at least partial control of the Ruhr. EDC negotiation did not involve such desperate necessity and became a target of nationalist sentiment and domestic political cleavages. Diplomatic burden from the failure of EDC became, in turn, a basis of further initiatives. Fast increase of European economic interdependence, loosening ties with the colonies, and the settlement of German issues under the transatlantic military alliance led to the recalculation of the French national interest. European integration could have been the best means available to maximize the French national interest at the given moment.

The French road to the Treaty of Rome focused less on the conditions of acceptance but more on the costs of non-acceptance. For France, the European Community was more economically inevitable than politically desirable.

References

Primary Sources
"Draft Treaty Embodying the Statute of the European Community Adopted by the Ad Hoc Assembly," March 11, 1953.
"Le plan Schuman à l'Assemblée nationale," dans la brochure B.E.D.E.S., Bureau d'étude et de documentation économique et sociale, 27 décembre 1951. Archives du ministère des Affaires étrangères, Paris, Cabinet du Ministre - Robert Schuman, vol. 144, ff. 622-24.
"Lettre de Konrad Adenauer à Robert Schuman, 18 avril 1951." Archives du ministère des Affaires étrangères, Paris, Coopération économique, vol. 520, f. 42.
"Lettre de protestation du Comité central d'Entreprise de l'Union sidérurgique du Nord de la France (USINOR) contre le plan Schuman à Marcel Plaisant," président de la Commission des Affaires Etrangères du Conseil de la République, 28 novembre 1951. Archives du ministère des Affaires

étrangères, Paris, Papiers d'agents - Papiers Plaisant, vol. 144, ff. 411-14.
"(Jean Monnet) Memorandum to Robert Schuman and Georges Bidault," May 1950.
"Note à propos de la participation de l'Allemagne à l'Autorité internationale de la Ruhr, annotée de la main de Robert Schuman, 3 décembre 1949." Archives du ministère des Affaires étrangères, Paris, Cabinet du ministre Robert Schuman, vol. 68, ff. 61-62.
"Note du Commissariat au Plan relative aux effets du plan Schuman sur les industries du charbon et de l'acier en France, 8 février 1951. Archives du ministère des Affaires étrangères, Paris, Secrétariat général, vol. 60, ff. 147-77.
"Protocol Modifying and Completing the Brussels Treaty," Paris, October 1954.
"Resolution Adopted by the Ministers of Foreign Affairs of the Member States of the ECSC," Messina, June 1955.
"Statute of the Council of Europe," London, May 1949.
"The Treaty of Economic, Social and Cultural Collaboration and Collective Self-Defence," Brussels, March 1948.

Secondary Sources
Bossuat, Gérard. *La France, l'aide américaine, et la construction européenne.* Paris: Comité pour l'Histoire Économique et Financière de la France, 1992.
Diebold, Jr., William. The Schuman Plan: A Study in Economic Cooeperation, 1950-1959. New York: Praeger, 1959.
Dumoulin, Michel, ed., 2000. *The European Defence Community: Lessons for the Future?* Brussels: Peter Lang Publishing, 2000.
Gillingham, John. *European Integration: 1950-2003.* Cambridge: Cambridge University Press, 2003.
Guedry, Michel R. France and European Integration: Toward a Transnational Polity? Westport: Praeger Publishers, 2001.
Guyomarch, Alain, Howard Machin and Ella Ritchie. *France in the European Union.* New York: St. Martin's Press, 1998.
Hitchcock, William. France Restored: Cold War Diplomacy and the Quest for Leadership in Europe, 1944-54. USA: University of North Carolina Press, 1998.
"Le Plan Shuman: Une nouvelle architecture pour l'Europe? 1950/2000," Colloque organize par l'Institut Historique Allemand et le Centre d'Information et de recherché sur l'Allemagne contemporaine (CIRAC) avec le soutien de la Fondation Robert Bosch (Stuttgart), Paris, les 28 et 29

avril 2000, AHF-Information No. 20, Volume 21, 2001.3.21.
Lynch, Frances M. B. *France and the International Economy: From Vichy to the Treaty of Rome.* London and New York: Routledge, 1997.
Mioche, Philip. *Le Plan Monnet: Genèse et élaboration, 1941-1947.* Paris: Publications de la Sorbonne, 1987.
Moravcsik, Andrew. *The Choice for Europe: Social Purpose and State Power from Messina to Maastricht.* Ithaca: Cornell University Press, 1998.
Petermann, Simon. "The ECSC, the EDC and the Messina Conference: Realities and Hopes," (2001). Online at www.edc.spb.ru/conf2001/Petermann.htmle.
Ruane, Kevin. *The Rise and Fall of the European Defence Community: Anglo-American Relations and the Crisis of European Defence, 1950-55.* Houndsmill, UK: Palgrave Macmillan, 2000.
Salmon, Trevor. *Building European Union: A Documentary History and Analysis.* Manchester, UK: Manchester University Press, 1997.
Story, Jonathan and Guy de Carmoy. "France and Europe" in Jonathan Story, ed., *The New Europe: Politics, Government and Economy since 1945.* Oxford: Blackwell Publishers, 1993.
Tuominen, Jarkko. "The European Defence Community 1950-1954: The second uneasy step towards the United States of Europe," (1997). Online at www.valt.helsinki.fi/kvtok/1997/3181.htm.
Van der Harst, Jan. "The European Defence Community: A Failure in High Politics Integration," Jean Monnet lecture, University of Manchester, March 7, 2003.
_____. *The Atlantic Priority: Dutch Defence Policy at the Time of the European Defence Community.* UK: European Press Academic Publishing, 2003.
Wall, Irwin M. *The United States and the Making of Postwar France, 1945-1954.* New York: Cambridge University Press, 1991.
Young, John W. *France, the Cold War, and the Western Alliance: French Foreign Policy and Post-War Europe, 1944-1949.* New York: St. Martin's Press, 1990.

CHAPTER 5

GERMANY AND EUROPEAN INTEGRATION: CONSOLIDATION OF THE POLITICAL SYSTEM AND ITS NORMS

Yuichi MORII

1. Introduction

Germany has been not only an eager supporter of European economic integration, but also an important adherent of the political integration since its foundation in 1949.[1] In this sense, Germany contributed much to the development of European integration and other regional cooperation regimes in Europe. But until Germany regained its sovereignty in 1955, Germany's options were very limited by both international constraints and domestic political conditions.

International constraints are, needless to say, the legacies of World War II. The restriction of the German sovereignty by the four powers (the United States, Great Britain, France, and the Soviet Union) continued until

---

[1] In this chapter analyzing the European integration policy of the "Federal Republic of Germany," "Germany" refers to "the Federal Republic of Germany (FRG)," the so-called "West Germany." The "German Democratic Republic (DGR)" or "East Germany" is stated as such.

German unification in 1990.[2] And as a country at the front of the East-West confrontation in the Cold War, the Federal Republic of Germany had to and was willing to embed itself in the Western system, namely in the NATO alliance and in European economic integration.

Domestic politics also restrained the foreign policy of Germany. The German reunification question, which was constrained by the Cold War environment, caused major difficulties for the political leadership of Germany until the end of the 1950s. But until the foundation of the European Economic Community, a fairly firm political consensus was formed among major political parties in Germany. That is namely the political commitment to the "West": the protection of the democratic free Western political system became the most important political goal for Germany. And second only to this political goal was the maintenance of peace in Europe. A third goal was German reunification. This hierarchy of political norms since the 1950s has been firmly embedded in the German political system. And for this goal, membership in the NATO alliance and European integration was an incontestable political choice.

The norm of democracy and freedom were internalized and became consensual in the 1950s. The norm of European integration is, in Germany, also internalized and almost totally consensual among all established political parties.[3] These norms were gradually but steadily constructed in the 1950s. These constructed beliefs of Western democracy and European integration became the core norms of the Federal Republic.

---

[2] The Two-plus-Four Treaty signed on September 12, 1990 by the USA, Britain, France, Soviet Union, FRG and the German Democratic Republic (GDR) cleared the way to the German unification in foreign policy area. The treaty defined the German international status (border, alliance membership, etc.) and legally abolished the reserved rights of the allied powers of the World War II.

[3] In the first legislature period of the national parliament, Bundestag, there were 11 political groups and 2 independent members in the Bundestag. After the 3rd Bundestag election in 1957 there were only 4: the Christian Democrats (CDU/CSU), Social Democrats (SPD), Free Democrats (FDP) and the German Party (DP). After the 4th election in 1961 there were only 3 political groups : CDU/CSU, SPD and FDP in the Bundestag. As the political consensus emerged, the party system converged in the three-party-system.

5. Germany and European Integration: Consolidation of the Political System and its Norms

This chapter examines how these political goals were set in Germany in the early period of European integration and how these norms of Western European integration were embedded in the political system. If we look back at the post-World War II foreign policy or the integration policy ("*Europapolitik*"), we discover how important these political norms are in the political system of Germany. The long-term influence of the political commitment toward the European integration expressed on many occasions by German political actors should not be disregarded.

Of course this does not mean that Federal Republic abandoned the goal of realizing its own national interest. What is crucial to understand is that the country's leaders tried to realize Germany's interests within the framework of European integration. To realize its interests meant often to construct the European institution in an ideal way, as the Federal Republic could not base its political assertions on its interest, but had to base its claims upon democratically legitimate modern political philosophy. As a consequence, German political opinion attached high normative value to the consolidation and democratization of European institutions. In the German European integration policymaking, this aspect — the existence of and influence by ideals of integrated democratic Europe — is highly significant. Without taking this point into account, we cannot explain well why the German government usually set a maximum goal at many treaty making or amending negotiations in the history of European integration.

Even if we stress the importance of general consensus toward European integration and the importance of the norm, we must at the same time point out that the decision-making process of the Federal Republic has another face. As Simon Bulmer points out, in Germany, the daily decision-making process of each issue area — like agriculture — is sectoralized. And the central coordination by the Chancellor is usually problematic and weak.[4] This daily sectoral policymaking has sometimes a negative impact on the so-called "*history-making*" (treaty amending or institution building) European policymaking of the federal government. It means that the sectoral political interests — such as agriculture, labor, and

---

[4] Simon Bulmer and William Paterson, *The Federal Republic of Germany and the European Community* (London : Allen & Unwin, 1987), Chapter 2.

environment — collide with the general goal of European integration policy of Germany to build more democratic and effective European institutions.

In the following sections it will be discussed how the domestic political consensus on European integration was formed, especially from 1949 to 1955. By discussing the period we especially pay attention to the interplay between the German political interest and the interests of the Allied Powers.

In the first section we discuss the formation of the political system during the period of occupation. After reviewing the foundation of the Federal Republic, we further analyze the negotiation of the Schuman Plan in the second part, a plan that was without question the decisive turning point for Germany. In the third part we discuss the consolidation period of the "Western European integration" in the mid 1950s until the foundation of the European Economic Community. Finally, we analyze how the course setting until the end of the 1950s influenced German European integration policy in the following period, especially in relation to its direct neighbor, France, and to Germany's Atlantic relations.

2. The Desire to Restore Sovereignty and Territorial Unity

The occupation of Germany, divided in four sectors, made the political development and reconstruction of the state far more difficult than that of the equivalent loser of World War II, Japan. Even among the western allied powers — the USA, Britain, and France — the occupation policies, such as reparation, denazification, and democratization were very different.[5] Under these circumstances Germany had to build a new democratic political system and regain control over its own territory.

---

[5] For further details of the division of the sectors and the policies of Western powers toward these sectors, see Theodor Eschenburg, *Jahre der Besatzung 1945-1949* (*Geschichte der Bundesrepublik Deutschland*, Band 1) (Stuttgart: Deutsche Verlags-Anstalt, 1983), pp. 77-105.

2.1. The Allies and the Occupation Policies

Even after the United States announced the Truman Doctrine and the Marshall Plan and it became quite evident that the confrontation with the Soviet Union was unavoidable, France took a fairly harsh occupation policy toward its German occupation sector. Though France was formally a winner of the war, it was economically in deep trouble. France tried to cut its occupation zone (Württemberg-Hohenzollern, Baden and Rheinland-Pfalz) from others parts of Germany. France wished to control its zone for its own political and economic interests. France cut out the Saar — a highly rich tributary of the Mosel in southern Germany — from the French occupation zone and integrated it into the French economic zone. As the Saar was responsible for one third of French coal production, France relied on the Saar for its economic recovery.[6] Thus the French policy toward the Saar was quite coercive in the early years.

Compared with the policy of France, the USA and Britain turned their occupation policies into modest one in early stages of the occupation. U.S. Secretary of State James Byrnes announced in September 1946 the intention of giving Germans their sovereignty back so as to establish a new German state. Byrnes and the British Minister of Foreign Affairs Ernest Bevin agreed in December 1946 to establish a united economic zone, the "Bi-Zone" in 1947, turning the U.S. and British zones into a single economic area.[7]

2.2. The Establishment of the Federal Republic

The currency reform of June 1948 in the western sectors and the following Berlin blockade made the unification of the four sectors decisively difficult, virtually impossible. As a consequence, the division between West Germany and East Germany became gradually fixed from this time

---

[6] It was the Iron Curtain that divided East Germany and West Germany. According to this analogy France made a silk curtain between its zone and the other zones in West Germany. Ibid., pp. 95-102. From the standpoint of French interest, France had to have a different occupation policy toward Germany than that of the USA or Britain.

[7] Manfred Grötemaker, *Geschichte der Bundesrepublik Deutschland: von der Gründung bis zur Gegenwart* (München: C.H. Beck, 1999), pp. 37-40.

forward. The allies agreed in London to make the western zones independent from the Soviet zone in June 1948. The constitutional assembly was called and it drafted a provisional constitution, the Basic Law, without using the term "constitution" to show its reluctance to the provisional establishment of a German state without solving the unification issue. The new German political system, the Federal Republic of Germany, was later established in May 1949.

The political system of the Federal Republic was constituted to overcome the problems that destroyed the democratic system of the Weimar Republic from inside. Of course, basic human rights were guaranteed in the first part of the Basic Law; but it was the federalism and the constitution of the federal government that made the new political system especially different from that of the former Weimar Republic.[8] For example, once the chancellor was elected, he could not be easily forced to resign by a vote on nonconfidence in parliament. Likewise, dissolution of the parliament was only to occur in very extreme circumstances. The plebiscitary elements that destabilized the Weimar Republic were excluded from the new system.[9]

Though Germany acquired its political institution, the Federal Republic was not fully independent and was under the control of the High Commissioners of the Western allied powers.[10] Symbolically the

---

[8] For detailed discussion of the constitution making process, see Karlheinz Niclauß, *Der Weg zum Grundgesetz: Demokratiegründung in Westdeutschland 1945-1949* (Paderborn: Schöningh, 1998).

[9] The plebiscites were excluded at the federal level, many of the German Länder have the plebiscites in their Länder constitution. Discussing the stability of the German political system, the 5-percent Clause, which does not allow a party to get proportional distribution of the parliamentary seats, if it did not get more than 5 percent of the vote at the federal level, is often mentioned. But the 5-percent Clause in today's sense was introduced since the second federal election. The first election's 5-percent Clause was applied at the Länder level and thus it was relatively easy for smaller parties to acquire seats in the parliament.

[10] "At the beginning, there were the allies." Haftendorn stresses the importance of the allies in the formation period of the Federal Republic. In the German contemporary history, the Arnulf Baring's expression "At the beginning, there was Adenauer" is well

5. Germany and European Integration: Consolidation of the Political System and its Norms

"provisional" Federal Republic was situated in the provincial capital city of Bonn, not in the former imperial capital Berlin, and it had neither a foreign nor defense ministry.

This birth of the Federal Republic without full sovereignty made European integration necessary and indispensable for Germany. And in this stage, cooperation with other European neighbors was not easy, because the Federal Republic was not in a position to cooperate as an equal partner. As is often cited, at the first visit of Konrad Adenauer, the newly elected first chancellor of the Federal Republic on September 21, 1949, the French, British, and U.S. Commissioners *on the carpet* were to hand over the occupation statute to Adenauer, who was then to step off the carpet. But as this symbolic inequality irritated Adenauer, he boldly stepped on the carpet. The goal of the first chancellor of the Federal Republic, Konrad Adenauer, was to regain equal status, not only in diplomatic formalities, but substantially in the European and international arena.[11]

Soon after the establishment of the Federal Republic, it was allowed to become a member of the International Ruhr Agency and the Organization for European Economic Cooperation (OEEC). But it was a long way off from becoming a member of the politically more significant European organization to restore its sovereignty.

The role of the United States during the formation period of the Federal Republic was huge. The U.S. government was from the early state in favor of a tolerant occupation policy and as the confrontation with the Soviet Union became severe, with the assent of Britain, the United States supported efforts to make the western part of the occupied Germany

---

known. Haftendorn warns to neglect the role of the allies and to overstress the independency of Germany during the early construction period. Helga Haftndorn, *Deutsche Außenpolitik zwischen Selbstbeschränkung und Selbstbehauptung: 1945-2000* (Stuttgart: Deutsche Verlags-Anstalt, 2001), pp. 17-26.

[11] Germany was controlled at the federal level by the Allied High Commission for Germany; at the zones level (later Länder), by each High Commissioner. Even after 1950 there were thousands of allied civil bureaucrats. See further; Grötemaker, op. cit., pp. 103-4.

independent. For the United States, the cost of supporting the occupied sector was regarded as too high. It was France that was very cautious with the status of the International Ruhr Agency and the nature of the would-be formed political system of Germany.[12] But especially after the Berlin blockade of 1948, the fate of Berlin and West Germany became directly connected with the fate of the allies. The German population also gradually accepted the allies. At the private level, U.S. High Commissioner John McCloy and Adenauer could understand each other well and their relationship built on trust had a positive impact on the U.S.-German relationship.

3. The Schuman Plan as a Decisive Turning Point

There was strong general support among almost all the parties in Germany for the vague concept of "federal Europe" after the end of World War II. After the experience of Nazi rule, the newly gathered political leaders found their hope not in a national institution but rather in a federal democratic Europe. But each party had a different interpretation of "federal Europe" and how such a state should be realized.

Adenauer was one of the eager supporters of European integration. He wrote, for example, in August 1949: "In the area of foreign policy, our principle is concrete. First of all the relationship to the western neighbor states and especially with the USA must be constructed. We'll make every effort to make Germany accepted in a European federation with equal rights and equal obligations."[13] Adenauer made not only the need for European integration clear, but he also stressed the importance of the "Western" integration with a strong tie to the United States. In this point his opinion collided with that of his political opponents, the Social Democrats, who preferred a rather independent Europe as a third power

---

[12] Wilfried Loth, *Die Teilung der Welt: Geschichte des Kalten Krieges 1941-1955, Erweiterte Neuausgabe* (München: DTV, 2000), pp. 229-36.

[13] Hans-Peter Schwarz, *Die Ära Adenauer: 1949-1957* (Geschichte der Bundesrepublik Deutschland Band 2), (Stuttgart: Deutsche Verlags-Anstalt, 1981), p. 55.

5. Germany and European Integration: Consolidation of the Political System and its Norms

between the United States and the Soviet Union.

Yet Adenauer's desire for German sovereignty and national interest was also clearly stated. To be equal with equal obligation with other members of the international community was from the beginning his goal for semi-sovereign Germany under the High Commissioner's control. But it was not at all easy for Adenauer to reach his goal under both domestic and international constraints.

3.1. Domestic Constraints

Domestically, Adenauer's policy goal was not supported by all of the important actors when he became the chancellor of the Federal Republic. Upon his election as first chancellor, his governing coalition parties' majority was not stable. In the parliament he had only one vote majority against the opposition parties. Even in his own party, the Christian Democratic Party, he faced strong opposition to his policy goal from people such as Jakob Kaiser, Minister for German Affairs, and Gustav Heinemann, the Interior Minister. Kaiser's preference for German unification outshone Adenauer's (both as a representative of Berlin, the symbol of the tragedy of post-war Germany, and as a minister for all German affairs).[14] Heinemann, on the other hand, represented one group of Protestants inside the Christian Democrats.[15]

The leader of the main opposition Social Democratic Party (SPD), Kurt Schumacher, shared with Adenauer a hatred of communism, but he also took a very different standpoint to "Western" European integration. Schumacher placed much more weight on German unification and independence.[16] Though Adenauer tried to make the Federal Republic

---

[14] This ministry for all German affairs (Ministerium für gesamtdeutsche Fragen) was responsible for the intra-German, i.e. East-West German, relations. But as the intra-German question is actually an international matter and the four allied powers were ultimately responsible, the real authority of the ministry was limited.

[15] For further elaboration of the party internal politics of the Christian Democrats the analysis by Bösch is indispensable. Frank Bösch, *Die Adenauer-CDU: Gründung, Aufstieg und Krise einer Erfolgspartei 1945-1969* (Stuttgart: Deutsche Verlags-Anstalt, 2001), pp. 118-127.

[16] Schumacher's foreign policy concept changed according to the development of the

more independent from the High Commissioners, the opposition leader Schumacher regarded him as a chancellor of the allies, not a chancellor of the Federal Republic, because his attitude toward the High Commissioners was too moderate and was not adamant enough from a national perspective.

The starting conditions for Adenauer were not only politically taxing but also economically complicated. During the winter of 1949-50, the rate of unemployment soared and economic recovery stagnated. The people's dissatisfaction helped the SPD and put the incumbent government in a difficult position. As history will attest, the miracle recovery under the "Social Market Economy" of Economic Minister Ludwig Erhard had to wait until the international economic boom after the beginning of the Korean War.

3.2. International Constraints

Germany's relationship with the United States, Britain, and France was not equal, and thus lacked cordiality. The Franco-German relationship was especially complicated. France controlled the Saar — which today is called Saarland — and the Saar did not even belong to the French occupation zone. The Saar essentially became detached from Germany under French control. In the winter of 1949 France wanted to make this Saar an autonomous region. France proposed that the Saar and the Federal Republic join the newly constituted Council of Europe. This "Saar question" aggravated the national sentiment of the German opposition and strained the Franco-German relationship. Adenauer perceived that France would make the Saar, by its convention of March 1950, into a French protectorate or even a colony.[17]

Adenauer tried to escape from this dead end relationship by launching a plan for a federal union between Germany and France. It was suggested that the union should be a core of further European integration.

Cold War. For detailed discussion of his foreign policy, see Christian Hacke, *Weltmacht wider Willen; die Außenpolitik der Bundesrepublik Deutschland* (Frankfurt am Main: Ullstein, 1993), pp. 34-47.

[17] Schwarz, op. cit., p. 93.

However, except for Charles de Gaulle, no French politician gave thought to Adenauer's idea at the time. Until just before the launching of the Schuman Plan in May 1950, the political constellation in Germany and the fate of the first chancellor were far from stable.

In the same winter, the Federal Republic confronted another dilemma. With the support of the Soviet Union, East Germany was founded in October 1949. It was allowed to establish a foreign ministry, and promptly opened diplomatic relations with the Soviet Union.[18] Now the Federal Republic had to compete with a new rival in the international stage.

3.3. The Schuman Plan and the German Rearmament Issue

The French foreign minister, Robert Schuman, launched his plan for building a new European institution to control the Coal and Steel sector under a supranational scheme on May 9, 1950. Adenauer, who had been informed of the plan on the previous day, welcomed it. The Schuman Plan fundamentally changed the political climate around Germany and launched a new era of German-Franco reconciliation.[19] For France this plan provided an answer to its international stalemate under the Cold War environment. By initiating a new original plan to solve the German question in a European framework, France tried to catch up with the demands from the United States to integrate the German economy in the European framework and to use its power for Western Europe.[20]

For the Federal Republic, this initiative was a solution both to the Ruhr and Saar problems. And being accepted as a member in a newly formed international organization as an equal partner could be regarded as a great step toward the regaining of sovereignty in a European framework. Social Democrats objected to this plan as they saw a possible danger being France's misuse of the system to advance solely French interests. But the

---

[18] However, this did not mean that the Soviet's Military Administration (SMAD) gave full sovereignty back to the East Germany. SMAD's declaration on November 11, 1949 stated reservation of East Germany's foreign and domestic decisions.

[19] For further information, see Schwarz, op. cit., pp. 96-97.

[20] Haftendorn, op. cit., pp. 29-30.

powerful Federation of German Trade Unions (Deutscher Gewerkschaftsbund, or DGB) joined Adenauer's side. The DGB wanted to be free from the High Commission's control and welcomed the "co-decision system" in the steel industry, which guaranteed labor's participation in the management of the industry.[21]

But soon after the announcement of the Schuman Plan, the political constellation drastically changed once again after the beginning of the Korean War in June 1950. For Adenauer the military threat from the Communist, dictatorial East was obvious. Since the establishment of the Federal Republic, he pointed out the danger of the so-called police forces in the German Democratic Republic. Over there paramilitary police were rapidly being built. Adenauer perceived the overwhelming conventional ground force of the Soviet block as a real threat to Germany.

Thus, Adenauer tried to create equal partnership at the security level by contributing to defense. He proposed a plan to rearm Germany by building up a federal police force of 150,000 personnel. In this rearmament issue, he had to confront opposition on two fronts. In his cabinet, Interior Minister Gustav Heinemann was against Adenauer's rearmament strategy; he later left Adenauer's cabinet. In parliament, the SPD sharply opposed his strategy.

In this stage there were alternative possibilities to the German rearmament. In the three powers' foreign minister conference in New York in September 1950 one possibility to admit Germany into the NATO alliance was discussed. During the negotiation process the problem of German sovereignty and the rearmament issue were gradually merged. The French "Pleven Plan" of October 24, 1950, which planned to construct a European Defense Community (EDC), was not as warmly welcomed in Germany as the Schuman Plan was. For Adenauer, the plan was a risky one both for German sovereignty and for achieving equality in the international arena because the status of German forces in the EDC was not clearly defined. Compared to the NATO alliance solution, in which Germany would be treated as an equal sovereign partner, the

---

[21] Christoph Kleßmann, *Die doppelte Staatsgründung* (Göttingen: Vandenhoeck & Ruprecht, 1986), pp. 226-35.

5. Germany and European Integration: Consolidation of the Political System and its Norms

solution through military integration had to be more carefully scrutinized.

The popular "*ohne mich*" ("without me") movement at the beginning of the 1950s symbolized the plain pacifist sentiment among the German people against any German military contribution. The movement influenced the local elections in 1951. At this time, Adenauer was in difficult defensive position. He had to confront the popular movement. In the end, he chose the European integration solution so that Germany could contribute militarily within the European framework.

The negotiations of the ECSC, later of the EDC and other agreements to regain sovereignty, were conducted with grave difficulty. During the negotiation of the ECSC, the major problem was rather an economic one for Germany, because the High Commission had political control over Germany. Politically, Germany had more to gain than it had to lose. Economically, Germany had to agree to dissolve the Coal Selling Association (DKV) and forbid the formation of a cartel. Yet, the economic recovery contributed much to the political stabilization of the country. The beginning of the Korean War in June 1950 helped the early stage of recovery of the German economy. The recovery of the export industry was indispensable. Along with the socio-economic stabilization through the economic recovery, the gradual realization of Social Market Economy *à la* Erhard contributed to the political stabilization. The German mixture of a market economy and socially just distribution of welfare gradually swept the dark shadow of modern history away. Germany stood at the beginning of its period of "economic wonder." In this overall socio-economic environment, Adenauer's political course became gradually popular from the end of 1952.

4. The Consolidation of the "West" European Integration Policy in Germany

The pre-1953 first four-year legislative period was one of uncertainty and instability for the governing coalition. The ratification process of the EDC treaty was very complicated. In that first period, Adenauer had to overcome many obstacles both in his coalition party and in parliament.

Part II: National Visions and Experiences of Cooperation in Europe and Asia

But things changed after the 1953 federal election. During the second election of the Bundestag, Adenauer's CDU posted a sounding victory with a stable majority. The domestic political situation gained stability and thus the political preference of Adenauer became the government's preferred course. The success of the social market economy, the success both in foreign and European policy, and Adenauer's personal popularity contributed to this election victory in 1953.

Also in the minds of many Germans was the Soviet Union's crushing of the labor uprising in East Germany in June of that same year. The brutal use of military force against its own people shaped the understanding in West Germans that they were far better off than their East bloc brethren; the clear choice of the "West" stood out as a better option than any third way alternative that drifted between West and East.

Though the failure to ratify the EDC treaty in France extremely disappointed Adenauer, the negotiation to solve the German rearmament and independence issue by using the West European Union (WEU) and NATO was completed in less than two months. This smooth change of course owes much to the United States. The acceptance of the Federal Republic to NATO in 1955 gave back the Federal Republic most of its sovereignty and independence,[22] as the High Commissioners became ambassadors.

The failure of the EDC extinguished the possibility of the "United States of Europe" in the near term. Though the integration through federal institutionalization was once given up, German insistence to the European institution was not easily surrendered.

In the economic ministry under Ludwig Erhard, the discussion about European economic cooperation and integration began in early 1955. From the German perspective at the time, the functional economic integration was believed to be better if combined with the institutions, for the ECSC institutions were seen as models for further economic integration. In Germany the ideas of Jean Monnet for further functional integration in areas such as transport, energy, and nuclear energy were

---

[22] The Federal Republic regained full sovereignty without any reservations only after the unification in 1990.

5. Germany and European Integration: Consolidation of the Political System and its Norms

rather skeptically perceived because the experience of functional integration within the ECSC was not satisfactory, at least not for Germany. Germany wished beyond the function oriented integration for more rapid overall market integration.

Hence, Germany supported the abolition of the tariff barriers among the European states as proposed by the Netherlands' foreign minister Beyen. It also supported overall market and extensive economic integration. In this regard, support to the Atomic Community was lukewarm because Germany had none of its own uranium resources and had to work together with the United States. However, the common market idea was very positively accepted because of the export possibilities of the German industrial products.

The domestic constellation in Germany was very favorable to the European Economic Community (EEC) and the European Atomic Energy Community (Euratom) projects. The governing parties and most of the opposition parties shared almost the same position and generally supported the project.[23] The public opinion played virtually no role during this process.[24] Though Germany, under the lead of the Walter Hallstein in the foreign ministry, wanted further institutional integration, the ratification in France had to be taken into account, so Germany did not demand the maximum from the common market project. As a consequence, the German foreign ministry placed importance on the establishment of the Court of Justice. The Court and its progressive pro-integration interpretation of the EEC treaty contributed much to the later development

---

[23] The Free Democratic Party (FDP), which was still a national conservative party in the 1950's, was against the EEC treaty. As the leading opposition party SPD was for the treaty, the overall majority in the parliament was for the EEC treaty.

[24] Since this EEC negotiation the German public opinion played very minor role in the European integration issue. As the firm general support for the European integration existed and the consensus among the major political parties did not politicize the general course of the European integration. Since the final stage of the negotiation of the Treaty on European Union in December 1991 when the German people found out that the German Mark would be replaced by the single European currency, the public opinion gradually began to play a bigger role also in this issue area.

of the EEC.[25]

After the smooth and rapid ratification of the EEC and Euratom treaties, Adenauer was again elected by federal election in September 1957. The Christian Democrats secured 50.2 percent, a record high for support in the history of the Federal Republic. The Social Democrats could not propose any attractive alternates to Adenauer's policies. Adenauer's election slogan *"Keine Experimente!"* ("No Experiments!") emphasized the legitimacy of his policy and failure of the Social Democrats' alternatives. His decision became the course of the Federal Republic and until this election the political norms of Germany became clear: the integration of Germany into Europe and further development of integration for a free and democratic Europe. The German constituency chose no experiment, no neutral Germany, no instability. The course of the European integration became, along with the social market economy, the core norm of the Federal Republic.

5. Germany between France and the Atlantic

Since the European Economic Community treaty negotiation, the German attitude toward European integration has been consistent. Though there were slight differences on how to realize the European economic integration among the federal ministries, the general course of the federal government's European integration policy (*Europapolitik*) remained consistent. For example, the Economic Ministry under Erhard put more weight on the compatibility of the European Common Market with the worldwide liberalization of trade under the GATT regime. The Foreign Ministry and the Chancellors Office put more weight on the further institutional development of European integration. But the German commitment to the European integration process usually exceeded the reality and as the other member states, especially France, did not want the

---

[25] For the political importance of the Court of Justice of the European Communities and the legal system of the EC, see Marlene Wind, *Sovereignty and European Integration: Towards a Post-Hobbesian Order* (New York: Palgrave, 2001).

5. Germany and European Integration: Consolidation of the Political System and its Norms

supranational development of the EEC, the minor differences of the vision of the future European integration among the domestic actors did not become a serious problem. Since this time, the normative commitment of the parliamentary political elites and the economic elites to European integration has experienced no change.

But the existence of the general consensus did not mean that Germany had no difficulties realizing the Common Market. In each policy area of the European Economic Community, especially in the Common Agricultural Policy issue, sectoral German interests collided sometimes with that of other member states. And in those sectoral policy areas, the tangible German interest played a major role.[26] The pro-European attitude was often forgotten. In this sense, Germany was not different from other EEC member states. Yet, this did not mean that one decision in a policy area would shake the overall policy toward European integration.

In the 1960s the general policy preference of the Federal Republic was to realize the Common Market and to promote more institutional integration, strengthening the democratic legitimacy of the European Parliament and to enhance cooperation also in the area of foreign policy. Germany usually stood along with Belgium, the Netherlands, Luxemburg, and Italy on the institutional pro-integration side.

In the 1960s French policy under the leadership of Charles de Gaulle mainly influenced the German policy. The friendship between Adenauer and de Gaulle since September 1958 put the German-Franco relationship into its second stage in the post-World War era. This summit meeting method influenced the German European policy until Adenauer retired in 1963. The idea of closer political cooperation outside of the EEC announced by de Gaulle in 1960 placed hardship on the federal government because the reform of NATO and a drastic change in its relationship to the United States were not desirable for Germany. At the beginning of the 1960s, Germany's relationship with Britain also became a controversial issue because in Germany the exclusion of Britain from the EEC was regarded as a construction failure of the European integration. As de Gaulle used a veto against Britain, Germany had no alternative but

---

[26] See Bulmer and Patterson, op. cit.

to accept, but it was always regarded as a misconstruction of the European institution.

As it became clear that the Benelux states did not support the idea of political cooperation around the Franco-German axis on the European continent, Germany agreed to conclude a bilateral treaty with France. In reality, looking at the intensive political contacts between France and Germany, it was not necessarily important to institutionalize or formalize the Franco-German consultation framework. But Adenauer wanted to formalize the Franco-German relationship so that the intensive consultation would survive after he left the German political scene. The 1963 signing of the Elysee Treaty by France's Charles de Gaulle and Germany's Adenauer did not only formalize the diplomatic consultation but also extended the close cooperation to cultural policy areas, such as education and youth exchanges.

But the Elysee Treaty was not wholly accepted in Germany. Economic Minister Erhrad and supporters of free trade and British EEC membership harbored reservations concerning the new Franco-German treaty. The domestic reservation represented by the so-called "*Atlantist*" both in the governing Christian Democrats and in the opposition Social Democrats to the Elysee Treaty was convincingly strong. Thus Adenauer had to make a compromise to allow a pretext to the ratification law of the treaty. The pretext stressed the importance of the partnership with the United States, the NATO alliance, the further integration through the EEC, the British membership in the EEC, and the Kennedy-round.[27] The Adenauer era ended with this treaty and the close cooperation with de Gaulle faded away with the resignation of Adenauer. With the emergence of the next chancellor, Erhard, the transatlantic relationship gained steam in the government and began to sail in the mid 1960s.

6. Conclusion

Looking back at the beginning of the European integration, the role of the

---

[27] Schwarz, op. cit., pp. 295-96.

5. Germany and European Integration: Consolidation of the Political System and its Norms

first chancellor Konrad Adenauer was immense in German politics, especially in the realm of foreign and security issues. This came on the one hand from his political maturity and his political confidence in Western European integration, rejecting a neutral Germany. It also represented the structure of the German foreign policy decision-making process. Adenauer virtually monopolized negotiations with the High Commissioner, and in the later period the foreign and security policy decision making. Until March 1951, there was not even a ministry of foreign affairs. The chancellor's office was in charge of all international negotiations. And even after the establishment of the ministry in 1951, Adenauer was the foreign minister until 1955.

During the 1950s, the controversy on the course of the country faded away and Adenauer's course was established as a base for foreign and European policy. As was symbolized by the convergence of the political parties, the political courses converged on Western European integration. The political structure of the Federal Republic contributed further to make these norms more and more stable, as the party system and the parties established themselves. The policy discourse of European integration had been firmly embedded in the stable political system.

There is no question that Germany had France as its most important direct neighbor. But at the same time, since its economy depended on world trade, and since its geographical location situated it on the doorstep of the geopolitical East-West confrontation, the United States was Germany's most significant guardian, and later, partner. Thus, the Federal Republic had to balance its policy between European integration and transatlantic cooperation.

Even after the Social Democrats joined the federal government in the grand coalition in 1966, and even after they came to power in the federal government under Chancellor Willy Brandt in 1969, the basic course of European integration remained unchallenged. Willy Brandt opened new relationships with Germany's Eastern Bloc neighbors and to East Germany via his renowned "*Ostpolitik*." Nonetheless, he was also an eager supporter of the European integration. Brandt was one of the initiators of the 1969 "relaunch" of the stagnated European Communities and supporters of British membership in the EC. Brandt's successor, Helmut

Schmidt, preferred a pragmatic and efficient way for European cooperation by establishing the European Council together with his French counterpart Valéry Giscard d'Estaing. During the 1970s, the Federal Republic's foreign policy acquired other arena as both the Federal Republic and the German Democratic Republic (East Germany) joined the United Nations in 1973. Along with the European institutions, the United Nations became one of the most important institutions for orientation of German foreign policy. The Conference on Security and Cooperation in Europe (CSCE) in 1975 added yet another important arena as well.

When the Christian Democrats came back to power in 1982, Chancellor Helmut Kohl stressed the significance of Adenauer's course and put much weight on the further development of European integration. Thus German foreign and integration policies became symbols of continuity. Germany became a reliable partner both in its transatlantic relations and in the context of European integration. Even the unification of 1990 and the full recovery of the sovereignty did not change this continuity. The post-Cold War change of the foreign and security policy environment forced Germany to adapt to the new environment in the 1990s. And yet Germany still continued to follow the traditional course.

When the Social Democrats and the Greens built the coalition in 1998, Chancellor Gerhard Schröder and Foreign Minister Joschka Fischer tried to retrace the traditional foreign policy course, with the German participation in the NATO military action in the Kosovo conflict a clear symbol of this continuity.

However, new challenges to this continuity do appear on the horizon. The enlargement of the European Union to twenty-five countries in 2004 and the further deepening of the EU present new challenges to German foreign policy. Through the development of the EU, Germany has acquired a system in which it can satisfy its political and economic interests. The enlargement will no doubt further extend this secure environment. But this new situation influences the perception of the international environment and as a consequence the decision making of the Federal Republic. Likewise, the crisis of U.S.-German relationship in 2002-2003 stemming from the most recent U.S.-led war on Iraq might imply that a change is looming in this long continuity of German foreign policy.

References

Bösch, Frank. *Die Adenauer-CDU: Gründung, Aufstieg und Krise einer Erfolgspartei 1945-1969.* Stuttgart: Deutsche Verlags-Anstalt, 2001.
Bulmer, Simon and William Paterson. *The Federal Republic of Germany and the European Community.* London: Allen&Unwin, 1987.
Eberwein, Wolf-Dieter and Karl Kaiser, eds. *Germany's New Foreign Policy: Decision-Making in an Independent World.* Hampshire: Palgrave, 2001.
Eschenburg, Theodor. *Jahre der Besatzung 1945-1949.* Geschichte der Bundesrepublik Deutschland, Band 1. Stuttgart: Deutsche Verlags-Anstalt, 1983.
Grötemaker, Manfred. *Geschichte der Bundesrepublik Deutschland: von der Gründung bis zur Gegenwart.* München: C.H. Beck, 1999.
Hacke, Christian. *Weltmacht wider Willen; die Außenpolitik der Bundesrepublik Deutschland.* Frankfurt am Main: Ullstein, 1993.
Haftendorn, Helga. *Deutsche Außenpolitik zwischen Selbstbeschränkung und Selbstbehauptung: 1945-2000.* Stuttgart: Deutsche Verlags-Anstalt, 2001.
Katzenstein, Peter, ed. *Tamed Power; Germany in Europe.* Ithaca: Cornell University Press, 1997.
Kleßmann, Christoph. *Die doppelte Staatsgründung.* Göttingen: Vandenhoeck & Ruprecht, 1986.
Knodt, Michèle and Beate Kohler-Koch. *Deutschland zwischen Europäisierung und Selbstbehauptung.* Frankfurt am Main: Campus Verlag, 2000.
Loth, Wilfried. *Die Teilung der Welt: Geschichte des Kalten Krieges 1941-1955.* Erweiterte Neuausgabe, München: DTV, 2000.
Niclauß, Karlheinz. *Der Weg zum Grundgesetz: Demokratiegründing in Westdeutschland 1945-1949.* Paderborn: Schöningh, 1998.
Schwarz, Hans-Peter. *Die Ära Adenauer: 1949-1957.* Geschichte der Bundesrepublik Deutschland Band 2. Stuttgart: Deutsche Verlags-Anstalt, 1981.
Schwarz, Hans-Peter. *Die Ära Adenauer: 1957-1963.* Geschichte der Bundesrepublik Deutschland Band 3. Stuttgart: Deutsche Verlags-Anstalt, 1983.
Weidenfeld, Werner. *Zeitenwechsel; von Kohl zu Schröder.* Stuttgart:

Part II: National Visions and Experiences of Cooperation in Europe and Asia

Deutsche Verlags-Anstalt, 1999.
Wind, Marlene. *Sovereignty and European Integration: Towards a Post-Hobbesian Order*. New York: Palgrave, 2001.

CHAPTER 6

BRITAIN AND EUROPEAN INTEGRATION: SOME IMPLICATIONS FOR EAST ASIAN COUNTRIES

Won-Taek KANG

1. Introduction

> *We are with Europe but not of it. We are linked but not comprised. We are interested and associated, but not absorbed. We do not intend to be merged in a European federal system.*
>
> Winston Churchill

Britain has been widely known as an "awkward partner" or "reluctant partner" in terms of European integration.[1] Its uncomfortable position is in stark contrast to that of France and Germany, which have been a major force for integration. In the quote above, Churchill summed up in 1953 the ambivalence of Britain's position.[2] In the early stages of European

---

[1] S. George, *An Awkward Partner: Britain in the European Community*, 3rd edition (Oxford: Oxford University Press, 1998); Michael Franklin (with Marc Wilke), *Britain in the European Community* (London: Royal Institute of International Affairs, 1990), p. 7.

[2] John Turner, *The Tories and Europe* (Manchester: Manchester University Press, 2000) p. 46.

integration, Britain declined to join the European Coal and Steel Community (ECSC) and led an alternative group of the European Free Trade Area (EFTA). However, this is ironic given that it was Winston Churchill that advocated the building of a "United States of Europe" in a speech on September 19, 1946. His idea of an integrated Europe had not borne fruit for Britain's constructive role in building a "united Europe." Even since Britain joined the European Community (EC) in its third attempt, it has been very reluctant to "deepen" the level of integration. Britain still stays outside the Euro zone. Although Prime Minister Tony Blair publicly expressed his wish for taking Britain into the Euro zone, it still looks uncertain in the near future.

To many member states of the European Union (EU), Britain has inevitably been a pain in the neck, but at the same time, the Europe issue has been a very thorny problem for British domestic politics. It has been a source of intra-party division and conflict, which has been described as "one of the dominant and most divisive issues of modern British politics."[3] British political parties have swapped places with one another. The Labour Party has moved from opposition to muted enthusiasm ("constructive engagement"), while the Conservatives have moved from support to scepticism to outright hostility.[4] That is, the Labour Party is becoming more Euro-enthusiastic, while the Conservatives are becoming even more sceptical.

The purpose of this paper is two-fold. Firstly, it aims to analyze the reasons for Britain's "lukewarm" attitude toward European integration and pays attention to Britain's historical and constitutional uniqueness. In addition, a "special relationship" with the United States is examined. Secondly, on the basis of the analysis of the British experiences, this paper will attempt to identify implications for East Asian countries. Although regional integration has occurred in many parts of the globe, it seems that

---

[3] David Baker and David Seawright, eds., *Britain For and Against Europe* (Oxford: Oxford University Press, 1998), p. 1.

[4] Philip Cowley, "British Parliamentarians and European Integration," *Party Politics*, vol. 6, No. 4 (2000), p. 465.

regional integration in East Asia is never seen as an easy task. Difficulty from an "awkward partner" could come up in the course of integration if it occurs. Each country in East Asia has developed historical, political and even cultural uniqueness that cannot be easily bridged. It is hoped that the analysis of the British case carried out in this paper can provide meaningful lessons to help resolve possible problems of regional integration in East Asia.

2. Britain and European Integration: An Awkward Partner

When the integration began, Europe had in mind an explicit political goal of building a union, which was shared by many of its people. Experiences of destruction and cruelty from the two world wars made many Europeans willing to accept an idea of a "united Europe," which could mean a pooling of sovereignty covering a variety of policy spheres including political issues. In the heart of the integration, there was the "German question." Part of the process of European integration has been closely related to the peaceful restructuring of Germany and its being re-incorporated in the "Western world." Accordingly, there was political determination, desperation and a strong will of the pioneers for resolving the "touchy and urgent" issue. However, Britain did not share the vision and dream of an integrated Europe. Three reasons can be identified for the unwillingness of Britain with respect to European integration.

2.1. "Exit options" of Britain: the Commonwealth

European integration has depended on successful cooperation between France and Germany, despite the two nations having had a long history of mistrust and conflict, which had been the root cause of both world wars. France and Germany set up the ECSC and laid the foundation for the European Union to avoid another war and to "institutionalize peace." Many pioneers of European integration like Jean Monnet, Robert Schumann, and Konrad Adenauer thought that Franco-German hostility would be eliminated through integration, which would eventually serve for establishing peace in Europe. That is, many advocates on the Continent shared an imminent and desperate need for integration. The creation of the ECSC in 1951 was an outcome from this view. The ECSC aimed at integrating the administration of the most important raw materials for building not only factories but also war ships and tanks. Besides, they hoped that their combined strength could provide a crucial bulwark against Soviet expansionism.

By contrast, Britain was never keen on integrating with other European countries although it did not explicitly oppose the integration of Europe. Above all, Britain lacked such a desperate and imminent need for integration as France and other Continental countries. Britain is an island that is geographically separate from mainland Europe and, unlike its neighbors, had not been subject to foreign invasion, defeat, occupation and conquest in recent times. Attempted invasions made notably by Napoleon and Hitler were all abortive; as a consequence, the British tend to boast that basic freedom had been preserved. This unique experience has had a great impact on various aspects of the British way of life. At Brugest in 1988 then Prime Minister Margaret Thatcher emphasized that Britain's national identity had been particularly sustained by an historic defense of freedom. She wanted to stress the importance of Britain's different political, cultural, and historic traditions compared with other member states.[5]

In addition, when World War II was over Britain still had strong ties with countries outside Europe. Although the British Empire broke up after 1945, Britain still retained links with its former colonies, especially those in the British Commonwealth. In other words, Britain saw its interests in terms of three overlapping spheres of influence: those of the Empire, the United States and Europe. In fact, Britain's financial interests and traditional relationships gave it stronger overseas links than the Continental countries. Britain's overseas interests would produce a structural conflict of interest with the Continental members whose trade and culture were much more centered on Europe itself.

As a matter of fact, Britain was enthusiastic about the immediate economic goals such as the creation of a customs union or common

---

[5] Turner, *The Tories and Europe*, p. 5.

6. Britain and European Integration: Some Implications for East Asian Countries

market in goods and services among member states. However, Britain worried that joining the Community would jeopardize its trading relationships with the Empire and Commonwealth countries and North America. In Hirschman's terms, Britain had "exit" options.[6] However, by the early 1960s, it became apparent that economic growth was falling behind the rates of Britain's main European competitors and the European Economic Community (EEC) was proving to be more successful than the EFTA that Britain led. Britain then became keen to share its prosperity and development, and applied to join the EEC.

This implies that imperial preference had been abandoned. The relationship with the Commonwealth countries had been transformed. For instance, the Commonwealth countries no longer looked to Britain for protection. This was demonstrated in 1951 when Australia and New Zealand concluded a defense pact with the United States, from which Britain was excluded on the grounds that Truman did not want to give Congress the impression that the United States was committing itself to defending British colonies.[7] Thus, the reasons for Britain's joining the Community were very practical. Europe was crucial to Britain for defining its post-imperial national identity when the imperial legacy was shattered. In fact pro-European Conservative leaders like Macmillan and Heath in the 1950s and 1960s saw Europe as a way of restructuring the British economy and society. They needed to move the party away from the memory of the "good old days" in the Imperial age to modernization. Britain's historical experiences of avoiding invasions as well as the legacy of the Imperial period were attributed to becoming "a reluctant partner." When the links with the Commonwealth had been weakened, Britain decided to join the Community to share the economic fruits it produced.

---

[6] Albert Hirschman, *Exit, Voice and Loyalty* (Cambridge, Mass.: Harvard University Press, 1970).
[7] Howard Temperley, *Britain and America since Independence* (Basingstoke, UK: Palgrave, 2002) p. 193.

2.2. Challenges to Britain's Framework of Institutions

> It is the character of the people which determines the institutions which govern them and not the institutions which gives people their character. It is about being British and about what we feel for our country, our Parliament, our traditions, and our liberties. Because of that history, that feeling is perhaps stronger here than elsewhere in Europe.[8]

Europe has developed in an unprecedented way toward new forms of international cooperation, redefining for member states traditional notions of national sovereignty and independence. The significance of the creation of the ECSC lies in the fact that this is the first European organization to have a supranational structure, which has powers above that of any individual nation state.

Instead, Britain has much preferred intergovernmental decision making rather than forms of supranational or federal decision making through supranational bodies within the EU. This is why Britain refused to become a founding member of the EC, and attempted to establish a free trade area. Britain as well as six other countries outside the EEC formed the EFTA in response to the creation of the EEC. This did not establish a supranational authority but a free trade area to dismantle barriers to trade within the bloc. In other words, British participation in European integration was acceptable only so long as it confined itself to extending free trade, but there was always the possibility of conflict once European integration went beyond that.

This implies that Britain has a very strong commitment to sovereignty in comparison with other European countries. That is, the idea of a united Europe caused confrontation with the notion of British identity. It is noteworthy that Britain's "exceptionally" strong commitment to

---

[8] Margaret Thatcher, December 10, 1991. Quoted from Mark Aspinwall, "Structuring Europe: Powersharing Institutions and British Preferences on European Integration," *Political Studies*, vol. 48 (2000), p. 415.

sovereignty and consequent hesitant attitude toward European integration is firmly related to its constitutional framework.

Firstly, a strong commitment to sovereignty is closely associated with the notion of "parliamentary sovereignty." In the British system of government supreme power lies in the Parliament, which has direct and exclusive control over legislation and indirect control over the actions of the executive and the central administration. There is no constitutional restriction in its authority.[9] The concept of parliamentary sovereignty is one of the cornerstones of the British constitution and the British identify sovereignty with the British institution of an all-powerful national Parliament.

However, joining as a member of the EC in 1973 has had an impact on a wide range of domestic politics, particularly in terms of parliamentary sovereignty. When Britain joined the EC, it was required to sign the existing treaties in which British law must be consistent with European law and British courts must both accept and enforce European law. In the case of disagreement the European Court of Justice has the final say.

This means that membership in the EU formally and legally limits parliamentary sovereignty. Many Britons tend to think that a loss of power from the Westminster Parliament is seen as a loss of national power. As Turner said,

> Europe has imposed a voluntary limitation on national sovereignty and the prerogative of the national veto. . . . Clearly, states are no longer sovereign in the traditional sense of the word, namely in the retention of national institutions as the expression of the nation state through the country's ability to make its own laws.[10]

Secondly, Britain is a strong unitary state, and a central government in London retains a centralized and concentrated power. A first-past-the-post electoral system as well a two-party system effectively works for creating

---

[9] Anthony Birch, *The British System of Government*, 10th edition (London: Routledge, 1998), p. 22.

[10] Turner, *The Tories and Europe*, p. 3.

a single-party government and a strong executive. In terms of territorial politics, Parliament has the power to reform or reduce the functions performed by local governments, as it could even pass a law abolishing all local authority outright. Unlike many other European neighbors, Britain has a long tradition of single-party government, and is not familiar with the concept of federalism, which many Euro-enthusiasts want to ultimately establish at a European level.

However, Britain fears that Europeanization would undermine the centralized and concentrated nature of its power. Regional policies of the EU that tend to provide more autonomy to lower level governments as well as create a weakening of sovereignty would accelerate demands for devolution and even independence from constitutional parts of the United Kingdom (UK) such as in Scotland. For instance, a policy of "independence in Europe" was officially launched in 1988 by the Scottish National Party (SNP), which ardently pursued a separation of Scotland from the UK. In Europe—as well as the poll tax under the Thatcher government—the SNP was setting the pace in Scottish politics.[11] Rising nationalism in Scotland yielded devolution by the Blair government in 1997, which created an autonomous Scottish Parliament.

As a consequence, to some Britons, European integration and devolution were seen to diminish Parliament's position and Britain's unitary state. This was taken quite seriously especially in the minds of politicians. As Westminster members of Parliament (MPs) are directly affected they tend to be the most resistant to transfers of responsibility to the supranational institutions of the EU. Many British politicians, especially among the Conservatives, do not share the vision of Euro-enthusiasts like Jean Monet, Robert Schumann, and Jacques Delors and so on who look forward to the creation of a European "super-state."

Due to these controversial effects on the nature of British constitutions, membership in the European Union has consistently caused

---

[11] James Mitchell, "Territorial Politics and Change in Britain," in Catterall et al., *Reforming the Constitution: Debates in Twentieth-Century Britain* (London: Frank Cass, 2000), p. 243.

tension not only between political parties but also within parties. In the beginning, the Labour Party was suspicious of the EC, regarding it as a rich capitalist club serving primarily for trade and corporate interest, particularly of West Germany. In the 1960s the moderate and pragmatic leadership of Harold Wilson changed the party's view closer to that of Europe. However, Labour was again led by Euro-sceptics in the wake of the 1979 election defeat and a subsequent breakaway of pro-European senior party members like the "Gang of Four." Labour promised complete withdrawal from the EC in the 1983 general election, which contributed to its disastrous electoral defeat. A sea change came after the 1983 election defeat, for which Labour's anti-European policy was partly blamed. Its attitude toward Europe has again been changed. For example, currently the Blair government supports the single currency.

The Conservatives are now severely divided over the Europe issue, but anti-European sentiment has prevailed. It is also ironic given that it was the Conservative government under Macmillan that attempted to join the Community for the first time. The Conservatives remained fairly in favor of integration until the Heath government. Since the Thatcher period, the Conservatives drastically moved to the opposite side. Current party leader Michael Howard is also a committed anti-European. He believes Britain should never adopt a single currency. He has talked openly of leaving the union altogether and joining the North American Free Trade Agreement (NAFTA).[12]

Consequently, Britain's reluctance to integration—particularly affecting sovereignty—is closely related with its constitutional institutions.

2.3. Britain and the United States: The Atlantic versus the Continent

Geographically, Britain is undoubtedly part of Europe. London is as close to Paris as Washington is to New York. However, Britain often chooses a role "apart from Europe."[13] As mentioned earlier, Britain refused to become a founding member of the EEC.

---

[12] John Stevens, *The Guardian*, November 21, 2003.

[13] Temperley, *Britain and America*, p.192.

One reason for this is clearly related to its cultural and historical connections to the United States. It seems understandable that for reasons of language and popular culture, shared war experience and continuing strategic interest, many British people, particularly of the old generation, still relate more readily to America than to the rest of Europe. Even at the governmental level, the consciousness of America's strategic importance as an ally and partner has caused successive governments to seek to sustain the "special relationship" between Britain and the United States.[14] For example, Harold Macmillan made a controversial nuclear deal with President John F. Kennedy in 1962 amid the discussion of entry into the Community. Britain also remains a staunch supporter of the United States in critical moments such as the Iraqi conflict in 1990 and the most recent Iraqi war in 2003. Britain has almost always been an "Atlanticist" rather than a European at the governmental level.

This feature is clearly illustrated in a MORI poll in 1999. The poll results revealed that when asked "In a crisis, which of these, Europe, the Commonwealth or America-do you think would be Britain's most reliable ally?" a total of 59 percent of Britons chose America over Europe (16 percent) and the Commonwealth (15 percent). Similarly, respondents believed that they could learn more about the workings of government and democracy from America than from any of their European neighbors.[15] This survey clearly shows how close Britain feels to the United States.

Apart from cultural affinity, there are historical and political reasons as well. When World War II ended in 1945 Britain portrayed itself as a major victor in the war, with its vestige of colonies and a close relationship with the United States. Britain thought that it could sustain a world role either militarily or economically, although its economic resources were insufficient to support such a role. In this sense it tended to see itself retaining the status of a world power superior to that of France and Germany. This illusion deterred Britain from building a closer relationship with other countries in Europe in the early stages of integration.

---

[14] Franklin, *Britain in the European Community*, p. 9.
[15] Temperley, *Britain and America*, p. 194

6. Britain and European Integration: Some Implications for East Asian Countries

It was not until the Suez crisis in 1956 in the wake of Gamal A. Nasser's decision to nationalize the Suez Canal that this illusion began to be shattered. A humiliating withdrawal from the failure of military invasion suggested that the "special relationship" with the United States was limited when it came to crucial matters of international relations and reflected how frail the "special" relationship was. Britain realized that it was the United States that was a world power with global responsibilities. That is, the Suez crisis provided an opportunity for Britain to realize the fact that it could no longer retain the image of a superpower.[16] That is, Britain realized that its status in international politics had been changed from that of a world power to a medium-sized power much on a par with France and West Germany.

Britain's assumptions about its special relationship with the United States have often disturbed many European countries. For instance, Charles de Gaulle vetoed Britain's entry into the EC twice. He suspected that Britain would play the role of a "Trojan horse" for the United States, and British membership would lead to the EEC being dominated by Anglo-American interests.

Emphases on the special relationship with the United States have been considerably weakened especially in the economic sphere. Instead, British interests toward a "European" rather than an "Altlanticist" or a global perspective has gained significance. However, it seems that the Trans-Atlantic or Anglo-Saxon link still remains intact particularly in terms of security and international politics. As Franklin aptly pointed out, among ministers and officials, divisions have surfaced between "Atlanticist," who are often involved with security-related issues, and "Europeans," who are concerned more with economic issues.[17]

Thus, a special relationship outside of Europe has made Britain reluctant to cooperate with other European neighbors.

---

[16] Turner, *The Tories and Europe*, p. 51.
[17] Franklin, *Britain in the European Community*, p. 9.

3. Implications for East Asia

Those who aspire to create an "ever-closer" union do not welcome the British attitude toward the process of European integration. However, its ambivalent attitude could provide valuable lessons for East Asian countries, which have just begun to undertake a similar experiment. It has been widely said that East Asian countries need to promote economic cooperation and integration through trade and investment liberalization in order to meet the substantial challenges from globalization. However, it is very difficult to attempt to simply transplant the European experiences to East Asia. There are differences between Europe and Asia in terms of historical and cultural backgrounds. Besides, the desperation and political will to pursue the goal in East Asia does not seem to match that of its European predecessors. There is no urgent agenda that is shared by potential member countries in the Asian region. Rather, the immediate concern in East Asia seems to aim simply at the removal of trade barriers for encouraging trade and investment. Countries in the region may simply have in mind the forming of an intergovernmental body. If this is true, the notion seems similar to the British preference in the process of European integration. Therefore the British experience could provide some useful insights for the possibility of East Asian integration.

3.1. Sovereignty and Nationalism
The creation of a single market like that in Europe means that capital, goods, services and labor move freely without legal, institutional (and non-institutional) barriers. The making of an economic and monetary union and the adoption of a common currency have accelerated and consolidated the single market, and have further weakened the capability of a nation-state over its monetary policy. This signifies that the integration may begin with purely economic purposes but its consequences should extend to broader areas including political matters.

These are the kind of problems that Britain encountered in the early stages of European integration. As already mentioned, while it recognized the need for integration, Britain feared that it could eclipse its sovereignty.

6. Britain and European Integration: Some Implications for East Asian Countries

Parliamentary sovereignty has been an important institutional barrier for the British commitment to European integration. Besides, a strong unitary state and a centralized system of government also affected its cautious attitude. Britain instead led an intergovernmental body of the EFTA in the 1960s, which reflects its ambivalence toward supranational integration. In a sense, what Britain has been concerned about with regard to the development of European integration is "how far" the integration proceeds. Britain was ready to accept an intergovernmental scheme like the EFTA but it resisted any attempt at encroachment on national sovereignty.

A similar formula can be applied to the East Asian case. It is plausible to assume that East Asian countries have a similar attitude to that of the British in the 1960s. With an improved outlook from the increasing integration of the region, East Asian countries vigorously seek a model for taking the most advantage of their opportunity within the region. That is, their concern lies only in the economy, not on other areas beyond the economic sphere. Even though East Asian countries seem to understand the importance of regional cooperation to reap gains from the recent boom in trade, it still remains to be seen if East Asia can do more than simply reduce tariffs, and ultimately form a more integrated "economic community." As a matter of fact, various regional organizations in East Asia are much less institutionalized in comparison with those in Europe. In other words, East Asia does not look ready to create a kind of "supranational body," such as a common regulatory scheme, which just sets a common external tariff by creating a customs union, not to mention a common currency. As a result, it seems that their chosen mode of interaction is very likely to be intergovernmental.

Like in Britain, strong commitment to national sovereignty in East Asian countries will make them reluctant to proceed any further than intergovernmental cooperation. South Korea, Japan and China are all unitary states with a centralized government. In addition, the economies of East Asian countries are also more explicitly state-led. Japan served as a role model of the developmental state, and South Korea followed suit. China has unarguably a strong state, and the Communist Party commands supreme power. China gives non-democratic monopoly of political power to the Communist Party.

Part II: National Visions and Experiences of Cooperation in Europe and Asia

The strong commitment to statehood in this region is reinforced by historical legacies. Nationalism in Europe was roughly equated with the concept of self-determination and often identified with linguistic and ethnic communities. However, nationalism in East Asia, particularly China and South Korea, more or less reflects a sentiment of resistance and bitter memories of national humiliation and wounded pride. That is, nationalism in East Asia is related to its colonial pasts and tends to lead to an emphasis on independent statehood. In that sense, reactive nationalism in East Asia might be inculcated by the state. No matter what the case, anti-Japanese sentiment is still quite strong in South Korea as well as in China, which will be an intractable psychological problem for regional integration. Even though Japan's state-centered nationalism has disappeared since World War II, Japan repeatedly agitates its neighboring countries like South Korea and China with nationalistic behavior such as visits to the Yasukuni Shrine by ministers including the prime minister and the use of textbooks that may not adequately cover Japanese atrocities during World War II. As a consequence, reactive nationalism has been reproduced.

As a matter of fact, the force of globalization has already weakened and eclipsed the sovereignty, which has been regarded as supremacy within a nation-state since the Westphalia treaty in 1648. However, if regional integration proceeds to the point that a supranational scheme is required for further development, it is very unlikely that the peoples in East Asia will accept "a pooled sovereignty" between former archrival countries.

With its past history, Japan can be a barrier to further integration. In the future, though, China may become another. It looks certain that China will play a central role in the economic integration of East Asia and continue to be an important driver for trade as its large economy opens up following its entry into the World Trade Organization (WTO). China already accounts for half of Asia's economy measured in terms of purchasing power and China's share of global exports has tripled while its share of world imports has doubled from 1990-2002,[18] according to the World Bank's research report in 2003.

---

[18] Online at english.peopledaily.com.cn/200306/07/eng20030607_117813.shtml.

6. Britain and European Integration: Some Implications for East Asian Countries

This implies that Asian countries should take advantage of China's emergence as a major world and regional economic player. This raises not only opportunities but also challenges for its neighbors as they strive toward closer economic and trade links.

The emergence of China as a major economic power also awakens fears of its dominance in the region. With the contested nature of Asian regionalism and the historical legacy of mistrust among China, Japan, and South Korea, one nation cannot endure the dominance of another state. In contrast to Japan, which has self-imposed limitations, a growing number of people are worried about the possibility that China can become a hegemon with its growing economic strength.

Like the British concern, the relationship between political and economic integration can be easily intertwined. Even when a single currency promotes regional economic prosperity, the possibility of dominance by the Japanese Yen or Chinese Yuan could provoke nationalistic sentiment that reflects worries about eclipsing sovereignty— or about surrendering economic sovereignty to Japan or China. This is not a matter of economics but a matter of politics. This is one of the important reasons that the Miyazawa initiative to create a Yen bloc in the midst of the financial crisis in Asia was not warmly accepted and widely debated.

Like Britain, East Asian countries still strongly stick to statehood— and reactive nationalism—and as a consequence they are not willing to yield some of their national sovereignty even if necessary.

3.2. Relationship with the United States: Something Special?

As noted earlier, a "special" relationship with the United States accounts for the ambivalence of Britain. The special relationship has often had negative effects, as recently seen in the dispute among some European countries over the Iraqi War in 2003.

In the early stages of European integration, Europe did not—and could not—intend to stand against the United States. Rather, the integration process would not have been possible without tacit agreement from the United States, even though the basic impetus came from European states. The United States needed a politically and economically strong "Western Europe" to defend against the Soviet bloc. This view of the United States was in line with its decision to rearm West Germany. Then Western European countries apparently recognized the influences and interests of the United States in Europe, and accepted its leading role in international politics.

However, the drive for an integrated Europe was more or less related to the growing recognition by Europeans that Europe could not compete with the United States without uniting together. The special relationship with the United State that Britain has maintained has often been at odds with this perspective.

The relationship with the United States can also be an important factor for regional integration in Asia. The United States has played the role of a stabilizer in East Asia since World War II. Regional peace has been established with the direct military involvement of the Unites States in the region. Particularly, Japan and South Korea have been conventionally strong allies with the United States. South Korea and Japan recognize the leading role of the United States in East Asia with respect to regional security and defense, and have stayed under the security umbrella of the United States. In spite of some changes in recent years, the fundamental framework of the relationship remains intact.

China, too, has managed to have a good relationship with the United States but only when it comes to economic issues. China's relationship with the United States seems to reflect its strategic and practical preferences. However, China was not, is not and will not accept a leading role of the United States in East Asia particularly in terms of military or security issues. This means that the attitudes toward the United States are different among China, South Korea and Japan.

In the process of European integration the American factor has not been crucial. Even though former French president de Gaulle refused the British entry into the Common Market twice, seeing it as an "American Trojan horse," the United States has never directly intervened in the integration process.

By contrast, the United States has been a key player in East Asia. The way that the American factor can affect East Asian integration is twofold. First, Japan and South Korea have respectively built a bilateral "special" relationship with the United States since World War II. This implies that it is not likely that East Asian countries give priority to Asia over the United States unlike the way that European countries did in the course of integration. Even though the asymmetrical nature of the relationships between the United States and South Korea and between the United States and Japan is likely to fuel nationalism, Japan and South Korea do not want to establish a regional cooperation by isolating the United States. Attitudes of these two countries are more similar to the British one.

Second, it is unlikely that the United States will let East Asia form a regional cooperation without its involvement. Unlike the European experiences, the United States will not remain a bystander. Rather, it will want to preserve its interests and dominant influence by getting directly involved in the regional cooperation of East Asia. For example,

> We can think about the rivalries between the 'Asia-Pacific' and 'East Asian' conceptions of region in terms of the role of the US in the former and the signals sent by the latter to exclude not only the US, but also the likes of Australia and New Zealand from the equation. The leading role of the US in APEC could be seen as an attempt to impose a particular conception of capitalist development. East Asian regionalism, on the other hand might be seen as an attempt to defend the 'Asian way' or the 'developmental state' model of capitalism.[19]

This attitude of the United States could sometimes be at odds with East Asian countries when they attempt regional integration. The United States is worried that if integration proceeds, China will play a central role in the economic integration of East Asia. U.S. concern is not limited to an economic sphere. With remarkable economic growth, China can modernize its armed forces and enhance its capacity to become an international military power.

---

[19] Ben Rosamond, "Regional Integration in Europe and Asia," ASEF University Library (2002), online at www.asef.org/asef-uni/3_infohub/infohub_m_library.html.

China has a potential to become a valuable, cooperative, constructive member of the Asia-pacific economic community; but it could also become the opposite—a fearsome, aggressive, and militaristic power.[20]

Japan also feels similar pressure from the United States in terms of forming a regional cooperative body. For example, the "United States ambivalence is evidenced, for example, by its hesitance to let Japan create a regional economic grouping without the United States like the East Asian Economic Conference or a regional monetary institution with money facility, aside from the International Monetary Fund."[21]

In the course of European integration, the U.S. factor was relevant only with the British insistence on the "special relationship." By contrast, the United States will be a much more important and assertive player in East Asia in terms of regional integration. It cannot be neutral or indifferent, which implies that the process of East Asian integration would be more complicated and would go beyond simply a regional matter.

3.3. Possibilities of an "Exit" Option

As mentioned earlier, there existed desperation among European countries. Integration was seen as an essential step for preventing another war, for resolving "the German question" and for rebuilding the economy. That is, when European integration began, there were few options available to the founding countries on the Continent. By contrast, Britain had another option: the Commonwealth countries and North America.

In comparison with the situations in the 1940s and 1950s, current international circumstances have been greatly changed. Because of the

---

[20] John Tkacik, Jr.,"Strategic Risks for East Asia in Economic Integration with China," (2002), p.10, online at www.heritage.org/Research/AsiaandthePacific/WM171.cfm.

[21] Takashi Inoguchi, "Possibilities and Limits of Regional Cooperation in Northeast Asia: Security and Economic Areas," in Tai-joon Kwon and Dong-Sung Kim, eds., *World Order and Peace in the New Millennium* (Seoul: Korean Association of International Studies, 2000), p. 297.

"unfettered forces" of globalization and remarkable technological progress of information and communications, bilateral or multilateral free trade and attempts at regional integration are not unusual. That is, globalization and regionalization dismantle barriers of nation-states. The former is mainly promoted by international organizations such as the WTO while the latter is brought forth through negotiations among individual countries and regional economic organizations. Although regional economic cooperation has been making progress in East Asia, it seems far behind bilateral free trade agreements. This means that each country can have other options besides regional integration.

This is especially true of China. China's role is unrivalled in East Asian integration. A freer trading environment, China's accession to the WTO and its emergence as a key global player have raised opportunities and challenges for its neighbors as they strive toward closer trade and economic links. For example, the Association of Southeast Asian Nations (ASEAN) and China agreed to begin talks to create a free trade area (FTA) in 2002. China and ASEAN have already launched a free-trade zone based mainly on tariffs.

Besides, the FTA cannot be limited to a neighboring region. Singapore has gotten a head start in this area of development. It has made a free trade pact with the United States. Its free trade agreement signed with New Zealand came into effect and it has also been making similar efforts with Japan, Mexico, Canada, Australia, India, South Korea, and Chile. In addition, Japan has been engaging in trade agreement negotiations with New Zealand, South Korea, Australia, and the United States. Japan has agreed to trade talks with Malaysia, Thailand, and the Philippines. The United States recently announced that it would begin free trade talks with Thailand. South Korea also made a free trade agreement with Chile.

This means that the need for regional cooperation between neighboring countries may not necessarily be a top priority. Each country has many options beyond a geographical boundary. Like Britain in the early stages, this kind of "exit" option, in Hirschman's terms, available to each country may slow down the process of integration among East Asian countries or lessen the drive for it.

4. Conclusion

Even if the British experiences as an "awkward partner" reflect the idiosyncratic features of British society, they provide some useful lessons for East Asian countries with respect to regional integration. It is widely recognized that East Asian countries should take actions to promote formal economic cooperation through trade and investment liberalization consistent with a strong development orientation. Essentially, there exists strong motivation for regional integration.

As noted earlier, in East Asian countries there are some similarities to the factors that have made Britain reluctant to get involved in integration. The most serious concern is on how far the integration proceeds. As long as East Asian countries seek to set up an intergovernmental body like the EFTA, no country in the region is likely to become reluctant. However, if East Asian countries attempt to emulate their European predecessors and form a supranational institution, there could emerge a country playing the role that Britain did during European integration.

All in all, it could be problematic to compare the European experiences including the British one with the East Asian case. The international environment has changed greatly, and political, cultural, and historical conditions are very different. Above all, the interest and intentions of the United States are different. Regional rivalry between East Asian countries also differs from that of Europe. For this reason, some might say that the concept of ASEAN+3 (+3 are the nations of South Korea, China, and Japan) could be a convenient space for regional integration rather than pursuing a different agency for East Asian countries.

Nevertheless, regional cooperation and integration have become an inevitable trend of international trade and investment with globalization. The regional integration of East Asia has already gained serious attention from both within and outside the region. Lessons from the British experiences will help promote a smooth process of integration in East Asia when it occurs.

References

Aspinwall, Mark. "Structuring Europe: Powersharing Institutions and British Preferences on European Integration," *Political Studies*, vol. 48 (2000), pp. 415-42.

Baker, David and David Seawright, eds. *Britain For and Against Europe.* Oxford: Oxford University Press, 1998.

Birch, Anthony. *The British System of Government*, 10th edition. London: Routledge, 1998.

Cowley, Philip. "British Parliamentarians and European Integration," *Party Politics*, vol. 6, No. 4 (2000), pp. 463-72.

Dixon, Joy. "Further Economic Integration in Asia: Some Lessons from the European Experiences," (2000). Retrieved January 14, 2004. Online at unpan1.un.org/intradoc/groups/public/documents/ apcity/unpan012137.pdf.

Eltis, Walter. *Britain, Europe and EMU.* London: Macmillan, 2000.

Franklin, Michael (with Marc Wilke). *Britain in the European Community.* London: Royal Institute of International Affairs, 1990.

Gavin, Neil. "Imagining Europe: Political Identity and British Television Coverage of the European Economy," *British Journal of Political and International Relations*, vol. 2, No. 3 (2000), pp. 352-73.

George, S. 1998. *An Awkward Partner: Britain in the European Community,* 3rd edition. Oxford: Oxford University Press, 1998.

Hirschman, Albert. *Exit, Voice and Loyalty*. Cambridge, Mass.: Harvard University Press, 1970.

Inoguchi, Takashi. "Possibilities and Limits of Regional Cooperation in Northeast Asia: Security and Economic Areas," in Tai-joon Kwon and Dong-Sung Kim, eds., *World Order and Peace in the New Millennium.* Seoul: Korean Association of International Studies, 2000.

Mitchell, James. "Territorial Politics and Change in Britain," in Catterall, et al., *Reforming the Constitution: Debates in Twentieth-Century Britain.* London: Frank Cass, 2000.

Rosamond, Ben. "Regional Integration in Europe and Asia," ASEF University Library (2002). Online at www.asef.org/asef-uni/3_infohub/infohub_m_ library.html.

Shahin, Jamal and Michael Wintle, eds. *The Idea of A United Europe: Political, Economic and Cultural Integration since the Fall of the Berlin Wall.* London: Macmillan, 2000.

Strange, Gerad. "British Trade Unions and European Integration in the 1990s: Politics versus Political Economy." *Political Studies*, vol. 50, No. 2 (2002), pp. 293-312.

Temperley, Howard. *Britain and America since Independence.* Basingstoke, UK: Palgrave, 2002.

Tkacik, John Jr. "Strategic Risks for East Asia in Economic Integration with China," (2002). Online at www.heritage.org/Research/AsiaandthePacific/WM171.cfm.

Turner, John. *The Tories and Europe.* Manchester: Manchester University Press, 2000.

Whitely, Paul, Patrick Seyd, Jeremy Richardson, and Paul Bissell. "Thatcherism and the Conservative Party," *Political Studies*, vol. 42, No. 2 (1994), pp. 185-203.

CHAPTER 7

OVERCOMING HISTORY:
GREECE, TURKEY, AND THE EUROPEAN UNION

Machiko HACHIYA

1. Introduction

Whether one may be pro or con for regional integration, a well-recognized fruit of the European integration is that it has made the rapprochement between France and Germany come true; the two countries that had gone through century-long confrontations are now regarded as the two front wheels of European integration. The fact that the two major confronting countries of Europe have attained a relationship for a war to be unthinkable between them is certainly a great achievement. This shift of relationship from insecurity to security was realized within the framework of European integration. If the integration of Europe has such a "peace-building" function, it should be edifying for other countries in confrontation. It is only more so if the countries are within the framework of European integration. In this regard, the enlarging European Union (EU) may present a significant test case for Greece and Turkey.

Turkey's long standing application for the EU was finally granted the status of "a candidate country" in 1999. It was made possible duly by the change of the Greek attitude not to use the veto against the Turkish issue. The two countries, after a century-long confrontation, finally seem to be

Part II: National Visions and Experiences of Cooperation in Europe and Asia

reaching a point of rapprochement. If the European experience in regard to the relationship of France and Germany offers a historical precedent, revisiting the Franco-German experience may help Greece and Turkey construct a stable relationship.

This chapter will try to envision a possible rapprochement between Greece and Turkey by tracing the Franco-German experience within the framework of European integration. Three factors will be examined to see how the shift in each one's relationship was initiated and stabilized in the hopes of applying the Franco-German case to relations between Greece and Turkey: national interest, institutional setting, and political leadership. National interest at a given time provides the initial motivation for any act or decision of a government. Institutional setting provides a sphere or an occasion where different interests merge into a common interest. Political leadership is indispensable for significant decisions. It is expected that this examination will uncover a potential role for regional integration for the countries with confrontational histories. Consequently, the second purpose of the chapter, although implicit, is to consider the significance of Turkey's EU membership from the standpoint of the "peace-building" function of regional integration.

2. A History Overcome

2.1. Franco-German Rapprochement

As it is well known, when a new intra-European organization to manage coal and steel was proposed by then French Foreign Minister Robert Schuman in 1950, then Chancellor of West Germany, Konrad Adenauer announced immediately his agreement to accept the plan. He manifestly declared that the Federal Republic of Germany (West Germany) would act as a country of Europe, but would never intend a Europe of Germany. The Schuman Plan proposed to include Germany as a member state with equal status, above all with France.¹ Of course, one of the purposes of the plan was to contain Germany within the framework of Europe under a multigovernmental system, for European stability had been shaken whenever Germany had begun to act unilaterally. History also taught that it was just as important to find a way to convince France not to take a sanction-based attitude toward Germany. The tragic consequences such an attitude would bring were already experienced throughout Europe during the first half of the 20th century.

As the Korean War broke out in June 1950, the Cold War seemed to have prevailed practically in every corner of the world. For the West, a strong Germany was needed, but the fear that such a Germany would become a new threat to the neighboring countries also loomed large. Against such circumstances, as Mattli rightly describes, "Europe needed to create a new institution to cement economies of individual governments into an interdependent regime out of which independent aggressive action by a single country would be impossible."²

Thanks to Jean Monnet, a concrete task of the above was worked out as the European Coal and Steel Community (ECSC). Monnet chose coal and steel because these were the central resources of the problem of security.³ In order to turn the source of insecurity into a common destiny, Monnet was convinced of the need for a "supranational" authority with real decision-making power, something learned from his previous experience as an international civil servant. ⁴ The concept of

---

[1] The U.S. gave approval and support to it. This U.S. attitude was vital to include West Germany whose sovereignty was limited and was under observation of the four powers in the scene of international relations in 1950. Jean Monnet, *Mémoires* (Paris: Fayard, 1976), pp. 447-8.

[2] Walter Mattli, *The Logic of Regional Integration* (Cambridge: Cambridge University Press, 1999), p. 69.

[3] Frederic J. Fransen, *The Supranational Politics of Jean Monnet: Ideas and Origins of the European Community* (Westport, Conn.: Greenwood Press, 2001) p. 103.

[4] Leon N. Lindberg and Stuart A. Scheingold, *Europe's Would-Be Polity* (New Jersey: Prentice-Hall, 1970) p. 15.

"supranationality" and creation of "European sovereignty" over coal and steel were thus explored as the key to "a post-war edifice in Europe."[5]

2.2. Enabling Settings

Even though an overall situation surrounding Europe required a new approach toward the intra-European relationship, the idea alone would not suffice to realize a new approach. In this section, we will examine three elements as components of enabling settings.

2.2.1. National interest

As chapters four and five of this book argue, both France and Germany had distinct national priorities at the time of the post-war era. For France, it was modernization of the national economy, for which German coal was crucial to France's energy resource security. At the same time, for French national security, Germany's industry had to be subjected to international control.[6] France would consent to equal status of Germany only as long as German industry was placed under control that prevented the emergence of new cartels.[7] For Germany, the foremost priority was to recover its full sovereignty and to be treated as an equal among other European countries. German foreign policy was formed around the issue of recovering German sovereignty, for which the integration project provided a legitimate framework. The ECSC accommodated the national interest of both countries at the beginning of 1950s.

2.2.2. Institution[8]

---

[5] Henri Brugmans, *L'idée Européenne 1920-1970* (Bruges: De Tempel, 1970), p. 166.
[6] Fransen, op.cit., supra note 3, p. 94.
[7] For this aim, the French had written an anti-trust provision into ECSC Treaty. Fransen, ibid., note 6, p. 110.
[8] The term "institution" is defined in a broad sense to include both procedures and organizations. A procedure allows the interactions between organizations as well as individuals to take place. An organization refers to a clearly ruled power structure and a cluster of routines. This understanding of "institution" is based upon the definitions

7. Overcoming History: Greece, Turkey, and the European Union

The initial institution that integrated coal and steel owes much to Monnet's imagination. The ECSC was comprised of four organizations: the High Authority, Common Assembly, Council of Ministers, and Court of Justice, the basic structure of which has remained till today in the EU. The High Authority was assured of its supranational nature while the power of the Council of Ministers was limited.

Fransen explains that according to Monnet's idea, such institutional structure would prevent war from breaking out among the members as the High Authority would be able to separate industrial policy from political tensions by preventing one country from increasing production of raw materials without bringing the others along with it.

> If France required increased steel for a war in Indochina, it could increase its purchases on the European market, thereby driving up prices. It could demand, in the Council of Ministers, that production be increased to raise the supply and lower the price. Since each country would be equally affected by the higher prices, the Council might request that High Authority increase production. The High Authority, however, would have full "sovereignty" over any decision about where the production increases would occur. It might, therefore, choose to increase output from German facilities, rather than French ones.[9]

The nature of the ECSC institution was innovative in coupling the supranational power of the High Authority with the limit on national sovereignty over coal and steel. For France, it provided a means of controlling German industry, while for Germany, sovereignty was offered to establish equality. Thus, the different interests were given a sphere to

---

given by Robert Boyer, although he distinguishes between institution and organization. Robert Boyer, "Les institutions dans la théorie de la régulation, no 2003-08," retrieved from *www.cnrs/*, Tableau 1, p. 13.

[9] Fransen, op.cit., supra note 3, p. 108.

merge toward a common destiny.

As integration expanded to economic policy under the framework of the European Economic Community (EEC), the Council of Ministers was the final decision maker, and the supranational power of the European Commission, not High Authority, was rather weakened. However, the Commission as a supranational executive body began to try and link national interests to bring forward the European interest by establishing networks through consultation committees broadly and at various levels. Such a committee system provided other opportunities for different interests to merge and transform into a common interest.[10] It also contributed to the development of a common feeling as "Europeans" through the discussion of European issues.

2.2.3. Political leadership
When the initial effort of integration started, France was under the regime of the Fourth Republic. The Fourth Republic was not only short-lived (1946-58) but also suffered from "*immobilisme*." Under such circumstances, the Schuman Plan was proposed and put into effect almost entirely through the leadership of Monnet, with the support of Americans. It was only after the return of de Gaulle as President in 1958 that France began to take strong initiative in the integration.

On the other hand, (West) Germany under its first Chancellor Adenauer manifested every possible policy for its goal to regain full sovereignty and equal status. Adenauer was determined to secure Germany's place within a European federation.[11]

The rapprochement between France and Germany regenerated the impetus after the first meeting of de Gaulle and Adenauer in 1958. They agreed to set up a permanent scheme of consultation on the foreign

---

[10] For example, it is one aspect of "comitology." Machiko Hachiya, "Who Implements Integration?" *Journal of EU Studies Association* (Japan), No. 20 (2000), pp. 72-90.

[11] See Chapter 5 of this book.

policies, and to promote a common market.¹² The diplomatic relation between the two countries was reinforced and deviated slightly from its course from Europe when the bilateral Treaty of Elysée was signed in 1963. But the importance of an integrated Europe for both remained unchanged, although the reasons might not have been the same.

While Adenauer's attitude toward the integration was drawn from the concern on his own country, de Gaulle's view of the integration was backed by a more global concern.¹³ As a realist, de Gaulle regarded any politics not built upon the basis of states or peoples as an empty dream. For him, the emerging American hegemony in the free world was far from acceptable and a stronger Europe under French leadership should be created to resist the Americans. In this sense, he never deviated from the idea of European integration. He understood that France alone would not be able to reconstruct the tormented world; a united Europe was needed. "*Construir l'Europe, c'est-à-dire l'unir.*"¹⁴ He believed in a united Europe to create a third power in the emerging bipolar system at the end of 1950s, a Europe under French leadership.

The two leaders' determination to create a united Europe—however different the causes might have been—made them choose not to break away but to arbitrate problems. This was demonstrated at the crisis of the "empty chair" caused by the Common Agriculture Policy (CAP) reform proposal in 1965.¹⁵ Arbitration was possible largely due to German concession, which was a typical way to settle a dispute during the early stages of integration. Adenauer's Germany decisively placed the priority on foreign policy over domestic interest.

During the later and more recent stages, when the differences between the two turned out to be persistent—as in the case of the

---

[12] Shuichi Kawashima, "Erize Joyaku no seiritsu to sengo no Doitsu-Fransu Kankeishi," *The Hokkaido Law Review*, vol. 1, No. 51 (2000), p. 290.
[13] Douglas Webber, ed., *The Franco-German Relationship in the European Union* (London: Routledge, 1999).
[14] Brugmans, op.cit., supra note 5, pp. 253-4.
[15] Webber, ed., op.cit., supra note 13, p. 116.

economic and monetary union (EMU) controversies[16]—the leaders of both countries made a point of trying to frustrate one another. However, they acted in good faith with the European policy and were able to mediate their differences.[17] The pattern of settlement changed but the commitment has not wavered. France and Germany have become allies and indispensable partners in the European integration project.

2.3. Summary

Projects for integration in Europe can be observed repeatedly throughout history. Yet, what could be the most innovative aspect of the post-war integration may be found in Jean Monnet's determination for a supranational executive power. What is more, he wisely chose coal and steel, the very causes of insecurity, to be placed under the control of a supranational power so that the factors of insecurity would be transformed to that of security by preventing one country from making any unilateral decision.

Monnet's choice for coal and steel to be placed under the supranational control also helped to separate raw materials and industrial production, which prevented a strong cartel from emerging in Germany. Such institutional setting was accepted by Germany only because the ECSC offered equal status to Germany. The French agreed mainly because it guaranteed to subordinate the German industry while providing opportunities to modernize the French economy. Thus, the institutional

---

[16] Germany insisted on the strict convergence conditions prior to the launch of EMU and an independent European Central Bank (ECB), while France urged the introduction of a common currency. The difference persisted between "the content" and "the timetable." French President Mitterrand conceded to the independent ECB, and Chancellor Kohl promised to join the ECB when France was to convert the French Bond market to Euro. Meanwhile, Kohl succeeded to adopt "Euro" as the name of the common currency instead of "Ecu" which was an ancient French currency unit.

[17] Jonathan Story, "Monetary Union: Economic Competition and Political Negotiation", in Douglas Webber, ed., *The Franco-German Relationship in the European Union* (London: Routledge, 1999), p. 36.

setting provided for both countries to promote primary national goals.

The original setting basically continues along the development of European integration from the ECSC to the European Community, then to the EU. The leaders of France and Germany were fully aware of the significance of the integration framework for both of their national goals to be realized and arbitrated the differences at critical moments, although they may have been differently motivated.

The European integration prepared a sphere for the Franco-German rapprochement by linking their national interests, transforming the factors of insecurity into those of security under a new institution. This initial setting has been maintained and the political leadership was exercised within it to attain a Franco-German relationship that was later coined "the couple."[18]

3. A History to be Overcome

3.1. Overview of the Relationship between Greece and Turkey

In this section, we will review the history of Greco-Turkish relations from the time of the independence of Greece from the Ottoman Empire in the 19th century up to this day in order to examine the causes of disputes between the two countries. We find that the disputes were mostly over national pride rather than any substantial benefits, and that the lop-sided relationship shared between Europe and Greece often increased the tempo of the tension between Greece and Turkey.

3.1.1. Until the end of World War II

The Republic of Turkey was first recognized by the world with the signing of the Treaty of Lausanne on July 23, 1923 and was named "The Republic of Turkey" on October 29, 1923. This young republic was built on the

---

[18] For example, *The Economist* often uses this expression. *The Economist,* January 31, 2004, p. 49.

ruins of the Ottoman Empire.[19] The empire, allied with the Germans, was defeated in WWI, which marked the end of its 650-year history. Yet, for the past few centuries, the decline of the Ottoman Empire was evident, and in 1830 the London Protocol recognized the independence of Greece from the empire, after which the Ottoman recognized Greek independence in 1832.

Between 1918 and 1923, Turkey was in a de-facto divided situation. The Allied powers of Britain, France, and Italy occupied the cities and areas beneficial for them. Greece was invited to participate in the Versailles peace conference in 1919, and by claiming a dominant Greek population it started to occupy the Aegean Anatolia, Aegean islands, and western Anatolia. It was a revival of the *megari idea* to "recover" all the Greek residing territories, which was supported by Britain and France.[20] Turkey claimed its right over the same territory as inherited from the empire, thus the two countries fought a harsh war that lasted over three years (1919-22). It was against this experience that a strong "Turkish" nationalism emerged, one that would persist throughout the history of the new republic as a legacy of Kemal Atatürk.

Atatürk is said to be a man full of contradictions, but he never lost his vision of the final goal.[21] Atatürk, or Mustafa Kemal, was chosen as the Turkish president when the republic was declared. He implemented the institutional reforms in every sphere of life: abolition of the Caliphate; enactment of the new Constitution and establishment of the Grand National Assembly as "sole, rightful representative of the nation"; abandonment of the Islamic-based civil and penal codes to be replaced by secular codes based upon the Swiss and Italian codes; change of the writing system from the Arabic to the Latin alphabet.[22]

---

[19] Nicole and Hugh Pope, *Turkey Unveiled* (London: John Murray, 1997) p. 58.

[20] But Italy opposed it. The paragraph is after the narrative of Hale. William Hale, *Turkish Foreign Policy, 1774-2000* (London: Frank Cass, 2000), p. 44.

[21] Pope, op. cit., supra note 19, p. 51.

[22] Turkey has begun the reforms of its domestic systems already during the Ottoman Empire era in the end of the 18th century. The army and education systems were

7. Overcoming History: Greece, Turkey, and the European Union

Efforts were concentrated in the domestic matters to attain the goal of the new republic, that is, to raise Turkey to the level of contemporary civilization. The foreign policy was concentrated to make Turkey recognized as a "respected European state."[23] All these concerns were consequences of the deep-rooted trauma of the experiences at the end of WWI with the decomposition of the empire, symbolized in the Treaty of Sevre even if it was later replaced by the Treaty of Lausanne, which guaranteed the territorial boarders that we see today.

Atatürk later explained it: "The West has always been prejudiced against the Turks . . . but we Turks have always consistently moved towards the West. . . . In order to be a civilized nation, there is no alternative."[24]

Between Greece and Turkey, a population exchange took place in 1923 in accordance with the Lausanne treaty. It is reported that 900,000 of the Greek Orthodox population of Anatolia was exchanged for 400,000 Muslims in Greece.[25] This movement helped to homogenize the population structure in both countries, and kept their relations relatively peaceful. In addition, in the early 1930s, both countries faced a severe economic crisis that made economic cooperation necessary. One scholar also points out that the Italian expansionist policy was perceived as a common threat for both Greece and Turkey.[26]

The two countries signed the Treaty of Ankara in 1930 to enhance their peaceful relationship, followed by an agreement in 1933 to mutually guarantee their common frontier in Thrace, and also to consult one another on all questions of common interest. In 1934, the Balkan Entente was

---

"modernized," modeling themselves after the French system. Masao Ohki, "The Succession of the Foreign Laws in Turkey," (in Japanese) in *RIKKYO HOUGAKU 11* (1969), chapter 2.
[23] Hale, op.cit., supra note 20, p. 57.
[24] Ibid., p. 38.
[25] Ibid., p. 55.
[26] Cem Emrence, "Rearticulating the Local, Regional, and Global: The Greek-Turkish Rapprochement of 1930," *Turkish Studies*, vol. 4, No. 3 (2003), pp. 26-46.

signed among the four countries of Yugoslavia, Rumania, Greece, and Turkey on the agreed frontier lines. The interwar period marks a time of rapprochement over the history of Greece and Turkey, mainly because of the need to protect the countries from externalities. This peaceful relation continued until World War II.

3.2. Post-war Era
The post-war regime of the bipolar system pushed Turkey to ally with the West, in particular with the United States. Soviet Union was a historical enemy for Turkey, and now it posed a direct threat as a long frontier line stretched itself out between the two nations. The Soviet threat was also perceived by Greece, which put the two countries to continue their relationship of rapprochement after the war. Both Greece and Turkey joined the North Atlantic Treaty Organization (NATO) together in May 1951.

Prior to their NATO accession, Greece and Turkey had agreed on the transfer of Dodecanese to Greece in 1947, and also to demilitarize Dodecanese as the Greek Aegean islands had been under the Treaty of Lausanne.

A grave regional conflict in the Aegean occurred over Cyprus. Cyprus became independent from Britain in 1960 with a new Constitution guaranteed by Britain, Greece, and Turkey. Before the independence, Cyprus was first given to Britain from the Ottoman as a result of the Ottoman-Russia war in 1878 under the premise that in case of a Russian attack against the Ottoman, Britain would support the empire. Then it was officially annexed to Britain in 1914, which Turkey recognized under the Treaty of Lausanne in 1923. British rule was continued until Cyprus' independence.

In the mid-1950s, the movement for *enosis* (union with Greece) seemed to revive and started to gain the support among the Greek Cypriots as well as the Greeks in Greece. On the April 1, 1955, a Cypriot group

7. Overcoming History: Greece, Turkey, and the European Union

called EOKA[27] began the campaign for *enosis* with simultaneous explosions in the major cities of Cyprus. Their arms were supplied by Greece.[28] The British called a conference with Greece and Turkey but no agreement was reached. Turkish Prime Minister Menderes expressed Turkey's preference for continued British rule on the island. For Turkey, *enosis* would change the power balance in the Mediterranean, placing Turkey in a position of encirclement by Greece on two sides.[29]

Cyprus became independent on the basis of two agreements signed in 1959: the Zurich Agreement between Greece and Turkey over the future of Cyprus, and the London Agreement between Greece, Turkey, and Britain, joined by the representatives of the Greek and Turkish Cypriots on the amended form of the Zurich Agreement.

However, independence did not bring peace. The conflict between the two communities of the Greek and Turkish Cypriots never ceded. In December 1963, heavy fighting broke out between the two communities, and Turkey threatened to intervene.[30] In March 1964, the United Nations (UN) peace-keeping force (UNFICYP) was called in. In July 1974, the EOKA under a new leader attempted a *coup* against the Greek Cypriot President Makarios who, by then, had lost interest in the *enosis* movement. This time, EOKA was supported by the Greek military junta.

Shocked by the incident, Turkey asked Britain to intervene together with Turkey as the guarantor states under the Treaty of Guarantee of 1960, but was refused. Prime Minister Ecevit of Turkey acted quickly and sent the Turkish army to protect the Turkish Cypriots in the island, who

---

[27] EOKA stands for "the National Organization of Cypriot Fighters" in Greece.
[28] Alan James, *Keeping the Peace in the Cyprus Crisis of 1963-64* (Houndsmill, UK: Palgrave, 2002), p. 9.
[29] Hale, op.cit., supra note 25, p. 131.
[30] Turkey gave up intervention after a letter from American President Johnson. This letter was later referred to as "the most rude" in a diplomatic manner. Bruce R. Kuniholm, "Turkey and the West since World War II," in V. Mastny and R.C.Nation, eds., *Turkey Between East and West: New Challenges for a Rising Regional Power* (Boulder, Colo.: Westview, 1996), p. 55.

Part II: National Visions and Experiences of Cooperation in Europe and Asia

comprised about 20 percent of the population.[31] Having failed in the peace talks, Turkey sent its army for the second time in August. The first intervention won broad support within the international community, but the second one did not. The intervention gave Turkey military superiority on the island, but not political power.[32]

Progress was not made on solving the Cyprus situation, and the unilateral declaration of the Turkish Republic of Northern Cyprus (KKTC) in 1983 isolated Turkish Cyprus as well as Turkey from the international community. Meanwhile, the bilateral relationship between Greece and Turkey worsened not only because of the Cyprus conflict but also because of the series of disputes over the rights to the offshore minerals within the Aegean Sea.

The earlier rapprochement had been completely lost, and there was a need for the search for a second. The Cyprus problem overshadowed the bilateral relations so fiercely that the rivalry between Greece and Turkey was raised to the point where they regarded each other as enemies.[33]

3.2.1. Greco-Turkish relations within the EU

As we have seen, in the years following the establishment of the Turkish Republic until WWII, the relationship between Greece and Turkey was relatively peaceful. Europe, sharing its view with Americans, was aware of the importance to give equal treatment to Greece and Turkey. As a matter of fact, the two countries joined NATO at the same time. The EEC reopened its dialogue with Turkey after a short freezing period following

---

[31] At the previous clash in 1963, it is reported that 108 people died among the Turkish Cypriots while the victims among the Greek Cypriots numbered twenty-six. Jean-François Drevet, *Chypre en Europe* (Paris: L'Harmattan, 2000), p. 135.

[32] Hale, op.cit., supra 29, 159.

[33] The height of it was marked in January 1996 by a maritime accident at a tiny, uninhabited island called *Imia* in the Aegean over the national flags. It raised the strong nationalist feelings on both sides. Bahar Rumelili, "Liminality and Perpetuation of Conflicts: Turkish-Greek Relations in the Context of Community-Building by the EU," *European Journal of International Relations*, vol. 9, No. 2 (2003) p. 213-48.

the first military coup in Turkey in 1960 as Greece signed the Association Agreement in 1962. However, Turkey has been passed over for EU membership since its Association Agreement in 1963 while struggling to secure its status in Europe.

On the other hand, Greece was accepted as a member of the EU[34] in 1981, which only served to sour relations with Turkey by enabling Greece to block any European policy concerning Turkey. Greece also succeeded in linking the problem of Cyprus with major European decisions, a strategy that successfully brought the divided Cyprus its EU membership.

Turkey applied for EU membership in 1987, and was granted the status of candidate country in December 1999, overturning a previous opinion of December 1997, which practically excluded Turkey from accession. Turkey's attitude toward the EU as well as to Greece was very confrontational in 1997. Unlike the case of France and Germany, the European attitudes toward Greece and Turkey did not share equal footing, and it was a matter of national pride for Turkey as well as national security. At the time, the situation seemed to have hit a dead end.

Rapprochement was brought about by the unexpected incidents in 1999: the consecutive earthquakes that first hit Turkey in August, then Greece a month later. Tragic scenes stirred feeling of strong sympathy for and established international solidarity with Turkey. The post-earthquake assistance offered from the world is said to have changed the worldview of the Turks from conflict-oriented to amity-oriented.[35] Turkey's goodwill was demonstrated during the rescue activities at the site of the Greek earthquake, as Turkish rescue workers were the first foreign ones to arrive in Greece.

The tension between the two countries further abated after the arrest of Abudullah Öcalan, the leader of the Kurdistan Workers' Party (PKK)—

---

[34] As the EC became the EU by the Maastricht Treaty in 1993, Greece, legally speaking, joined the EC, the European Communities, but not the EU. However, in order to avoid the intricacy, the author will use "the EU" to include the EC.

[35] *Financial Times*, September 11-12, 1999.

a Marxist separatist group within Turkey—at the Greek Embassy in Kenya in February 1999. The Greek government dismissed their hardline foreign minister Pangalos and replaced him with George Papandreou, a son of the former prime minister. He was searching for opportunities to mend relations with Turkey as he had recognized the Öcalan arrest had badly damaged the bilateral relations by revealing Greece's underlying support of the PKK. Papandreou accepted the offer from the Turkish foreign minister Ismail Cem, and series of dialogues over the bilateral issues were held between the two.

These incidents in 1999 contributed to improve the general atmosphere and led the way for Turkey to achieve EU recognition as a candidate country for EU membership. In this case, Greece did not veto the Turkish issue. The dialogue between the leaders of Greece and Turkey continued despite the change of government in Turkey in November 2002.

3.3. Search for Rapprochement
The high time for establishing a Greco-Turkish rapprochement that lasts is nearing. If we take the Franco-German rapprochement as a precedent, a promising way for rapprochement would be to transform the sources of Greek and Turkish insecurity to that of security. The experience also suggests that transforming acts may take place more easily within the framework of European integration, as each country's national interest would be modified to accommodate the other. In this section, we will try to identify the sources of insecurity and to find out a possible approach to rapprochement in the light of the three elements taken up in this chapter.

3.3.1. National interest
Unfortunately, Turkish and Greek national interests sit on opposite ends of an unbalanced scale. Greece has been a member of the EU since 1981, which constrains partly its sovereignty but also provides many means for the country to fulfill its interests both domestically and diplomatically. On the other hand, Turkey holds on to the six principles of the republic manifested by Atatürk, which focused on the domestic reforms of westernization. The finality of the reform should raise the country's status in the international scene and be recognized as "a respected European

power." It was precisely in this respect that Turkey enthusiastically seeks EU membership. EU membership is also important to Turkey as Greece, its rival state at least until 1999, is a member. Turkish people believed Turkey's unfavorable position in Europe is because of the (non) EU membership.

Their rivalry displays itself most acutely over the Cyprus problem. Major powers such as Britain and the United States did not act with enthusiasm to solve the problem in the past but rather opted for the status quo. What is the implication of Cyprus for the national interest of Greece and Turkey? The geographical location of Cyprus finds the island only about 100 km away from the Turkish boarder, which is much closer than it is to Greece.[36] This geography serves as a strategic point for Greece and as a threat to Turkey, only if the two countries regard each other in a state of enmity. If amity is achieved, the geography of Cyprus will auspiciously become a crossing point of civilization.

Both Greece and Turkey regard it beneficial to expand their influence over the island. However, it is a difficult task to find any real benefit for either from the viewpoint of a divided Cyprus. The current status has persisted since 1974 and is not at all likely to shift toward absolute dominance for one side or the other. For Turkey, supporting Northern Cyprus is highly costly as the region is totally dependent on the Turks for things such as basic infrastructure to higher education. Turkey also pays to maintain an overwhelmingly superior military power against the Greek Cypriots on the island. For Greece, it is a place where the Hellenic culture and the orthodox religion are shared, but today *enosis* has completely lost its reality. As a matter of fact, Greece failed to bring a peaceful settlement to Cyprus on every occasion since the end of WWII, and was never able to implement a coherent policy toward Cyprus.[37] Consequently, Greece was never able to benefit from the richness of Cyprus.

---

[36] From the island of Rhodos, it is about 400 km away. From the western edge of the Greek territory it is still 300 km away.

[37] Drevet, op. cit., supra note 31, pp. 17, 302.

Part II: National Visions and Experiences of Cooperation in Europe and Asia

Up to this stage, the relevant parties seem to have spent their efforts only to keep the status quo, leaving behind the realistic welfare of the whole island. Unlike the case of France and Germany after WWII, there is no evident national interest for Greece or Turkey over Cyprus, but rather it is a question of national pride being explored over Cyprus.

3.3.2. Institution

Despite the fact that both Greece and Turkey are members of various international organizations, they do not have a common sphere for European policies. This has caused a complex problem concerning the accession right to NATO information facilities by the European Action Forces created in 1999.[38] Turkey, as a member of NATO but a nonmember of the EU, intended to veto the accession proposal for fear of being left aside regarding EU related issues in NATO. It took a good three years before a compromise was reached by arbitrating the Turkish contestation and the Greek counter-contestation. Turkey had ceded for agreeing on the accession of EU forces after it was assured of a systemic close consultation in the case of EU-related matters.

Unlike the Franco-German case, neither equal status nor a common framework is shared between Greece and Turkey in the regional integration.[39] The governments have to look for either a wider or indirect framework for dispute settlement. The geographical proximity of the two should in theory help exchanges among the peoples, thus complementing the shortcomings at the government level. Even if it did, the absence of an institution does not enhance the exchange effectively or may not be able to

---

[38] Although the European Action Forces was officially agreed on its establishment at the Helsinki European Council in December 1999, the discussion about the concrete ways and means of its operation had been going on prior to the official agreement. The relevant proposal was presented in April 1999 at the NATO Council. A. Birol Yasilada "Turkey's Candidacy for EU Membership," *Middle East Journal*, vol. 1, No. 56 (2002), pp. 94-111.

[39] The Customs Union is not sufficient to arbitrate any issues outside the exchange of goods.

solve problems in a fair and efficient way.

Turkey fights hard whenever it considers itself being marginalized or by-passed. Such an attitude tends to trigger a new phase of confrontation then creates causes of insecurity. Particularly when it comes to relations with Europe, as Greece being a part of it, the lack of common institution on an equal plane fails to provide a sphere to transform the insecurity but it may risk raising the degree of it.

3.3.3. Political leadership
Considering the significance of EU membership for Turkey, the negotiation for accession to the EU gives Turkey an overwhelming motivation to reform its domestic institutions. Since 2001, the Turkish government legislated a series of epoch making reforms in the hope of obtaining a starting date for accession negotiations. In particular, the current government under Prime Minister Erdoğan passed a reform law to lower military influence over domestic politics. It has also proposed a package of measures for the UN to reopen negotiations for the reunification of Cyprus.[40] The aggressive and decisive attitude of the current government led by Erdoğan toward Turkey's EU membership is unprecedented.

However, as was the case for France and Germany, Turkey may continue to take a conciliatory attitude only as long as it maintains hope for gaining equal status within European integration. It was largely due to the shift of Greek policy, especially with the change of its foreign minister, that Turkey was brought closer to the EU. The leadership in Turkey and Greece need to be secured within a wider framework in order to solidify Greco-Turkish rapprochement.

3.4. Summary
The case of Turkey and Greece do not present the same conditions as France and Germany for attaining rapprochement. The latter came about

---

[40] *Financial Times*, January 23, 2004.

based on need stemming from each one's national interest, while the former emerged from under a delicate balance of good will and regional security. However, for both cases, the institutional setting provides an incentive and opportunity to arbitrate the confrontation or transform it into a common destiny.

In this sense, a European Union stressing only Turkey's responsibility in solving the issue of divided Cyprus does not look like a wise tactic from the viewpoint of achieving Greco-Turkish rapprochement. Final rapprochement and settlement of the Cyprus issue are two sides of the same coin. If Europe is serious about reuniting the divided Cyprus, Turkey's cooperation is indispensable. The most powerful incentive for Turkey to shift toward finding a peaceful solution to the issue is membership in the EU. Hence, what is being tested here is European integration's ability to overcome history.

4. Implication of the European Experience

We have two clear cases of rapprochement in Europe: accomplished rapprochement between France and Germany, and unfinished rapprochement between Greece and Turkey. Both pairs share some commonalities: France and Germany are neighbors, as are Greece and Turkey; France fought fierce wars against German and so can be said of Greece and Turkey; France and Germany decided to ally with the West after World War II, as did both Greece and Turkey. The difference between the two cases lies in the countries' EU-membership status. Amending the Franco-German relation was started by placing the two countries on an equal base within a common framework of supranationality. It succeeded in linking each country's national interest, making each one indispensable for achieving their final goals by choosing the most critical field to be controlled by the supranational organization.

In contrast, the Greco-Turkish relationship lacks a common ground for arbitration. Greece has stood in a privileged position to that of Turkey, at least in regards to their regional rivalry. The unequal circumstance seems to have been the cause of increased confrontation whenever a

7. Overcoming History: Greece, Turkey, and the European Union

relevant issue for both sides was at stake. They inclined to take an exclusive decision to each other only to augment the degree of insecurity.

The two cases suggest the importance of institutional setting in building a common framework for attaining resolutions, as well as the importance of realizing equal status for the parties concerned. The cases also demonstrate the decisive role that political leaders play in shifting and promoting the course of policy toward rapprochement. In this regard, for the Greco-Turkish relationship to accomplish rapprochement, the most critical starting point seems to be to place the two countries on equal footing. As this is not yet realized, it will take political leadership to prepare such ground.

These European experiences suggest conditions needed for creating regional stability in cases where neighboring countries suffer from historical disputes and confrontations. The spreading regionalization may first require that areas of competence be clearly demarcated and institutional setting be prepared in order to take up the question of insecurity. Here, both the finished and on-going experiences in Europe may offer some worthwhile lessons.

References

Arai, Masami. *Toruko Kin-Gendaishi (Modern and Contemporary History of Turkey)*. Tokyo: Misuzu Shobou, 2001.

Athanassopoulou, Ekavi. *Turkey: Anglo-American Security Interests 1946-1952*. London: Frank Cass, 2001.

Black, Jeremy. *European International Relations 1648-1815*. Houndsmill, UK: Palgrave, 2002.

Brugmans, Henri. *L'idée Européenne 1920-1970*. Bruges: De Tempel, 1970.

Christiansen, Thomas and Emil Kirchner, eds. *Committee Governance in the European Union*. Manchester, UK: Manchester University Press, 2000.

_____., eds. *Europe In Change: Committee Governance in the European Union*. Manchester, UK: Manchester University Press, 2000.

Cowles, Green Maria, James Caporaso, and Thomas Risse, eds. *Transforming Europe*. Ithaca, N.Y.: Cornell University Press, 2001.

Drevet, Jean-François. *Chypre en Europe*. Paris: L'Harmattan, 2000.

Elmas, Hasan Basri. *Turquie-Europe Une Relation Ambiguë*. Paris: Édition Syllepse, 1998.

Emrence, Cem. "Rearticulating the Local, Regional, and Global: The Greek-Turkish Rapprochement of 1930," *Turkish Studies*, vol. 4, No. 3 (2003), pp. 26-46.

Featherstone, Kevin and George Kazamias, eds. *Europeanization and the Southern Periphery*. London: Frank Cass, 2001.

Fransen, Frederic J. *The Supranational Politics of Jean Monnet: Ideas and Origins of the European Community*. Westport, Conn.: Greenwood Press, 2001.

Hachiya, Machiko. "Who Implements Integration?" *Journal of the EU Studies Association* (Japan), No. 20 (2000).

Hale, William. *Turkish Foreign Policy, 1774-2000*. London: Frank Cass, 2000.

Henig, Stanley. *The Uniting of Europe,* 2nd edition. London: Routledge, 1997.

Höfert, Almut and Armando Salvatore, eds. *Between Europe and Islam*. Brussels: P.I.E.-Peter Lang s.a., 2000.

Hooghe, Liesbet and Gary Marks. *Multi-Level Governance and European Integration*. Lanham, Md.: Rowman and Littlefield, 2001.

James, Alan. *Keeping the Peace in the Cyprus Crisis of 1963-64*. Houndsmill, UK: Palgrave, 2002.

Katzenstein, Peter J. T*amed Power*. Ithaca, N.Y.: Cornell University Press, 1997.

Kawashima, Shuichi. "Erize Joyaku no seiritsu to sengo Doitsu-Furansu Kankeishi (1), (2)," *The Hokkaido Law Review*, vol. 51, No. 1 & 2 (2000).

———. "Politique étrangère et européenne du Chancelier Ludwig Erhard: l'initiative allemande 1964," *The Hokkaido Law Review*, vol. 53, No. 6 (2003).

Lindberg, Leon L. and Stuart A. Scheingold. *Europe's Would-Be Polity*. New Jersey: Prentice-Hall, 1970.

Mastny, Vojtech and R. Craig Nation, eds. *Turkey Between East and West*. Boulder, Colo.: Westview Press, 1996.

Mattli, Walter. *The Logic of Regional Integration*. Cambridge: Cambridge University Press, 1999.

Milward, Alan S. *The European Rescue of the Nation-State*. London: Routledge, 1992.

Monnet, Jean. *Mémoires*. Paris: Fayard, 1988.

Pope, Nicole and Hugh. *Turkey Unveiled*. London: John Murray, 1997.

Sandholtz, Wayne and Alex Stone Sweet, eds. *European Integration and Supranational Governance*. New York, N.Y.: Oxford University Press,

1998.
Stavridis, Stelios, Theodore Couloumbis, Thanos Veremis, and Neville Waites, eds. *The Foreign Policies of the European Union's Mediterranean States and Applicant Countries in the 1990s*. Basingstoke, UK: MacMillan Press, 1999.
Ugur, Mehmet. *The European Union and Turkey: An Anchor/Credibility Dilemma*. Aldershot, UK: Ashgate, 1999.
Watanabe, Hirotaka. *Furansu Gendaishi (Contemporary French History)*. Tokyo: Chuo Koron Sha, 1998.
Webber, Douglas, ed. *The Franco-German Relationship in the European Union*. London: Routledge, 1999.
Yamamoto, Eiji. *Kokusai Tsuka Shisutemu (International Monetary System)*. Tokyo: Iwanami Textbooks, 1997.
Yasilada, A. Virol. "Turkey's Candidacy for EU Membership," *Middle East Journal*, vol. 1, No. 56 (2002), pp. 94-111.

CHAPTER 8

CHINA: VISIONS FOR REGIONAL COOPERATION IN EAST ASIA

TING Wai

1. Introduction

Ever since the beginning of the open-door policy and economic reform a quarter of a century ago, the People's Republic of China (PRC) has been consistently trying to integrate her economy into the global capitalist system, irrespective of all the setbacks due to internal disorder, such as that of 1989, and external challenges imposed from the outside by other powers, such as the United States' attack on the Chinese Embassy in Belgrade in 1999. China's accession to the World Trade Organization (WTO) in December 2001 was claimed as a significant victory for Beijing, but it also denotes an important step in the western attempt in absorbing the Chinese economy into the world market economy. The accession of China to the WTO means that China has accomplished to a great extent her reform of economic, legal, and financial institutions after consistent and laborious efforts in the 1990s, and she is well prepared to link up her economy with world capitalism, despite the period of transition needed to pave the way for a total opening up.

With the further expansion of the Chinese economy, economically speaking, China's neighbors have started to experience the impact caused by such rapid growth. Apart from the very wide variety of imports from China, the country provides an enormous market, and is also becoming a source of foreign direct investment. China definitely has been becoming a significant regional power, exerting its influence in politics and economics. The realists in the East Asia region by all means would pay emphasis on the need of balance-of-power as well as deterrence elements to offset the possible "China threat." The liberalists on the contrary point out the positive effects due to international economic interdependence, and the absorption of China into various international institutions so that China has to abide by international norms, which are basically products of western and notably U.S. political culture. Apart from the conventional balance-of-power mode of thinking, resulting in a method of "checks and balances"—especially by the Japan-U.S. military alliance—the Chinese involvement in multilateral frameworks has also begun to be a matter of concern among Asian politicians. Can the behavior of the rising dragon be checked or at best "controlled" by the multilateral frameworks in military or political arena? How should this rising power be checked in order to maintain peaceful regional and global order? What are the visions and resulting policies of Beijing in conceiving its role within the multilateral frameworks?

Some earlier limited scholarly attempts in understanding the Chinese perceptions of multilateralism pay emphasis on the disquietude of Beijing facing multilateralism but nevertheless wanting to participate so as not to be secluded:

> The PRC's cooperation within ARF is primarily aimed at preventing anti-Chinese block-building while on balance, bilateral relations remain more important. After a long resistance against multilateral cooperation in security policy, China obviously concluded from a growing number of initiatives, that the tendency towards closer multilateral cooperation in Asia Pacific could not be stopped. From China's point of view, it would be a much

8. China: Visions for Regional Cooperation in East Asia

greater risk to be totally excluded than to accept selective participation.[1]

However, this passive attitude of China vis-à-vis those multilateral frameworks has been undergoing significant changes in the past few years. Not only is China becoming more enthusiastic in participating in various regional institutions, Beijing is performing much more actively in these frameworks. Does it mean that China actually seeks to exert more influence in the regional affairs, concomitant to its rising status as a prominent regional power? This paper tries to examine the Chinese conceptions of regionalism and regionalization, as well as analyze Chinese behavior in the practice of regional cooperation.

2. From Bilateralism to Multilateralism: China's Learning Process in her Formulation of Foreign and Security Policy

It is useful to unearth the characteristics of Chinese foreign policies now that the PRC entered a new century and has retrieved her confidence as a great nation and strong state. A Chinese scholar, Wu Xinbo, elaborates on five major characteristics that merit in depth study.[2]

First, the independent foreign policy implemented since the beginning of the 1980s has rendered China maximum freedom to maneuver. China has experience in forging alliance with great powers, in the 1950s with the Soviet Union, and in the 1970s aligning with the United States against the Soviet Union; but China's freedom to maneuver was constrained by these superpowers. Now with an equidistance policy, she

---

[1] See Julia Hurtzig and Eberhard Sandschneider, "National Interest and Multilateral Cooperation: the PRC and its Policies towards APEC and ARF," in Jorn Dosch and Manfred Mols, eds., *International Relations in the Asia-Pacific* (New York: St. Martin's Press, 2000), p. 233.

[2] See Wu Xinbo, "National Security and Chinese Foreign Policy after the Cold War," in Hsueh Chun-tu and Liu Shan, eds., *Zhongguo Waijiao Xinlun* (*New Dimensions of China's Diplomacy*) (Beijing: World Affairs Press, 1998), pp. 224-34.

can formulate her policies basing them only on her own national interests. Wu uses the Chinese position during the Gulf War in 1990-1991 as an example. China was against foreign interventions (Kuwait by Iraq and Iraq by the United States), but abstained from veto against U.S. military actions. As a result she could always maintain friendly relations with Iraq, but at the same time secure her relations with the United States. Some Chinese officials and scholars argue that these positions reflect the intelligent combination of a high degree of principle (against any hegemonism) and a high degree of flexibility (abstaining from voting for U.S. military actions against Iraq) in Chinese diplomacy. These are believed to yield the best results for Chinese interests. But China's actions can also be regarded as "opportunistic" because she wants to maintain relations with Iraq while not offending Washington. Her proposal requesting all the parties concerned to solve the crisis by peaceful means was by and large weak and resulted in nothing. China did have the freedom to maneuver in choosing her policies, but her influence was rather limited in the final outcome of the issue.

Second, in the post-Cold War era, China strives to create a balance of power that benefits her. For instance, in order to relieve the pressure imposed by the sole superpower (the United States) after the Cold War, China has established some kind of political and strategic relations with Russia, India, and Iran. Beijing also used the "market card" to attract the allies of the United States so that they would not be keen on supporting the strong policies of the United States against China. Strengthening the relationship with the Third World is considered an important asset in Chinese diplomacy. This is basically a typical *realpolitik* approach to international relations and is clearly a result of "de-ideologization" in contemplating the effects of China's diplomacy. But Wu also confesses that since the end of the Cold War, China's relations with the Third World have been affected to a large extent by Beijing focusing its attention towards modernization through seeking the assistance of developed countries.

Third, China strives to deal with other countries on a bilateral basis. The rationale, according to Wu, is that due to historical reasons, China lacks experience managing her relations with others within a multilateral

8. China: Visions for Regional Cooperation in East Asia

framework. It is also the natural consequence of past Chinese strategic thinking, which tended to bifurcate the other nations in a simplistic way, either as enemies or friends. However, Wu gives an interesting reason why bilateralism is preferred. If the partner is weak, then China could benefit from a more superior position, thus enabling her to seek more advantages (e.g., China's way of solving the South China Sea disputes). China only negotiates bilaterally with the states concerned. If the partner is stronger than China, China could at least try to press it not to use a multilateral forum or mechanism to attack China. While Beijing feels more at ease in bilateral relations, multilateralism has nevertheless become increasingly important in international affairs. China does pay attention to the role of Asia-Pacific Economic Cooperation (APEC) in promoting economic exchanges, and the ASEAN Regional Forum (ARF) and Council on Security and Cooperation in Asia-Pacific (CSCAP) as effective forums in discussing regional security issues. While multilateralism does pose challenges to the conventional bilateralism in Chinese diplomacy, the idea of "cooperative security," though still in a primitive stage, can be regarded as a new Chinese attempt to promote a new form of multilateralism.

The fourth point that draws our serious attention is the stipulation that China should aim to influence the formulation of the "rules of the games" in the interactions within the global community. Before the era of opening and reform policy, China avoided joining the numerous international agreements or institutions, as the Western capitalist countries created these international norms, norms that China believed were biased and unreasonable. This resulted in self-imposed isolation. As China opens, she cannot avoid participating in certain international institutions and abide by those international norms that mainly reflect the worldviews of the West. Such institutions and norms limit the Chinese freedom to maneuver on the international stage. However, a more confident China, for the sake of her national interests, should seek ways to reform or participate in the creation of international norms. For instance, while Beijing joined the Nuclear Non-Proliferation Treaty (NPT) in 1992 and the Comprehensive Test Ban Treaty (CTBT) in 1996, moves which underline the Chinese wish to join the world as a responsible partner and which aim to upgrade her international status, Beijing at the same time urges all the nuclear states to negotiate an international agreement for the "no first-use" of nuclear weapons as well as non-utilization of such lethal weapons against non-nuclear countries. While at present China's proposal is ignored by other nuclear powers, this is a clear signal that China wants to modify or at least participate in designing international norms.

Fifth, China continues its diplomacy of "*tous azimuth*," that is, maintaining good relationships with all countries. But Wu emphasizes it does not mean that Beijing pays equal attention to all parts of the world. In reality, two areas are particularly important. One is the developed world, and the other is neighboring countries. While the former is needed by China for her economic modernization, the latter is suspicious of the intention of a rapidly growing regional power in relation to their own security, so China needs to appease them. China promulgates the message that since she herself has long suffered from imperialism and hegemonism, she will never become a hegemon. Since 1993, China consistently accused the others, including the United States, Japan, and Southeast Asian countries in promoting the "Chinese Threat" theory, because they could not accept the reality of a rising China. But with China pursuing a more active role in the international community parallel to her rising economic and military power, it becomes difficult to dissipate the worries of others. It is even more intriguing if China accounts first of all for her national interests, or even tries to modify the international norms. The present world order is dominated by an "imperial power," the United States, which determines the international norms and is able to control numerous international institutions. Yet, would it be possible for China to become another "imperial power" that can challenge the leadership position of the United States, albeit not in the near future, given the historical reality of the Middle Kingdom, and the existence of the "Middle Kingdom mentality" that could easily be found among Chinese leaders when the country is growing stronger? If this is a possible scenario, the neighbors of China, whom she wants to appease, must feel perplexed and begin "preparing for the worst."

Thus, the characteristics of Chinese diplomacy can be summarized as follows:

8. China: Visions for Regional Cooperation in East Asia

- Maintain an independent foreign policy to assure maximum freedom of maneuver;
- Create a balance of power beneficial to China;
- Benefit from bilateral relationships but try to accommodate to multilateralism and to promote her concept of multilateral "cooperative security";
- Seek to influence the creation of or modify the international norms;
- Try to improve relations with the developed world and neighboring countries.

However, despite the successes of Chinese diplomacy based on the above characteristics, Beijing faces a lot of new challenges in this era of globalization: from independence to interdependence; from a balance of power (during the Cold War) beneficial to China to a power constellation balanced against China; from benefiting from bilateralism to the need for coping with multilateralism; from the wish to reformulate international norms to the potential repulsion from the West that strenuously defends the norms and regulations; and lastly, the emergence of a more hostile security environment contrary to the Chinese wish to maintain a peaceful relationship with her neighbors. All these challenges originate from two trends of development that underpin the transformation of the world: globalization resulting from complex interdependence, and the rising economic and military power of China.

3. On Multilateralism and International Regimes

Chinese conventional thinking on multilateral frameworks had undergone a significant degree of transformation in the 1990s. Until the mid-1990s, Beijing tended to be very skeptical about the ideas of multilateral framework, especially in the area of security, fearing that China would be "locked" and bound and its freedom to maneuver would be restrained. "Where Beijing is concerned there is a fear that it will be resistant to having its national concerns harnessed within multilateral frameworks that perforce lead to a diffusion of its power."³

Since the late 1990s, however, China has appeared to be more enthusiastic and assertive regarding regional cooperation and multilateralism, as China has become a rising economic power with its large market economy gradually integrating into the world capitalist system. In other words, China's position in the geopolitical and geo-economic global hierarchies has undergone a rapid and crucial change. China would be interested in building a free trade area for mutual benefits. The reason is simple, as indicated by two Korean scholars: "Those who would not be competitive, of course, do not want integration to happen, but those who expect to expand and sell to people in other countries may have an intense interest in breaking down barriers to economic exchange."⁴ Beijing is also interested in influencing the future formulation or transformation of the rules of the games (international norms) in international institutions or international regimes, especially in the security arena. Chinese analysts always point out the unreasonable, undemocratic, and unrighteous parts of the international system:

> In order to search for a more beneficial international status, every major power is formulating cross-century strategy. To strengthen the functions of international institutions is an important constituent part of the diplomatic strategies of major powers, and China is no exception. . . . [China] should participate in the revision and perfection process of international regimes, in order to make them more reasonable, legal, democratic, equal emphasis on efficiency and justice; participate in the formulation of new international regimes, and actively participate in the decision-making within the international institutions so as to play a role as a leading power. Currently China should be the active participating

---

³ Rosemary Foot, "Pacific Asia: The Development of Regional Dialogue," in Louise Fawcett and Andrew Hurrell, eds., *Regionalism in World Politics* (Oxford: Oxford University Press, 1995), p. 248.
⁴ Young Jong Choi and Nae Young Lee, "A Comparative Study of Regionalism in East Asia and the Americas," *Asian Perspective*, vol. 26, No. 3 (2002), p. 173.

country of international regime, and in the future should try to be a 'leading country', so as to give full play to China's role as a 'responsible state.' . . . China should perform better, no matter whether she considers from her national interests or from her international responsibility. China should actively and thoroughly participate in the design, perfection, and development of international regimes so that they would possess 'Chinese character.'[5]

This is in conformity with Chinese saying of practicing "great power diplomacy," and extending regional influence is a natural corollary. Chinese analysts stress that China as a great power should be responsible and constructive. Apart from "transforming" international regimes, Beijing analysts emphasize the need to make use of China's participation in these international regimes to fulfill her strategic interests. The focus of attention is shifted to serving national interests and domestic economic development.[6]

Participating in international institutions and adopting multilateralism in international affairs is also considered as an action against hegemonism:

> Though the arrangements made by international regimes possess a lot of unreasonable claims, they do help to maintain the peace and stability of the world. China has started to change from passive to active. Strengthening the multilateral diplomacy is being seen as a significant component of China's external strategy, i.e., making use of multilateralism to defend the interests of China and to fight against all kinds of hegemonism and great power politics.[7]

---

[5] Report published by the Research Center on Chinese National Environment, Tsinghua University, reported in *Hong Kong Economic Journal*, July 16, 2002, p. 10.
[6] See Zhang Youmin and Dong Jiangwei, *2003 Zhongguo Guoji Diwei Baogao* (*2003 Report on China's International Status*) (Shanghai: Far East Press, 2003), p.220.
[7] See Wang Jie, ed., *Guoji Jizhi Lun* (*On International Regimes*) (Beijing: Xinhua Press, 2002), pp. 451-52.

China definitely becomes a regional power and behaves actively thereafter in relation to her participation in international institutions. Given China's increasingly high profile and active participation in multilateral diplomacy, it is legitimate that her Asian neighbors express a certain degree of worry and skepticism. The logic of hegemony is to affect and try to modify the formulation of international norms. Would China become a regional hegemon, i.e., playing a dominant role in the regional development of the Asia-Pacific, and thus eclipse Japan? As a logical consequence, would the "Middle Kingdom mentality" re-emerge, as China is increasingly confident of becoming a great power? When the PRC was still relatively poor she was reluctant to join those international institutions or regimes, being afraid that her freedom to maneuver would be "locked" by the others led by the United States. Now as China is growing stronger, it seems that she is attempting to exert some kind of influence towards the design and function of the international norms that are imbedded in those international institutions. China does not like "institutionalization" of regional affairs, as she is always suspicious that she would be bound by these institutionalized mechanisms. But if she tries to exert a leadership role in those international institutions, she would think and behave differently. If this is the case, regionalism and regionalization would become an instrument for China and it is not illegitimate for the others to query whether Beijing would seek a leadership position in Asian affairs.

4. China and ASEAN: Towards a New Model in Regional Cooperation?

As China is fast expanding her market economy, she will definitely want to benefit from the advantages of regional economic cooperation, especially in enlarging the market in East Asia. This is a market-driven mode of regionalism, and both China and ASEAN do not seem to be very enthusiastic in having more institutionalized political mechanism to cope with economic cooperation. Yet, Beijing is keen to see the states playing an active role in extending the market and facilitate cohesion among the nation-states within the same region. Moreover, facing the challenges of globalization and the possibility of protectionism outside the region, China

8. China: Visions for Regional Cooperation in East Asia

and other East Asian countries including ASEAN share the same idea that trading within Asia would provide insulation from the forces of globalization, though China as a "world factory" benefits much more from the transfer of production bases to China as a result of globalization.

China would like to have alignments that are non-alliance, nonmilitary, and do not aim at a third party. Chinese diplomacy appears to be more proactive, in parallel with her process of becoming a rising power and starting to occupy a particular status within the structure of international society. On the other hand, Chinese style in diplomatic maneuvering appears to be subtle, flexible, and nonconfrontational. This sits well with the ideas of ASEAN countries that look for consultation as a means to solve their problems and full consensus as the basis for achieving final resolutions.

The key words that can usually be found in Chinese documents on regionalism and regionalization include "open, incremental, voluntary, consensus, development, mutual benefits, and common interests."[8] These words in sum reflect the attitude of Beijing in conceiving its expanding relations with her Asian neighbors. China welcomes alignments that are not directed against a third party, and she prefers full consensus based on thorough consultation when taking joint political actions. Other terms, which appeared lately when China acceded to the ASEAN Treaty of Amity and Friendship in October 2003, include the following words, which are alleged to represent the spirit of the treaty: "equal participation, gradual and incremental, consultation to arrive at consensus, seek for common cause while leaving the differences aside."[9] The latest terms that appear in Chinese diplomatic terminology are *"Mulin, Anlin, Fulin"* (good-neighborliness, securing the neighbors, enriching the neighbors).

---

[8] See the analysis by Wu Lingjun, "The APEC Strategy and Change of Role of China: A Neo-realist interpretation," *Wenti yu Yanjiu* (*Issues and Studies*), vol. 40, No. 3 (May-June 2001), p. 7.

[9] See the report by Dao Shulin et al., "Research Report on China's ASEAN Policies," *Xiandai Guoji Guanxi* (*Contemporary International Relations*), (October 2002), pp. 1-10.

These are considered to be important components of China's developmental strategies.[10]

Though ASEAN and China have a lot in common regarding the ways to achieve consensus in cooperation, the relationship between ASEAN and China remained lukewarm until the late 1990s. However, the politically authoritarian nature of most of the regimes in ASEAN is common with that of the PRC. Both sides want to defend the so-called "Asian values" facing the challenges of the West on human rights conditions in the respective societies. What is more, China wanted to have a stable security environment after the Cold War and cultivating good neighborly relations became her primary goal after 1990. In 1991, China began participating in multilateral regional dialogues, and since then, she showed a "willingness to discuss the Spratlys with ASEAN in multilateral fora."[11] In the past, she was willing to discuss this issue only on a bilateral basis, as she could enjoy her status as the stronger side. The Asian financial crisis provided a chance for China to exert a certain degree of influence towards her Southeast neighbors. The diagnosis of the International Monetary Fund (IMF) in close relation to the U.S. government led to a policy of cutting public expenditure among Southeast Asian states. Interest rate had to rise while currencies eventually were largely devalued, thus causing a further deterioration of the recession.[12] Based on a vast foreign currency reserve that amounted to US$403 billion by the end of 2003,[13] China did have the means to "support" other East Asian countries and this facilitated her better relationship with them. Disappointed by the American reaction towards the Asian economic crisis, the ASEAN countries were looking for more and better cooperation with East Asian countries, notably China, Japan, and Korea.

---

[10] See the speech of Premier Wen Jiabao during the summit on ASEAN business and investments held in Bali, Indonesia, *Ming Pao*, October 8, 2003, p. A22.

[11] See Alice D. Ba, "China and ASEAN: Renavigating Relations for a 21st Century Asia," *Asian Survey*, vol. 43, No. 4 (July/August 2003), pp. 632-33.

[12] Richard Stubbs, "ASEAN plus Three: Emerging East Asian Regionalism?" *Asian Survey*, vol. 42, No. 3 (May/June 2002), p. 448.

[13] *International Herald Tribune*, February 11, 2004, p. 8.

8. China: Visions for Regional Cooperation in East Asia

For the ASEAN countries, despite the fact that they support the continual commitment of the United States in Southeast Asia, it is true that, as one observer has said,

> . . . economic growth and growing trade tensions contributed to a greater willingness in ASEAN to explore alternative arrangement. . . . they also began exploring alternative political-security frameworks like the ASEAN Regional Forum (ARF), which aimed to address perceived insecurities stemming from regional imbalances of power, at the same time that such frameworks represented a move away from the U.S.-centered bilateral alliance system of the Cold War. As in the 1970s and 1980s, the prospect of a less-involved United States created the context for ASEAN to reconsider its relations with China and to engage Beijing.[14]

China hence has become a new trading partner. In addition, it also provides new investment and a nonthreatening diplomacy.[15]

In January 1992 the fourth ASEAN summit decided to establish the "ASEAN Free Trade Area" (AFTA) by 2008, but in the fifth summit held in December 1995, it was decided that the time interval to achieve the AFTA should be reduced to ten years. So 2003 became the final date for the establishment of the AFTA. However, though the tariff reaches only 2.3 percent in 2003 from 12.7 percent in 1993, ASEAN countries have to wait until 2010 to abolish all the tariffs. Besides, for the poorer latecomers like Vietnam, Laos, Cambodia, and Myanmar, the target date will be 2015.[16] And yet, this will be a difficult task, as there still exists a lot of non-tariff barriers among the member states of ASEAN.

---

[14] See Alice D. Ba, "China and ASEAN," p. 627.
[15] See Jane Perlez, "China Inroads in Asia Erode US Trade Edge," *International Herald Tribune*, October 20, 2003, p. 1.
[16] See the article written by the Secretary-General of ASEAN, Ong Ken Yong, "ASEAN Moves Forward to Build a Single Market," *Asian Wall Street Journal*, October 19, 2003, p. A11.

Zhongnanhai leaders consider the ASEAN+3 and ASEAN+1 models initiated in 1997 as new initiatives for regional cooperation based on newly-defined regional identity. These become an impetus that promotes the development of the free trade area and further "integration" of ASEAN. China seized this opportunity to push forward her plan in constructing a "strategic partnership relationship of Good neighborhood and Mutual Trust between China and ASEAN." Three pillars buttress this strategic partnership.[17] First, in terms of economic development, in November 2001 it was decided by Premier Zhu Rongji and leaders of ASEAN that an ASEAN-China Free Trade Area (ACFTA) would be established by 2010. Second, in terms of political relations, the two parties established a "strategic partnership" relationship in the China-ASEAN summit held in October 2003. Correspondingly Beijing also signed the "ASEAN Treaty of Amity and Friendship" in the same month. China is the first non-Southeast Asian country to have joined the treaty. Third, in terms of security and confidence-building measures, China and ASEAN countries signed a "Declaration on the Conduct of Parties in the South China Sea" in November 2002, which paved the way for a nonconfrontational approach to resolve their conflicts in the South China Sea.

On economic development and cooperation, the ACFTA incorporates not only the traditional content of a free trade agreement, the trade in services is also an important component in ACFTA. The banking industry, tourism, and engineering contracts are considered to be the "sunrise industries" in their mutual cooperation.[18] Other service industries like logistics and professional/infrastructure services including telecommunications and financial services are largely in demand in China. It is hoped that the ACFTA would provide opportunities for China's southeastern counterparts to play a role in the massive transformation of

---

[17] See Zhai Kun "A Brief Review of China's Accession to the Treaty of Amity and Cooperation in Southeast Asia," *Xiandai Guoji Guanxi* (*Contemporary International Relations*), No. 11 (November 2003), pp. 36-37.

[18] See Chen Dezhao, "A New Stage of East Asia Economic Cooperation," *Guoji Wenti Yanjiu* (*International Studies*), No. 6 (November 2003), p. 51.

8. China: Visions for Regional Cooperation in East Asia

China's economy.[19] It is estimated by Chinese analysts that by 2005 China will be the largest importer in the world, by 2010, the largest exporter, and by 2020, the largest trading nation in the world.[20] They are optimistic that ASEAN countries will benefit a lot from the rapid growth of China. Bilateral trade between China and ASEAN may reach US$70 billion in value in 2003. It is aimed to reach US$100 billion by 2005.

Concrete demarches are implemented rapidly under the umbrella of ACFTA. Both China and ASEAN have decided to implement an "early harvest" proposal. Starting January 1, 2004, tariffs for about 600 agricultural products will be gradually reduced, and in 2006 all tariffs will be abolished.[21] China has started to negotiate bilaterally with ASEAN countries to reduce tariffs for different kinds of products. For instance, China and Thailand agreed on June 19, 2003 to reduce the tariffs for the trading of agricultural products to zero, starting from October 1, 2003.[22] This is a challenge to agricultural products in China rather than from Thailand, as the cost of Chinese products are higher but the quality is lower. However, Beijing thinks that on the one hand, China is helping others, while on the other hand Chinese peasants are forced to compete with the better Thai products. The competition would certainly benefit China since the peasants will have to raise their productivity and improve their products.

During the ASEAN+3 meeting in November 2002 held in Phnom Penh, China announced that she would liquidate the debts owed by the poor ASEAN countries, including Vietnam, Laos, Cambodia, and Myanmar, as well as providing zero tariffs on most of the products imported by China from these countries.[23] China also dissolved the debts

---

[19] Zhang Bin, "The Economic Relations and Prospects between China and East Asia," *Guoji Wenti Yanjiu* (*International Studies*), No. 4 (July 2003), p. 55.

[20] Ibid.

[21] Jin Chunli et al., "Investigating the Prospect of China-ASEAN Agricultural Cooperation," *Liaowang Weekly* (*Outlook*), No. 18 (May 5, 2003), p. 39; See also *Ta Kung Pao*, December 18, 2003, p. A5.

[22] See *Liaowang Weekly* (*Outlook*), No. 44 (November 3, 2003), p. 25.

[23] Luo Jie, "Interview of Fu Yin, Secretary of Asia Bureau, Chinese Ministry of Foreign Affairs," *Shijie Zhishi* (*World Affairs*), No. 23 (December 2002), pp. 8-10.

valued at US$10.5 billion from African countries three years ago, and recently also declared that imports from more than thirty African countries would enjoy the privilege of zero tariffs (a result of Premier Wen Jiabao's visit to Africa in December 2003).[24]

Other initiatives in economic and financial cooperation include, first of all, the Chinese decision to invest in the development of the Mekong River region, as exemplified in the agreements signed in November 2002 between ASEAN and China on transport and trading of electricity in this region.[25] China assisted in constructing a 263-kilometer section of the Kunming-Bangkok Highway in Laos.[26] This is followed by the Chiangmai Initiative initiated in May 2000 for financial cooperation. This includes an "East Asia-wide currency 'swap arrangement', that would include a network of bilateral swap and repurchase agreement facilities"[27] among ASEAN countries, China, Japan, and South Korea, so as to supply in emergency hard currency resources to a partner country in terms of crisis in shortage of foreign currencies and deficit in balance of payment. China has signed such a bilateral swap arrangement with Thailand, Japan, South Korea, and Malaysia, and negotiations on the one with the Philippines has also been concluded.[28] Altogether eight such bilateral agreements have been signed among Asian countries, and six others are undergoing negotiation. This is an extension of the Miyazawa Initiative created by Japan in late 1998 to assist other Asian states that are suffering from financial difficulties. Japan in fact proposed the establishment of an Asia Monetary Fund (AMF), but Washington rigorously opposed this idea. The ASEAN+3 is also designing an early-warning mechanism on financial crisis, with the assistance of the Asia Development Bank (ABD).

---

[24] See *Hong Kong Economic Journal*, December 16, 2003, p. 14.

[25] Qiu Danyang, "East Asian Cooperation and China's Strategic Options," *Guoji Wenti Yanjiu* (*International Studies*), No. 3, (May 2003), p. 45.

[26] See Léon Vandermeersch, "Le monde vu de Chine," *Hérodote: Revue de Géographie et de Géopolitique*, No. 108 (1er trimestre 2003), p. 49.

[27] See Liu Fu-Kuo, "A Critical Review of East and Northeast Asian Regionalism," in Christopher M. Dent and David W. F. Huang, eds., *Northeast Asian Regionalism: Learning from the European Experience* (London: RoutledgeCurzon, 2002), p. 24.

[28] Chen Dezhao, "A New Stage of East Asia Economic Cooperation," p. 52.

8. China: Visions for Regional Cooperation in East Asia

On political and security aspects, the meaning of Beijing signing the ASEAN Treaty of Amity and Friendship is more symbolic than substantial, but ASEAN hopes to stimulate other regional powers like India, Japan, and Russia to accede to the same treaty. The treaty is also considered as a kind of legal protection to solve peacefully the territorial disputes of the South China Sea between China and ASEAN, while the document "Declaration on the Conduct of Parties in the South China Sea" signed in December 2002 has no legal binding power. China and ASEAN also achieved agreement on cooperation in a full range of nontraditional security issues, as this fulfills Chinese perception of a "new security concept," something that can be reflected by the "Joint Declaration on Cooperation of Non-Traditional Security Domain."[29]

Since 2002, both Singapore and Thailand have been very enthusiastic in the promotion of "ASEAN Economic Community." They plead for further integration of ASEAN in eliminating the numerous barriers that still exist along the borders. Their cause eventually led to the signing in October 2003 by ASEAN leaders of a declaration urging for the establishment of "East Asian Security Community," "East Asian Economic Community," and "East Asian Social and Cultural Community" by the year 2020.[30] China explicitly expresses her support of the ASEAN integration, as a more prosperous and unified ASEAN would not possibly become a source of things that would challenge China's security; instead, it serves Chinese interests since it would be a fast growing economic entity.

5. China and ASEAN Regional Forum (ARF)

According to Robert Scalapino, the ASEAN Regional Forum (ARF) is a kind of "regional dialogue" which is based on consultation and not on a

---

[29] Nontraditional security includes economic security, human security, and environmental security. The Chinese use a term "comprehension security" to denote security in all aspects, apart from the military aspect.

[30] See the report in *Ta Kung Pao*, October 8, 2003, p. A2.

formalistic process with legal binding agreements, thus can only be classified as "soft regionalism." China supports the dialogue nature, principle of consensus, and style of discussion within the ARF that suits China's new security concept. China is happy to see that the ARF has taken into consideration the "degree of comfort" of every nation-state. Beijing analysts are satisfied with the largely similar position expressed by ASEAN states on constructing a new international political and economic order. They also agree on the three-stage approach of the development of ARF: first, the establishment of confidence-building measures (CBM); second, the implementation of the mechanism of preventive diplomacy; and third, the measure for conflict resolution. For the CBM, some countries, including China, have publicized their white papers on national defense. Though what they have revealed is rather limited, China nevertheless regards them as important moves in enhancing transparency in the national defense.

The objective of ASEAN is to "bind" China so that she becomes a component within the Southeast Asian framework. As a result China could not go her own way, thus enabling her actions to be checked by her neighbors. However, Southeast Asian analysts remain skeptical on the eventual effect of whether China could be really engaged within a multilateral security framework designed by ASEAN. Nevertheless, ASEAN welcomes the following despite its capability to engage China: "only an ASEAN initiative made it possible that China could be included in a form of regional security cooperation, since any suggestions by the great power, USA, Russia or Japan would be considered as an instrument to contain China."[31] Interestingly, Chinese leaders think that it is better to participate in this forum instead of sit on the outside. There is no risk involved, as the ARF is based on the principles designed by ASEAN. For instance, human rights and other political issues are simply excluded in the discussion, and further institutionalization of the mechanism has not yet considered. This suits Chinese taste; thus China could always present a cooperative image and promote confidence-building measures to her

---

[31] See Hurtzig and Sandschneider, "National Interest and Multilateral Cooperation," p. 227.

8. China: Visions for Regional Cooperation in East Asia

neighbors, while at the same time she is able to check upon the collective behavior of ASEAN on whether it is trying to contain or engage China. Beijing has been consistently promoting her *xin an quan guan* (new view on security) and her ideas on nontraditional security. Since she shares with ASEAN the so-called "ASEAN way" and the significance of Asian values, China feels comfortable participating in the tribunes provided by the ARF.

The ARF seeks to develop and institutionalize regional confidence and security-building measures. However, China feels confident in participating in the ARF as it is possible for her to avoid major tricky and difficult issues such as territorial claims and the Taiwan problem. On the contrary, it enables her to raise concern over the Theatre Missile Defense (TMD) and security strategy of major powers.[32] China has been active in proposing new ideas and measures to facilitate the dialogue. In July 2002, China proposed a formal paper on its new security concept. In June 2003, China proposed to the ARF meeting to establish a new "Security Policy Conference" to be attended by senior military officers from member countries.[33]

6. Asia-Pacific Economic Cooperation (APEC) and Open Regionalism

The objectives of the Asia Pacific Economic Cooperation aims to sustain the growth and development of the region; strengthen the open, multilateral trading systems; and reduce barriers to trade in goods, services, and investments. Basically, APEC is only a "consociational" body with a set of regional economic norms and practices. It sets long-term liberalization goals in trade, investments, business operation, and even

---

[32] See Bates Gill, "China and Regional Cooperation and Security Building Measures," in Robert Ash, ed., *China's Integration into Asia* (Richmond, Surrey: Curzon, 2002), pp. 219-20.

[33] See Bates Gill, "China's Growth as a Regional Economic Power: Impacts and Implications," presentation before the U.S.-China Economic and Security Review Committee, U.S. Senate, Washington, D.C., December 4, 2003.

financial markets.[34] Indeed, the increasing trade transactions would create the need for institutions so as to pave the way for further integration. Some powers or even a single power may be needed as an engine that propels the regional endeavors towards integration. However, though Asian countries are not reluctant to evolve towards a direction of further economic cooperation, they are resistant to this potential process of economic integration being led by a hegemonic core, whether it is the United States, Japan, or China.

China's political objectives in participating in APEC are fourfold. First, she aims to ameliorate political relationships with Asia-Pacific countries. Second, in the security arena, Beijing would like to soften territorial disputes that have been sources of long-term serious problems between China and her Southeast Asian neighbors. Third, China would make use of the forum, especially the annual informal summit, to counter-attack the "China Threat" theory. Fourth, China seeks to reduce the influence of western hegemony within the region. China would like APEC to be a non-binding consultative mechanism. It should be open, flexible and pragmatic in nature. In short, China does not want "de-nationalization of statehood," which means the "hollowing out of national state apparatus with old and new state capacities being reorganized territorially and functionally on subnational, national, supra-national and trans-local level."[35] In other words, the sovereign states should play the key role.

For the East Asian and Southeast Asian states, the most crucial point is to have the rising dragon, China, incorporated into a regional multilateral framework, and to "socialize" China so that when she is integrating into the international community she will abide by the international norms. But for China, the best way to defend her economic and political-strategic interests is to participate in the formulation or transformation of international norms (or rules of the game). In other

---

[34] Foot, "Pacific Asia," p. 247.
[35] See Bob Jessop, "The Governance of Economies: the Dialectic of Globalization-Regionalization," in Glenn Drover, Graham Johnson, and Julia Tao Lao Po-Wah, eds., *Regionalism and Subregionalism in East Asia: The Dynamics of China* (Huntington, New York: Nova Science Publishers, 2001), p. 25.

8. China: Visions for Regional Cooperation in East Asia

words, it is beneficial to China if "regional agreements offer a kind of laboratory to transform national norms into international standard."[36] Through APEC, Beijing also seeks to open the access to the markets of industrialized countries. A reduction of barriers to products from developing countries would hopefully become a concrete result of APEC, through the application of nondiscriminatory principle. It goes without saying that APEC provides China an opportunity to have bilateral and multilateral contacts, while at the same time softens the American pressure vis-à-vis China and other developing countries.

Beijing appeared to take a rather low profile after China joined APEC in 1991, but started to take a higher profile in 1995, when President Jiang Zemin announced in the Osaka summit that China's average import tariff would be reduced from 35.9 percent to 23 percent in 1996. This has been further reduced to an average of 15 percent in 2000.[37] This demonstrates China's determination to liberalize the trading and denotes China's wish to open up further. Beijing insists that APEC should limit herself on economic issues, and American attempts to discuss political and security issues, like human rights, or to develop APEC into a kind of Asia-Pacific Security forum, has been consistently repulsed by China. The only exception is the anti-terrorist statement made by APEC leaders in the Shanghai summit in 2001, just after the September 11th terrorist attack on New York. China consistently stresses on the "APEC way" as the basic rule or principle for cooperation. This means recognizing the heterogeneity of the region, emphasizing the voluntary wish and autonomy of member countries, and dialogue plus consultation leading to full consensus should be the basis for making decisions.

China supports the 1994 Bogor Declaration of APEC members' commitment to liberalizing trade and investments by 2010 and 2020 for developed and developing countries respectively. China is rather satisfied with the concrete demarches on liberalization of trade and investments, but

---

[36] See Hurtzig and Sandschneider, "National Interest and Multilateral Cooperation," p. 224.
[37] Li Yuming, "The APEC Process and China," *Liaowang Weekly* (*Outlook*), No. 42, (October 15, 2001), p. 11.

is not happy with the little progress achieved in economic and technological cooperation due to the reluctance of developed countries to transfer the technologies.[38] Beijing leaders think that this is the domain that could lead the developing countries out from poverty. Though what Beijing could do is rather limited, since it is also striving very hard to improve her technology and create new industries, it did contribute a modest sum of US$10 million to set up an APEC foundation for scientific and technological development.

7. Shanghai Cooperation Organization under the "Leadership" of Beijing

Chinese strategic analysts have repeatedly demonstrated their repugnance toward the alliance system, and the concept and practice of collective security. Apart from reiterating the usual Five Principles for Peaceful Coexistence as the fundamentals for a new international political order, Chinese analysts since the mid 1990s have been discussing a new Chinese vision regarding international security. In the post-Cold War era, the concept of "international security" has undergone great changes, as the border between friends and enemies is blurred. Since the potential of another world war is nonexistent, the international community is keen to maintain a peaceful environment and facilitate economic exchanges. "Economic security" has particularly alarmed Chinese analysts, especially after the outbreak of the Asian financial crisis and the rapidly developing phenomenon of globalization. Chinese leaders also pay attention not only to the increasing number of religious and ethnic conflicts, but also to the role of culture and ideology in international relations, particularly the dominating influence of the "soft power" of the United States. The Chinese analysts are increasingly concerned with the tremendous impact of U.S. "soft power," as exemplified by Joseph Nye's usage of the term.[39]

---

[38] See Chai Penghong, "China and APEC," *Guoji Guancha* (*International Observation*), No. 4 (2001), pp. 40-42.

[39] Joseph S. Nye, Jr., *Bound to Lead* (New York: Basic Books), 1990.

8. China: Visions for Regional Cooperation in East Asia

They are also obsessed with the weakness of China in this aspect. The term "comprehensive security" is used to denote achieving security in all areas, including the increasingly important "economic security."[40]

Facing the paradoxical "consolidation" of bilateral military alliances (like the U.S.-Japan alliance) and multilateral alliances (NATO) even after the end of Cold War, Beijing proposes and promotes a new concept of international security. The achievement of bilateral or multilateral security can be obtained through mutual cooperation and by harmonizing the national interests of the partners concerned. China consistently insists that the traditional military alliances are not favorable to the construction of a more peaceful international environment. This kind of military alliance is always dominated by a superpower, thus the relationship among the partners is not equal. Not only may internal conflicts cause troubles to the proper functioning of these alliances, the sheer existence of the military alliance would arouse mistrust from other members of the international community, thus generating suspicion or even new conflicts. Strengthening military capabilities, locating a third party as potential enemy, and deterring against the potential enemy are characteristics of a military alliance. These are reminiscent of the Cold War and actually reflect the "Cold War mentality" of politicians in the West.[41]

As a substitute, the Chinese vision of international security can be characterized by the concept of "cooperative security." It emphasizes first of all the reciprocity and mutual benefits of the nations participating in such mechanism. It is non-antagonistic: instead of stressing on the binding power upon each partner in a military alliance, it is open and cooperative, and is not directed against a third party as a potential enemy. The concept

---

[40] For a succinct analysis of the Chinese views on international security and cooperative mechanism, see Su Ge, "New International Security Order and Cooperation Mechanism," *Zhongguo Pinglun* (*China Review*), No. 13 (January 1999), pp. 22-25. See also Chu Shulong, "Security in the Asia-Pacific Region: Concepts, Structure and Strategy," *Xiandai Guoji Guanxi* (*Contemporary International Relations*), No. 5 (May 1997), pp. 2-7.

[41] See Cheng Ruisheng, "On China's New Policies Towards Asia Pacific Security," *Guoji Wenti Yanjiu* (*International Studies*), No. 3 (July 1997), pp. 1-6.

of security should be broadened. Instead of being limited to strategic and military areas, it should also include political, economic, cultural, and societal security, as well as their inter-relatedness. China is particularly concerned about her own economic security when her economy is gradually opening up to the robust capitalist economies in the West. The new concept of cooperative security clearly reflects China's wish to protect her economy from outside attack by speculators. China believes that some kind of confidence-building measures built upon egalitarianism and increasing transparency based on mutual trust are useful mechanism for achieving cooperative security.[42]

This idea of cooperative security for facilitating regional security has been written into the Official White Paper on Chinese Defense published in July 1998. The agreement on "Strengthening Confidence in the Military Realm at the Border Region" signed by China, Russia, Kazakhstan, Tajikistan, and Kyrgyzstan in April 1996, as well as the Sino-Indian Agreement on Military Confidence-Building Measures signed in November 1996 are being boasted as successful examples resulting from the new Chinese vision on regional security. These agreements provide clear guidelines on the deployment of armies along the border and limiting the scope of military exercises in the border regions.[43] China has never been keen in joining any multilateral collective security framework in defense and security, since these institutional frameworks are always dominated by some big power, and Beijing does not want to be "locked" by multilateral frameworks that are conceived as constraining China's freedom to maneuver. But now China is promoting an alternative kind of framework under the banner of cooperative security. Being constructed on an egalitarian basis of sovereign states, it is more loosely organized and flexible. Although Chinese analysts agree that the loosely organized mechanism may not be very effective in solving the crises that burst abruptly, and it is unable to eliminate all the mistrust among neighbors, they deeply believe that this is a more viable way to promote international

---

[42] See Su Ge, "New International Security Order," p. 25.
[43] Office of the Press, State Council, PRC, "The Defense of China," *Renmin Ribao* (*People's Daily*), July 28, 1998, p. 1.

8. China: Visions for Regional Cooperation in East Asia

security. This can be seen as a new and bold move of Chinese leaders in trying to influence the "rules of the games," at least in the security arena of the international community. This can be regarded as a sign that China wants to become a credible great power parallel with her enormous economic success and the growing sense of nationalism among her people.

In the long run, China aspires to have a clear strategic vision and eventually hopes to shoulder her "global responsibility" through establishing some kinds of multi-layered mechanism on Asia-Pacific security based on the concept of "cooperative security," and actively promulgating proposals as well as participating in the multilateral activities of the United Nations.[44] The annual summit meeting of the "Shanghai Five" becomes a kind of diplomatic "mecca" for China, which assumes her role as the leader and promoter of a new practice in international interactions. The summit held in mid-June 2001 was boasted as a great success when new member Uzbekistan joined the Shanghai Five mechanism. As a consequence of the enlargement of the Shanghai Five, the mechanism was upgraded, and is now called the "Shanghai Cooperative Organization" (SCO).[45] The six nations also signed an agreement on counter-attacking terrorism, ethnic separatism, and religious radicalism.[46]

The Shanghai Six is now "institutionalized," with a secretariat established in Beijing since January 2004 under the leadership of China to become a regional, multilateral security and confidence-building mechanism between China and its Central Asian neighbors. Recent concrete actions include setting up a counter-terrorism center in Bishkek in Kyrgyzstan. China also started her joint military exercises with

---

[44] See Wang Yizhou, "Demands for Development, Sovereignty and Responsibility," *Shijie Zhishi* (*World Affairs*), No. 5 (March 1, 2000), pp. 8-10.

[45] See *Ming Pao*, June 15, 2001, p. B14.

[46] Numerous articles on Shanghai Five appear in Chinese publications, see for instance, Zhang Buren, "Regional Security: Keynote of 'Shanghai Five'," *Xiandai Guoji Guanxi* (*Contemporary International Relations*), (March 2001), pp. 27-29; Xu Tao, "Promoting 'Shanghai Five' Spirit for Regional Cooperation," *Xiandai Guoji Guanxi* (*Contemporary International Relations*), (May 2001), pp. 1-5.

Kyrgyzstan in October 2002, and with Russia, Kazakhstan, and Tajikistan in August 2003. The commonality of the member countries is that all are interested in checking upon American infiltration in Central Asia.[47]

8. On the Relationship between China, Japan, and South Korea within the Framework of Regional Cooperation

Japan, too, faces a dilemma. The proactive attitude of China vis-à-vis ASEAN nations has left Japan fearful of being eclipsed by China in the regionalization process. Tokyo worries that Beijing will dominate regional economic cooperation in East Asia. But if Japan follows China and establishes a free trade area with ASEAN, such an agreement would affect Japan's agricultural sector, which has always been resistant to market opening. This is part of a long-term problem Japan faces in resisting the restructuring of its national economy.[48] Japan already rejected ASEAN's 2001 proposal for establishing a free trade area. Nonetheless, it is reported that Japan is preparing to implement the "Economic Partnership Plan" with ASEAN in 2012.

As a result of Japan's anxiety about the growing influence of China, in December 2003 Japanese Prime Minister Koizumi had a special meeting with leaders of ASEAN in Tokyo. The "Tokyo Declaration" was signed subsequently, urging for the establishment of an "East Asia Community."[49] Japan will assist in providing US$1.5 billion in the next three years for human resources development and Mekong River Development. Japan also wishes to start negotiation in 2005—by the latest—on establishing a free trade area with ASEAN.[50] Political

---

[47] See Pang Guang, "From 'Shanghai Five' to Shanghai Cooperation Organization," *Dangdai Shijie* (*Contemporary World*), No. 7 (2002), pp. 10-12.

[48] See Lu Jianren, "The Flashpoints and Problems of East Asian Economic Cooperation," *Shijie Zhishi* (*World Affairs*), No. 21 (November 1, 2003), pp. 40-41.

[49] See *Ta Kung Pao*, December 13, 2003, p. A5.

[50] *Japan's FTA Strategy*, October 2002.

8. China: Visions for Regional Cooperation in East Asia

considerations regarding China's potential leadership in the region have obviously encouraged Japan's actions.

It seems that in the multilateral diplomacy of China, Beijing is fully confident in forging a comprehensive deal with ASEAN, but she is not so confident in dealing with stronger powers like South Korea and Japan. In other words, the three individual ASEAN+1 work well, but the more meaningful ASEAN+3 remains a forum without yielding anything really substantial, as the goals of the consortium remain unclear. This is related to the intricate problem of potential leadership within this region. ASEAN would like to be the "leader" and making use of the ASEAN+3 mechanism in absorbing China, Japan, and Korea to set up a free trade area that would eventually develop into an "East Asian Free Trade Area."[51] Thus, this consortium of small and medium nations could form a coalition that could play a leadership role, at the same time it could implement a balancing strategy among the strong powers. On the contrary, South Korea pays more emphasis on the effects of Northeast Asia Free Trade Area (NEAFTA), hoping that the NEAFTA would be established first with China and Japan, then absorb ASEAN to form an economic community. Korea would like to make use of China to improve its bargaining power during its negotiation in establishing a free trade area with Japan. Japan also wishes to establish bilateral free trade areas among China, Korea, and Japan, then extend to ASEAN in order to eventually form the "Northeast Asia Economic Cooperation Organization."

Despite the lack of concrete, serious actions, during the ninth ASEAN summit held in Bali in October 2003, Chinese, Japanese, and Korean leaders signed the "China-Japan-Korea Joint Declaration on Promoting Trilateral Cooperation."[52] They urged for more cooperation among the three nations, and pledged to examine the feasibility and implications of establishing a free trade area composed of the three nations.

---

[51] Li Chunming and Zhao Zhenlin, "On the Prospects and Challenges of the China-ASEAN Free Trade Area," *Shijie Jinji yu Zhengzhi* (*World Economic and Politics*), (November 2002), pp. 32-37.
[52] See *Hong Kong Economic Journal*, October 8, 2003, p. 22, and *Ming Pao*, October 8, 2003, p. A22.

Sino-Japanese relations, which could and should become the axis of Asian regionalization, are frequently in a state of apprehension as mutual political mistrust still lingers between the two sides. However, recent analyses made by Chinese analysts proclaim a "forward looking" attitude. On the one hand, they insist that the Japanese government should begin shouldering some responsibility by forbidding some actions that "harm Chinese people's sentiments" (e.g., such as stop denying the Nanjing massacre). On the other hand, China would like to see that "both China and Japan should not seek unilaterally or in cooperation with extra-regional state to play a leadership role in East Asian multilateral system. Instead, both nations should shoulder the responsibility in order to play a role as major East Asian powers, basing on the foundation of mutual respect and mutual trust." That is to say, the two nations should play a central role in solving East Asian problems. The principles for the construction of East Asian multilateral cooperation system should be :

- "Asianism": Asian problems should be solved by Asians themselves;
- Openness: multilateral cooperation system is not against non-Asian states;
- Equality of interest, mutual trust, consultation to achieve consensus, and not against any Asian states;
- Anti-hegemonism: great powers like China, Japan, and Indonesia should play a role to lead and consult, but not interfere in the domestic politics of the others.[53]

It seems that Beijing understands that China and Japan could be the joint leaders (like the so-called Franco-German axis in the European Union) in achieving regionalization in Asia, but Beijing wants Japan to get rid of its image as a "Western" state. Chinese sympathy to the "ASEAN process" as well as to Asian values emphasized by some ASEAN leaders would render this joint leadership extremely difficult to achieve in the short run. Nevertheless, the Japanese actions in helping her Asian

---

[53] See Ye Zicheng, *Zhongguo Da Zhanlue* (*The Grand Strategy of China*) (Beijing: Chinese Social Science Press, 2003), pp. 286-91.

8. China: Visions for Regional Cooperation in East Asia

counterparts during the Asian financial crisis, and the proposal made by Japan in creating an AMF—though aborted—are positive actions launched by Japan to promote a concerted development of this region,[54] and they are well appreciated by the PRC.

9. Conclusion

Two Chinese economists are quite explicit in expressing their vision towards the future of this region. They write that "China should make use of her strong economic, political and military capabilities to extend her influence southward and northward, so as to 'combine' the 'Northeast Asian Economic Cooperation Organisation' and ASEAN into the 'East Asian Union'; and change it to become the regional cooperation organisation dominated by the Asians."[55] China should facilitate the development of an "Asian Union." But what role then should China play in such a Union? If the "Middle Kingdom mentality" reemerges, all the Asian states have to ponder about how to cope with this newly emerging hegemon.

It seems apparent that China will become more active in the regional multilateral economic and security frameworks, such as ASEAN+1, APEC, ARF, SCO, all of which achieve unanimous consensus only through dialogue and consultation as a way of making decisions. As a result, China's freedom to maneuver is not bound by these organizations that aim at "open regionalism," but at the same time, she aspires to play a leadership role in these institutions. China is the first non-ASEAN nation

---

[54] For some Japanese views of China, see Tatsumi Okabe, "International Relations Theory and Chinese Foreign Policy," in Yoshinobu Yamamoto, ed., *Globalism, Regionalism and Nationalism: Asia in Search of its Role in the Twenty-First Century* (Oxford: Blackwell, 1999), pp. 142-53; and Shigeaki Uno, "China and Japan in Search of their Roles in the Twenty-First Century: Regionalism or Globalism?" in Yoshinobu Yamamoto, ed., *Globalism, Regionalism and Nationalism: Asia in Search of its Role in the Twenty-First Century* (Oxford: Blackwell, 1999), pp. 154-70.

[55] See Zhao Chunming and Liu Zhenlin, "On the Prospects and Challenges of China-ASEAN Free Trade Area," p. 37.

that signed the ASEAN Treaty of Amity and Friendship, and the first to agree to sign a free trade agreement with ASEAN. This stimulates other countries to follow, thus enhancing China's role as the engine that promotes a new brand of regionalization, which emphasizes equality, dialogue, confidence building, consensus, and mutual trust. A prominent Chinese scholar in Asia-Pacific studies even promotes the idea of setting up a regional organization, an "Organization of East Asian Cooperation" within three to five years to replace the ASEAN+ 3 mechanism.[56] Chinese analysts always proclaim that a great power should go the way of *Wandao* (benign leadership) instead of *Badao* (hegemony), and Chinese leaders are very keen about retrieving the *grandeur* of the Chinese civilization. If Chinese ideas are accepted for the further development of regionalism in Asia, it would be perceived as a sign of *grandeur* as China rediscovers her leadership role. Though Beijing insists that it will never become a hegemon, it should pay attention to the reactions of others toward Chinese political and diplomatic behavior. The logic of hegemony is that a great power exports or promotes what she thinks is good for others, but others may perceive this as a hegemonic measure being imposed upon them.

China welcomes the flexible, open, and non-binding nature of the above-mentioned institutions, since the sovereignty of all the states concerned is duly respected. Her increasingly developed market economy enables China to accept the concept of a free trade area, as she could benefit enormously. It is interesting to note that Chinese analysts voice out vehemently against the barriers that inhibit free trade. China would like to establish the East Asia Free Trade Area by 2020, an objective that is more realistic than the "East Asia Economic Community" proclaimed by Singapore and Thailand. The rise of China will certainly see China playing an extremely important role in stabilizing Asia's economy.

Many analysts agree that the SCO is marginalized by American penetration into the Central Asian states since the September 11th incident in order to oust the Taliban regime in Afghanistan. This American intervention has filled the power vacuum in this region after the collapse

---

[56] See Zhang Yun Ling, "East Asian Regionalism and China," *Issues & Studies*, (June 2002), p. 221.

of the Soviet Union. However, the strategic "loss" of China in this area is compensated by the increasing influence that China enjoys in ASEAN and East Asia cooperation. While China is still resistant to joining any multilateral security scheme, especially those dominated by the United States, the increasing influence of China in regional multilateralism poses a challenge to the dominance of the United States in the region. A rising China that exerts her influence upon the design and transformation of the international norms will become a subject of serious concern to Asian nations.

References

Ba, Alice D. "China and ASEAN: Renavigating Relations for a 21st-Century Asia," *Asian Survey*, vol. 43, No. 4 (July/August 2003), pp. 622-47.

Chai Penghong. "China and APEC," *Guoji Guancha* (*International Observation*), No. 4 (2001), pp. 40-42.

Chen Dezhao. "A New Stage of East Asia Economic Cooperation," *Guoji Wenti Yanjiu* (*International Studies*), No. 6 (November 2003), pp. 50-54.

Cheng Ruisheng. "On China's New Policies Towards Asia Pacific Security," *Guoji Wenti Yanjiu* (*International Studies*), No. 3 (July 1997), pp. 1-6.

Choi, Young Jong and Nae Young Lee. "A Comparative Study of Regionalism in East Asia and the Americas," *Asian Perspective*, vol. 26, No. 3 (2002), pp. 169-92.

Chu Shulong. "Security in the Asia-Pacific Region: Concepts, Structure and Strategy," *Xiandai Guoji Guanxi* (*Contemporary International Relations*), No. 5 (May 1997), pp. 2-7.

Chu Shulong and Geng Qin. *Shijie, Meiguo he Zhongguo: Xinshiji Guoji Guanxi he Guoji Zhanlue Lilun Tansuo* (*World, USA and China: Theories of International Relations and International Strategies in the New Century*). Beijing: Tsinghua University Press, 2003.

Dao Shulin et al. "Research Report on China's ASEAN Policies," *Xiandai Guoji Guanxi* (*Contemporary International Relations*), (October 2002), pp. 1-10.

Dosch, Jorn and Manfred Mols, ed. *International Relations in the Asia-Pacific*. New York: St. Martin's Press, 2000.

Drifte, Reinhard. *Japan's Security Relations with China since 1989*. London: RoutledgeCurzon, 2003.
Economy, Elizabeth and Michael Oksenberg, eds. *China Joins the World*. New York: Council on Foreign Relations, 1999.
Fawcett, Louise and Andrew Hurrell, eds. *Regionalism in World Politics*. Oxford: Oxford University Press, 1995.
Gill, Bates. "China and Regional Cooperation and Security Building Measures," in Robert Ash, ed., *China's Integration into Asia*. Richmond, Surrey: Curzon, 2002.
Gurtov, Mel. *Pacific Asia? Prospects for Security and Cooperation in East Asia*. Lanham, Maryland: Rowman & Littlefield, 2002.
Hsueh Chun-tu and Liu Shan, eds. *Zhongguo Waijiao Xinlun* (*New Dimensions of China's Diplomacy*). Beijing: World Affairs Press, 1998.
Jessop, Bob. "The Governance of Economies: the Dialectic of Globalization-Regionalization," in Glenn Drover, Graham Johnson, and Julia Tao Lao Po-Wah, eds., *Regionalism and Subregionalism in East Asia: the Dynamics of China*. Huntington, N.Y.: Nova Science Publishers, 2001.
Johnston, Alastair Iain and Robert Ross, eds. *Engaging China*. London: Routledge, 1999.
Kim, Samuel, ed. *East Asia and Globalization*. Lanham, Md.: Rowman & Littlefield, 2000.
Li Chunming and Zhao Zhenlin. "On the Prospects and Challenges of the China-ASEAN Free Trade Area," *Shijie Jinji yu Zhengzhi* (*World Economics and Politics*), (November 2002), pp. 32-37.
Liu Fu-Kuo. "A Critical Review of East and Northeast Asian Regionalism," in Christopher M. Dent and David W. F. Huang, eds., *Northeast Asian Regionalism: Learning from the European Experience*. London: Routledge Curzon, 2002.
Luo Jie. "Interview of Fu Yin, Secretary of Asia Bureau, Chinese Ministry of Foreign Affairs," *Shijie Zhishi* (*World Affairs*), No. 23 (December 2002), pp. 8-10.
Mearsheimer, John J. *The Tragedy of Great Power Politics*. New York: Norton, 2001.
Nye, Joseph S. Jr. *Bound to Lead*. New York: Basic Books, 1990.
Office of the Press, State Council, PRC. "The Defense of China," *Renmin Ribao* (*Peoples's Daily*), July 28, 1998, p. 1.
Okabe, Tatsumi. "International Relations Theory and Chinese Foreign Policy," in Yoshinobu Yamamoto ed., *Globalism, Regionalism and*

Nationalism: Asia in Search of its Role in the Twenty-First Century. Oxford: Blackwell, 1999.
Ong, Eng Chuan. "Anchor East Asian Free Trade in ASEAN," *Washington Quarterly*, (Spring 2003), pp. 57-72.
Ong, Russell. China's Interest in the Post-Cold War Era. Richmond, Surrey: Curzon, 2002.
Qiu Danyang. "East Asian Cooperation and China's Strategic Options," *Guoji Wenti Yanjiu (International Studies)*, No. 3 (May 2003), pp. 42-47.
Schulz, Michael et al., eds. *Regionalization in a Globalizing World.* New York: Zed, 2001.
Song Chengyou and Tang Chongnan, eds. *East Asian Regional Consciousness and Peaceful Development.* Chengdu: Sichuan University Press, 2001.
Stubbs, Richard. "ASEAN plus Three: Emerging East Asian Regionalism?" *Asian Survey*, vol. 42, No. 3 (May/June 2002), pp. 440-55.
Su Ge. "New International Security Order and Cooperation Mechanism," *Zhongguo Pinglun (China Review)*, No. 13 (January 1999), pp. 22-25.
Uno, Shigeaki. "China and Japan in Search of their Roles in the Twenty-First Century: Regionalism or Globalism?" in Yoshinobu Yamamoto, ed., *Globalism, Regionalism and Nationalism : Asia in Search of its Role in the Twenty-First Century.* Oxford: Blackwell, 1999.
Vandermeersch, Léon. "Le monde vu de Chine," *Hérodote: Revue de Géographie et de Géopolitique*, No. 108, (1er trimestre 2003), pp. 43-64.
Wang Jie, ed. *Guoji Jizhi Lun (On International Regimes).* Beijing: Xinhua Press, 2002.
Wang Yizhou. "Demands for Development, Sovereignty and Responsibility," *Shijie Zhishi (World Affairs)*, No. 5 (March 2000), pp. 8-10.
Wang Yizhou et al., eds. *2003: Quanqiu Zhengzhi yu Anquan Baogao (2003: Report on Global Politics and Security).* Beijing: Social Sciences Documentation Publishing House, 2003.
Wu Lingjun. "The APEC Strategy and Change of Role of China: A Neo-realist Interpretation," *Wenti yu Yanjiu (Issues and Studies)*, vol. 40, No. 3 (May-June 2001), pp. 1-20.
Xu Tao. "Promoting 'Shanghai Five' Spirit for Regional Cooperation," *Xiandai Guoji Guanxi (Contemporary International Relations)*, (May 2001), pp. 1-5.
Yang, Richard H. et al., eds. *Chinese Regionalism: the Security Dimension.* Boulder, Colo.: Westview, 1994.
Ye Zicheng. *Zhongguo Da Zhanlue (The Grand Strategy of China).* Beijing: Chinese Social Science Press, 2003.

Part II: National Visions and Experiences of Cooperation in Europe and Asia

Zhai Kun. "A Brief Review of China's Accession to the Treaty of Amity and Cooperation in Southeast Asia," *Xiandai Guoji Guanxi* (*Contemporary International Relations*), No. 11 (November 2003), pp. 36-37.

Zhang Bin. "The Economic Relations and Prospects between China and East Asia," *Guoji Wenti Yanjiu* (*International Studies*), No. 4 (July 2003), pp. 54-59.

Zhang Buren. "Regional Security: Keynote of 'Shanghai Five'," *Xiandai Guoji Guanxi* (*Contemporary International Relations*), (March 2001), pp. 27-29.

Zhang Youmin and Dong Jiangwei. *2003 Zhongguo Guoji Diwei Baogao* (*2003 Report on China's International Status*). Shanghai: Far East Press, 2003.

Zhang Yun Ling. "East Asian Regionalism and China," *Issues & Studies*, (June 2002), pp. 213-23.

CHAPTER *9*

THE DEVELOPMENT OF KOREA'S REGIONAL STRATEGY IN NORTHEAST ASIA

Cheol-Hee PARK

1. Korea's Place in the World

Over the past decades, the Republic of Korea (ROK, also referred to hereinafter as Korea or South Korea) has made remarkable progress in the world. On the one hand, Korea has climbed up the vertical ladder of success via its rapid economic development.[1] With the institutionalization of democratic political order since the mid-1980s, Korea joined the club of democratic market economies. On the other hand, Korea continued to widen its geostrategic and diplomatic horizons. Korea, which had diplomatic relations with only seven nations in 1954, has established diplomatic relations with 186 nations as of 2003.[2]

However, despite Korea's advance in the world, few serious attempts

---

[1] Jung En Woo, *Race to the Swift* (New York: Columbia University Press, 1991); See also, Bruce Cumings, *Korea's Place in the Sun* (New York: Norton, 1997).
[2] Ministry of Foreign Affairs and Trade, *White Paper on Korean Diplomacy* (Seoul: MOFAT, 2003), p. 494.

were made to discuss Korea's regional strategy. Some even cynically say that Korea has not had any regional strategy. However, the Roh Tae Woo regime's "*Nordpolitik*" and the Roh Moo Hyun administration's idea of a Northeast Asian Business Hub suggest otherwise. Still, it is undeniable that Korea's regional strategy has been somewhat vague.

There might be two reasons for the lack of discourse on Korea's regional strategy. One may be that Korea's focus has been lopsided toward bilateral relations, especially U.S.-ROK relations. When Korea touches upon its regional diplomatic strategy, it has long been a custom that bilateral relations be a starting point of discussion. However, putting bilateral relations in a regional setting has rarely been tried. A second may be that when regional areas are referred to, it has often been the case that the focus of discussion be narrowed down to a single issue area. The lack of a comprehensive scheme that goes beyond specific issue areas characterizes the discussion on Korea's regional strategy.

This does not imply that Korea has not coined a regional strategy at all. Korea is geographically located in Northeast Asia with powerful neighbors surrounding the country. It has long been told that the so-called "Big Four"—the United States, Russia, Japan, and China—have been instrumental in deciding the fate of Korea. Regional strategy, whether Korea pursues it consciously or not, has been a core of its external and diplomatic strategy to guarantee its physical survival and economic prosperity.

What is needed is a renewed look at the assumptions that have long been taken for granted in the discussion of Korea's regional strategy. As the bilateral alliance with the United States was pivotal for Korea's political and economic development, Koreans have long been accustomed to looking at the world affairs through the prism of the United States. Korea's strategy was closely intertwined with U.S. strategy toward East Asia. In other words, Korean strategy was viewed from the angle of "outside-in." However, Korea has developed loosely defined regional strategic approaches to realize its national interest.[3] An "inside-out" approach is needed in order to grasp the essential features of the historically evolving regional strategy of Korea.

It is noteworthy that, unlike European countries, Korea did not necessarily design its diplomatic strategy with a reference to the region it physically belonged to. Though there is no denying that Korea is an Asian country, Asia was not a unified whole historically. Asia was more of a geographical term and not a culturally and politically integrated entity. Accordingly, regional powers in the eyes of Koreans are not confined to geographically adjacent nations. The lack of intra-regional integration in turn led to the extension of Korea's regional angle to extra-regional power. Hence, the boundary of the term "regional" should not be limited to intra-regional but encompass extra-regional power.[4] In other words, extra-regional dynamics should be brought in to grasp the nature of intra-regional dynamics in Asia.

Together with the U.S.-Korean relations, Korea's relationship with the Democratic People's Republic of Korea (DPRK or North Korea) has set the boundaries for its regional engagement strategy. Since its inception, Korean governments have been preoccupied with the issue of how to deal with North Korea. How to peacefully coexist with North Korea without inviting another war on the peninsula has been a priority concern for the governments. How to reunify the country has been a national aspiration. The issue of how Korea should engage with external powers has been closely intertwined with the North Korean question. It is not an exaggeration at all that Korea's regional strategy has been designed and implemented with the prism of strategic considerations concerning the inter-Korean relationship. Hence this chapter also aims at analyzing Korea's regional strategy in Northeast Asia in close connection with the development of the inter-Korean relationship.

---

[3] Koo Youngnok, *Hanguk kwa Kukka Iik* (*Korea and the National Interest*) (Seoul: Bupmunsa, 1996).

[4] This may be a difference between Asian and European regionalism.

Part II: National Visions and Experiences of Cooperation in Europe and Asia

On the basis of these renewed assumptions, this chapter attempts to survey the historical development of Korea's regional strategy in Northeast Asia since its liberation from Japanese colonial rule. The focus of the discussion will be laid on three points. First, this chapter tries to show when and why Korean political leaders designed regional strategies under discussion Political leaders tend to make their choice under structural and circumstantial constraints while taking best advantage of unfolding opportunities. Understanding the logic of those bounded strategic choices is the first purpose of this chapter. Second, this article aims at sketching out historical trends and distinctive features of the Korean approach to engage in a regional order. Though each period revealed a justifiable logic of taking a particular strategic stance, one can identify a few characteristics that run through different periods. Third, by highlighting Korea's strategic approach to Northeast Asia, this chapter tries to grasp the possibilities and limitations of regional cooperation in Northeast Asia.

2. Period One: Virtual Absence of Regional Strategy
— from 1945 to the mid-1960s —

It is no wonder that Korea lacked a regional strategy in a true sense of the word under the Rhee Sung Man regime. Unilateral reliance on the United States represents Korea's geo-strategic approach till the end of the 1950s. A divided nation after the liberation from colonial rule followed by the devastating Korean War set the stage for this strategic alliance with the United States.

Theoretically, Korea had three strategic options at that time. One was neutrality. Becoming a Switzerland of Asia was conceivable. However, the division of the Korean peninsula into two blocked its chance to take a neutral position when the cold war situation was in progress. Surrounded by big powers, Korea faced a moment of choice rather than that of neutrality. Another possible strategic choice was self-reliant autonomy. Diplomatic isolation was a theoretically possible choice, but never a practical one for Korea. To be independent, Korea had to have an

9. The Development of Korea's Regional Strategy in Northeast Asia

abundance of natural resources as well as the means to defend national sovereignty. However, Korea was deficient of such natural and financial resources, especially after the colonial rule and devastating war.

Korea was obliged to take a third option, which was the strategy of aligning with the major powers. The United States, which was instrumental in liberating the country and also helped Korea during the war, became a natural choice for Korea. Alliance with other regional neighbors was not feasible then. Ever since the liberation from Japanese colonial rule, Japan was a country to antagonize, not engage. Anti-Japanese sentiment constituted a source of national identity.[5] Japan was perceived as a country not only to stay away from but also to despise. Likewise, after the Korean War, China turned out to be a resentful nation to Koreans, for it helped North Korea invade the South. Cultural affinity that many Koreans had with China faded away rapidly. Under the cold war structure, China was looked upon as an enemy. Russia, which was a central pillar of the Socialist bloc, was also a target of antagonism.

Though Korea could not develop friendly ties with neighboring countries due to the cold war structure and aftereffects of the Korean War, it faced an urgent need for obtaining effective means to acquire national security and economic rehabilitation. Korea made a strategic choice to forge an alliance with extra-regional security guarantor, the United States. United States provided not only a nuclear umbrella in the bipolar world order but also a conventional security backup against North Korea. President Rhee persistently requested a security guarantee offered by the United States as a condition for accepting an armistice with North Korea.[6] On October 1, 1953 right after the Korean War, a U.S.-Korean security treaty was signed. On top of it, the United States gave the country massive

---

[5] Jim Morley pointed out that the most resentful was not necessarily communists but the Japanese. James Morley, *Japan and Korea: America's Allies in the Pacific* (New York: Walker & Co., 1965), p. 54.

[6] Park Sil, *Hanguk Oegyo Bisa (Hidden Stories of the Korean Diplomacy)* (Seoul: Jungho Press, 1984), p. 244.

amounts of aid, which worked as a lifeline that would allow for the economic revival of Korea after the war. Between 1948 and 1960, the United States provided US$1,214 million worth of economic assistance to Korea, which constituted almost 80 percent of the Korean national budget.[7]

Anti-communist ideology and anti-Japanese sentiments worked as building blocks for national sovereignty. Disengagement from intra-regional powers made Korea heavily dependent on its extra-regional alliance partner. Though Korea was not alienated from all the countries on the globe, it is hardly deniable that Korea was isolated from the regional powers. It is not an exaggeration that Korea lacked any significant regional strategy in this period. The United States was Korea's strongest and virtually only reliable ally.

Korean diplomacy under the Rhee regime can be characterized as follows. First, the national priority in the 1950s was essentially physical survival and national security. To realize this goal, Korea opted for unilateral reliance on the United States as a way to guarantee its national security as well as to obtain external aid for reviving its economy.

Second, Korea under Rhee took anti-communism as the first and uncompromising principle of diplomacy.[8] Rhee did not even drop the rhetoric of militarily advancing into North Korea. North Korea was an immediate and visible enemy. While deepening ties with the liberal camp, Korea closed its doors to the socialist countries.

Third, the Rhee regime placed nationalism as a foundation for its diplomatic strategy. For example, despite America's repeated persuasion to normalize relations with Japan, Rhee persistently refused to engage in any serious talks with Japan. In addition to the strategic concern, Rhee Sung

---

[7] Jung Won Kim, *Divided Korea: The Politics of Development 1945-1972* (Cambridge: Harvard University Press, 1975).

[8] Heo Man, *Hanbando wa Oegyojungchaekron* (*Korean Peninsula and Foreign Policy*) (Seoul: Gyoyuk Kwahaksa, 1988), p. 135.

Man's personal career deeply affected the decision.⁹

In other words, Korean diplomacy in this period was structured and deeply influenced by historical memory of colonial rule, the Korean War, as well as the global development of the cold war.

3. Period Two: Trilateral Alliance under the Cold War Setup — from the mid-1960s to the late 1980s —

3.1. The First Phase: The Park Chung Hee Era
Park Chung Hee, who assumed power through a military coup, placed a priority on two national goals. One was to strengthen the national security setup against North Korea. Inherited the legacy from the Rhee regime, anti-communism became a catch phrase for Park's political legitimacy. But he dropped the provocative rhetoric that South Korea would absorb North Korea by militarily force. Instead, Park Chung Hee put more emphasis on economically vitalizing the country. Getting out of the group of underdeveloped countries and advancing to "developing" status through active government guidance was the Park regime's mandate.

In line with this strategic choice, the Park regime upgraded diplomatic efforts to enhance economic growth in addition to diplomacy for regime survival and national security. Korea, which was isolated from Asia while leaning extremely toward the United States, felt a need to return to Asia.¹⁰ This move reflected situational changes surrounding Korea. Since the early 1960s, Korea, Japan, and the United States faced a strategic need to forge a new type of alliance among one another. The Korean government was in need of an alternative source of economic

---

⁹ Rhee, before he assumed the position of president, was a nationally well-known and respected independence movement leader during the colonial period. He symbolized Korea's resistance against Japan.
¹⁰ Joon Young Park, *Korea's Return to Asia: South Korean Foreign Policy 1965-1975* (Seoul: Jin-Heung Press, 1985).

Part II: National Visions and Experiences of Cooperation in Europe and Asia

assistance because the United States began sharply reducing its foreign aid. U.S. grants in 1962 reached US$165 million, but it was reduced to US$88 million in 1964. Japan, however, with its revitalized economy after the Korean War, sought for a place to invest its money for furthering economic expansion. On the part of the United States, it wanted Japan and Korea to cooperate with each other to build up a strong bulwark against the communist threat in Asia.[11]

Park Chung Hee, who fashioned his pro-Japanese attitude in his early years, looked at Japan not only as an object of denunciation but also as a model of economic development. Most of all, he saw positive strategic advantages for Korea if it normalized relations with Japan. Normalization of ROK-Japan relations would send a positive signal to Washington, which had made this request earlier. This would allow Korea to then acquire some space for diplomatic autonomy from the United States. It is noteworthy that diplomatic normalization with Japan was accepted together with the dispatch of Korean troops to Vietnam, which were two agendas that Washington requested of Seoul.[12] Also, in order to firmly establish political legitimacy, Park had to push economic development plans. What was most in need for that initiative was funding to launch a series of economic projects. External funding for economic rehabilitation was needed. Park saw Japan as one of those sources. The other was the United States once Korea dispatched its troops to Vietnam. Out of those strategic considerations, Park Chung Hee normalized diplomatic ties with Japan and dispatch combat units to Vietnam in 1965. After twists and turns, a Korea-Japan normalization treaty was signed on June 22, 1965. Japan gave Korea a total of US$800 million, including grants and loans.[13] Considering that Korea's total GDP at that time was around US$2 billion,

---

[11] Kim Jungwon, *Hanguk Oegyo Baljonron* (*Development of Korean Diplomacy*) (Seoul: Chipmundang, 1996), p. 125.
[12] As for American requests to Korea during this period, see ibid., chapter 7.
[13] A critical secret deal was made between Jong Pil Kim and Ohira to decide the amount of Japanese financial compensation to Korea in November 1962. Dosung Lee, *Park Chung Hee and Korea-Japan Talks* (Seoul: Hansong, 1995).

9. The Development of Korea's Regional Strategy in Northeast Asia

it goes without saying that the money from Japan contributed much to speeding up economic development.[14] In reality, Korea made rapid economic growth between 1965 and 1970, recording an annual average growth rate of 12 percent.

Korea's regional engagement entered a new phase after it normalized its diplomatic relationship with Japan. Despite the everlasting presence of anti-Japanese sentiment, political leaders incorporated Japan as an alliance partner. When Korea aligned with Japan, North Korea was predominantly an object of strategic concern among Korean political leaders. It was widely believed until the early 1970s that South Korea still lagged behind North Korea economically. To make Korea militarily strong and economically rich was an underlying motive of entering into such a trilateral alliance. To deter possible aggression from North Korea as well as to strengthen the nation's economic capability, Korea needed economic assistance and technological transfer from Japan. The United States also saw this as a plus as it could relieve itself of the burden of propping up the Korean economy by hopefully linking it with the Japanese economy.

U.S. President Nixon declared the "Guam Doctrine" in July 1969, whose message was basically that Asian problems should be solved by Asians. As an extension of this declaration, the Nixon administration delivered its will to withdraw part of its American forces in Korea in July 1970. In March 1971, the 7th division left the Korean peninsula and the size of American forces in Korea was reduced to 33,250 from 52,580 troops in 1969.[15] This presented a shock to Korean diplomacy, which had relied heavily on the United States. Moreover, Nixon secretly visited Beijing to normalize relations with China. Japanese Prime Minster Tanaka followed suit in September 1972. In place of the cold war atmosphere, the Sino-U.S. détente created a mood of reduced tension, opening a new horizon in the regional order.

---

[14] Ministry of Foreign Affairs and Trade, *Fifty Years of Korean Diplomacy* (Seoul: MOFAT, 1999), p. 48.
[15] Kim Jungwon, op. cit., p.179.

Despite regional changes, Korea could not change its stance toward China easily. China was an enemy since the Korean War. More than anything else, China remained a close ally of North Korea. Under the consciousness that Korea cannot align with China, Park switched his stance toward North Korea. On August 15, 1970, Park declared, "if North Korea stops making provocative military actions and if it renounces the policy of militarily overthrowing South Korea, South Korea is ready to make a path-breaking and realistic proposal for ameliorating inter-Korean relations in a phased fashion."[16] This was a fundamental switch of the ROK position toward North Korea in that South Korea for the first time acknowledged the North Korean government as a counterpart of negotiation and that it accepted North Korea as a competitor rather than an enemy. On the Korean side, this was the first move to flexibly respond to newly evolving global détente. Again in January 1971, Park made it clear that Korea would pursue an alliance partnership while strengthening friendly ties with neutral nations. He went further to announce that Korea would endeavor to make an interest-based approach to communist countries as long as they are not hostile to Korea."[17] As an extension, after several meetings for the making of secret deals with North Korea, South and North Korea announced on July 4, 1972, that unification should be achieved under the three principles of autonomy, peace, and national solidarity. Korea's ameliorating approach toward North Korea culminated when Park Chung Hee announced on June 23, 1973, that Korea would open its doors to all countries, including countries of different ideology and political systems, on the principle of reciprocity and equality. This declaration aimed at peacefully coexisting with North Korea until conditions for peaceful unification were ripe. Though the inter-Korean relationship had elements of both cooperation and conflict—before and even after Park's statements—since then Korea's strategic approach to

---

[16] *Donga Ilbo* (Seoul), August 15, 1970.
[17] Office of the Secretary to the President, *The 8th Collection of President Park Chung Hee's Speeches* (Seoul: Office of the President, 1972), pp.18-19.

9. The Development of Korea's Regional Strategy in Northeast Asia

North Korea fundamentally shifted in a sense that North Korea came to be perceived not simply as an enemy but as a competitor that South Korea could peacefully coexist with.

This strategic shift was the Korean way of adjusting to the newly evolving regional order under the awareness that diplomatic normalization with China or the Soviet Union was not easily feasible. Korea took a turn by taking a soft-line approach toward North Korea. However, this shift in regional strategy was initiated while maintaining close security and political ties with the United States. Also, Korea deepened economic ties with Japan. In that sense, the-then socialist countries like China and Russia were not seriously considered a part of Korea's regional strategy design.

Korea's awareness of the need to widen the scope of regional engagement came when Korea actively began expanding its export market. With a burgeoning high growth economy in the 1970s, Korea expanded contacts and transactions with major powers of the world. Foreign countries were perceived as potential markets for export goods. Korea did not dare open its doors to non-aligned nations; but it did begin establishing diplomatic ties with Asian countries throughout the 1960s (i.e., with Malaysia in 1960; Australia, 1961; and New Zealand, 1962; Indonesia, 1962; Burma, 1961, Pakistan, 1968; and Nepal, 1969). In the 1970s, diplomacy toward Southeast Asian countries became more active (i.e., Korea established ties with Cambodia in 1970; Indonesia, 1973; Laos, 1974; and Singapore, 1975). Korea also widened diplomatic horizon to South American countries during these two decades. Starting from diplomatic normalization with Mexico in 1962, Korea established diplomatic ties with twenty South American countries in the 1960s, and by the end of the 1970s, twenty-six of the twenty-nine South American countries had established formal ties with Korea. However, except for a few countries, strategic focus in establishing diplomatic ties with the third world countries lied in securing numerical superiority over North Korea in international organizations like the United Nations.

The Middle East has featured itself as a diplomatically meaningful region to Koreans since the 1970s. When Korea first opened diplomatic ties with Israel in 1962, the region was just one of those remote countries in the world. However, since the first oil crisis in the early 1970s, the

Middle East earned strategic leverage as an energy supply source. Oil-producing countries in the region accumulated huge amount of oil dollars, which drove them to speed up national redevelopment projects. At that time, Korean companies began sending a number of construction workers to the Middle East. Between 1966 and 1978, Korea earned about US$14 billion in the Middle East region by participating in the various construction projects. However, the Middle East was regarded simply as a commercial market and a source of foreign currency rather than as a region of critical geo-strategic interests.

In the late 1970s, the Carter administration's posture toward the withdrawal of U.S. forces in Korea provided momentum to reexamine Korea's over-reliance on the United States. That was a shock to Koreans—especially those in the security community, who blindly followed U.S. policy lines. It gave Korean political leaders a wake-up call to the idea that the United States might not be an eternal security guarantor for South Korea. However, considering the imminent threat from North Korea, leaders in Seoul strengthened their will to keep the United States as an ally.

Korea's regional strategy made important changes under the Park Chung Hee regime. First of all, Korea decided to partly return to Asia by normalizing relations with Japan. It was the first serious attempt to forge a virtual alliance with an intra-regional power. It is important to note that the development of the so-called trilateral alliance among the United States, Korea, and Japan was pushed by the key ally of Korea, the United States. In this sense, Korea's new regional strategy was not necessarily fashioned independently. The United States was the prime mover of Korea's regional strategy.

Second, Korea began pursuing economic diplomacy in addition to its security-focused one. Associating diplomatic reach closely with economic development of the nation was in the minds of Korean political leaders. In other words, economic betterment of people came to be intertwined with establishing diplomatic relations with foreign countries. This is especially so in the case of diplomatic normalization between Korea and Japan.

Third, Korea dropped the policy of not recognizing North Korea as a political entity. Though Korea maintained its policy of securing military deterrence against the potential North Korean threat, South Korea began pursuing the policy of peacefully coexisting with North Korea. It was possible on the premise that South Korea could recognize North Korea as a competitor in the international scene. On the one hand, this is the reflection of emerging Korean confidence over its competitor. On the other hand, Korea made a realistic U-turn because it could not knock the doors of key regional players like China and Soviet Union. In order to concentrate on national economic development, Korea faced a strategic need to reduce military tension with North Korea.

Finally, Korea widened its diplomatic horizon to the globe, including non-aligned nations. It established diplomatic ties with countries in diverse regions of the world as long as those countries were not hostile to Korea. Only communist countries remained out of diplomatic reach by the end of the 1970s. However, this does not necessarily mean that Korea actively pursued a systematically designed and well-coordinated global regional strategy. Rather, establishing diplomatic ties with many nations was led by the desire to gain diplomatic advantage over North Korea. Commercial interest to exploit new markets was a driving force to reach out to developing countries. Basically, however, Korea's primary concern lay with North America and Japan.

3.2. The Second Phase: The Chun Doo Hwan Era
It was in the era of President Chun Doo Hwan that Korea built a visible security alliance with both the United States and Japan. Chun, who had a troubled relationship with the United States in the course of assuming political power, tried to feature himself as a political leader deeply committed to the U.S.-ROK alliance. The United States faced a new challenge to its global security alliance in the newly unfolding security threat from the Soviet Union. In 1979, the Soviet Union invaded Afghanistan.[18] At a summit meeting between Chun and Reagan, the

---

[18] Robert Lockwood, "The Global Soviet Threat and U.S. Security Commitment to South Korea," *Asian Perspective*, vol. 6, No. 2 (Fall/Winter 1982), pp. 1-29.

Part II: National Visions and Experiences of Cooperation in Europe and Asia

United States promised that it would nullify its plan to withdraw American forces in South Korea, as well as endorse plans to modernize the Korean military. Close ties between Korea and the United States advanced in the area of security cooperation. Chun in turn asked for economic cooperation from Japan as a way to strengthen security ties. He first asked then Prime Minister Suzuki for a US$6 billion loan from Japan.[19] A final deal was made between Chun and Japanese Prime Minister Nakasone in January 1983, who consented to provide a US$4 billion loan to Korea over a seven-year period.[20] Nakasone made the first official visit to Korea in January 1983 before he flew to the United States. In return, President Chun visited Japan in September 1984, the first visit of a Korean president to Japan.[21] It symbolized the development of the bilateral relationship and brought it to a new stage. From then on, the two countries began substantially cooperating with each other on the security arena as well as on the economic front, going beyond the historical animosity.[22]

The unfolding trilateral security cooperation and rapidly growing Korean economy gave Koreans a sense of security parity with North Korea. Korea's annual GDP growth between 1980 and 1988 was a rate of 8.7 percent. Also per capita GNP went up from $1,640 in 1979 to $3,098 in 1987, and $4,040 in 1988.[23] With this elevated sense of confidence, Korea launched a dual policy of securing a competitive edge against North Korea while more positively incorporating it into South Korea's

---

[19] Chong Sik Lee, *Japan and Korea: The Political Dimension* (Stanford: Hoover Institute Press, 1985), pp. 145-47.

[20] About the role of Sejima to cut a deal between the two, see, Seijima Ryuzo, *Sejima Ryuzo Memoir* (Tokyo: Fushosha, 1995), pp. 149-445.

[21] When Chun visited Tokyo Japan, Japanese emperor was reported to say that it is indeed regrettable that there was an unfortunate past between us for a period of time in this century and I believe that it should not be repeated. *Asahi Shimbun*, September 8, 1984.

[22] As for cooperation between two countries despite historical animosity, see, Victor Cha, *Alignment Despite Antagonism* (Stanford: Stanford University Press, 1999).

[23] Economic Planning Agency, *Key Economic Indicator* (1989).

9. The Development of Korea's Regional Strategy in Northeast Asia

diplomatic world. The successful hosting of the 1988 Olympic Games was a symbol of Korea's overwhelming diplomatic advancement. On the other hand, Korean government suggested a summit meeting to North Korea in January 1981. Also on January 22, 1982, Korea made a comprehensive proposal based on the idea of national reconciliation and democratic reunification.[24] The basic premise of the new policy was to take a phased approach to reunification. Simply put, "peace first, unification later" was the essence of the policy. However, despite Korean efforts to take an eclectic stance, the North Korean attitude was not forthcoming. A North Korean terrorist attack on a South Korean delegation to Burma in October 1983 represented North Korea's true mind.

At the back of the tight security cooperation among the United States, Korea, and Japan, Korea began making utmost efforts to make inroads into Southeast Asia. As the importance of the Asia-Pacific region increased, Korean governments actively exploited diplomatic channels to Southeast Asia. In June and July of 1981, President Chun visited five ASEAN countries—Indonesia, Malaysia, Philippines, Singapore, and Thailand. Considering the abundant natural resources and cheap labor, ASEAN countries could contribute much to diversifying export and import channels and to revitalizing the Korean economy. Also, the president's visit to Southeast Asia aimed at obtaining support for the Korean approach to North Korea from those countries. Chun's visit to Southeast Asian countries signified Korea's expanding business relations in the region, where North Korea thought they had the advantage. At that time, North Korea turned not only defensive but also hostile toward Korea. Symbolic was North Korea's terrorist attack to assassinate Chun Doo Hwan and his close aides in Rangoon when Chun and his delegation visited Burma in October 1983.[25] Burma was the first country in a series of stops

---

[24] Han Kyo Kim, "South Korea's Unification Policies: A Reassessment," *Asian Perspective*, vol. 10, No. 1 (Spring-Summer 1986), pp. 3-19.

[25] Seventeen high-ranking Korean delegation members were killed including a chief of staff and foreign minister. Burma found that the North Korean embassy was deeply

throughout the region. Because of this incident, North Korea was designated as a terrorist country and further lost its diplomatic leverage on the international scene. The image of North Korea worsened when North Korean agents were found responsible for planting the bomb that destroyed Korean Airlines flight 858 as it flew across Southeast Asia on its way from Abu Dhabi to Seoul on November 29, 1987, killing all 115 passengers on board. As time went by, North Korea became more and more diplomatically isolated.

4. Period Three: Reaching Out to the Socialist Countries
— from the late 1980s to the late 1990s —

The year 1988 symbolized a new phase of Korean regional strategy. Korea achieved democracy after long years of authoritarian rule, the Korean economy was growing fast, and Seoul hosted the Olympic Games. Most of all, the Games demonstrated to the world that Korea was a mature country with democratic values. It also demonstrated that that South Korea excelled North Korea in every aspect of life. Together with Korea's global outreach, the international situation changed. The advent of the Mikhail Gorbachev regime in the Soviet Union and his strong initiative to reform socialist practices awarded an unprecedented diplomatic opportunity to Korea, which had long shut its doors to communist countries.

Taking advantage of this new opportunity, the Roh Tae Woo regime fashioned a new strategic initiative, policy called *Nordpolitik*. The July 7 declaration in 1988 provided a turning point. President Roh made it clear that North Korea was no longer an object of hostility, confrontation, and competition but a companion for reunification, or a part of a national community. He also announced that Korea would normalize relations with communist countries like China and Soviet Union while helping North

---

involved in this terror. It terminated diplomatic relations with North Korea in November 1983.

9. The Development of Korea's Regional Strategy in Northeast Asia

Korea to normalize relations with Korea's allies. Economic demands for diversifying export and import markets worked as an underlying motive for initiating the *Nordpolitik*.[26] The strategic aim of this policy was to pave the road to peaceful reunification of two Koreas by encircling North Korea.[27] Its aim was not necessarily one of isolation of North Korea, but it was certainly a pressuring tactic to induce changes in North Korea. This was a new development in that Korea linked regional diplomatic strategy with unification policy.[28] Increasing confidence over North Korea worked as a foundation for the *Nordpolitik*.[29] As of 1988, Korea had twice the population, six times the GDP, and twenty times the trade volume than that of North Korea.[30]

Korea normalized relations with Russia and China in 1990 and 1992 respectively. Also, South and North Korea joined the United Nations simultaneously in September 1991. By making diplomatic inroads into the socialist countries, Korea's regional strategy truly widened its horizon. Before reaching out to the socialist countries, Korea's regional contacts were only half realized. With the normalization of diplomatic ties with

---

[26] *Hanguk Oegyosa (Diplomatic History of Korea)* (Seoul: Chipmundang, 1995), p. 465.
[27] Hakjoon Kim, who was a senior secretary to President Roh, made it clear that the essence of the July 7 declaration was to show the way to achieve peaceful unification. He notes that President Roh used the expression, "As Pyongyang does not open its door, we have to knock on the door of Beijing and Moscow. We have to go to Pyongyang by way of Moscow and Beijing." Hakjoon Kim, "Essential Diplomatic Tasks of the 6th Republic," *Oegyo (Foreign Relations)*, vol. 24 (December 1992), p. 19.
[28] Sekyun Kim, "Northern Policy and Unification Policy," *The Korean Journal of International Relations*, vol. 29, No. 2 (1989).
[29] President Roh, in his book, said, "Korea is no longer a nation in the periphery. Korea now is one of the central states in the international society. . . . It is time for us to make an independent and nationalistic diplomacy and self-defense." Roh Tae Woo, *Uidaehan Botongsaramdeul eui sidae (The Era of the Great Middle Mass)* (Seoul: Ulyou, 1987), p. 192.
[30] Ministry of Foreign Affairs and Trade, *Fifty Years of Korean Diplomacy* (Seoul: MOFAT, 1999), p. 104.

Russia, China, and other socialist countries, Korea's regional reach drew full circle.

What is noteworthy is that China became a significant player in Korea's regional strategy. Until then, Japan was the only Asian ally to Korea in Northeast Asia. Trade ties between the two countries developed rapidly. In 1991, Korea's trade with China remained at $4.4 billion, but it skyrocketed to $25 billion in 1997. Within five years, China became Korea's third largest trade partner.[31] As Korea's new diplomatic initiative to target socialist countries overlapped with the end of the cold war, the United States had no reason to stop Korea's outreach to the world. Rather, Korea's efforts were seen as a visible example of the end of the cold war period. Even on the Korean peninsula—an island of cold war relics—it looked as if the ice of confrontation was melting.

Roh initiated a new unification policy called "A Scheme for Unifying the Korean National Community" in 1989. Based on the principle of autonomy, peace, and democracy, this scheme put the stage of federation as a step toward final unification. Repeated contacts between high-ranking authorities of South and North Korea succeeded in producing "Basic Accord between South and North Korea," announced on February 19, 1992. In the document, both Koreas officially agreed to proceed with exchange and cooperation on the principle of non-aggression. However, since the early 1990s, North Korea posed an unprecedented challenge to international society. The North Korean regime demonstrated symptoms of system fatigue that stemmed from the long-term autocratic rule combined with structural contradiction inherent in the socialist-type regime. The gap between South and North Korea became irreversible. As an adventure to defend its regime, North Korea pursued a hard-line option of developing nuclear weapons and directly confronting the United States through brinkmanship diplomacy.[32] After meandering through negotiations, the first North Korean nuclear crisis was resolved with the signing of the

---

[31] Ibid., p. 53.
[32] Ibid., p. 117.

9. The Development of Korea's Regional Strategy in Northeast Asia

"Agreed Framework" in Geneva in 1994.[33] But even after this accord was signed and energy assistance from the international community began to flow into the DPRK, North Korea had to call for international food assistance because excessive flooding and drought, coupled with structurally driven agricultural problems, drove the country into famine. The North Korean question remained a challenge not only for Korea but also for regional powers.

Korea's regional strategy in this phase made remarkable progress. First, Korean diplomacy became "multidirectional," encompassing socialist countries. During the Roh regime, Korea normalized diplomatic relations with forty additional countries, bringing the total number of countries with which it shared diplomatic relations to 165.[34] Opening diplomatic ties with China opened a new horizon for furthering economic exchange. It also made possible for Korea to obtain indirect channels of influence with North Korea. In that sense, Korea's regional landscape expanded rapidly while remaining intact with former allies.

Second, Korea approached North Korea with more confidence. The DPRK now was perceived not just as a competitor but also as a partner to be incorporated.[35] North Korea was not just another political entity that should coexist peacefully but was a part of Korean community where the two Koreas eventually be reconciled. This approach was based on overwhelming confidence over North Korea on diplomatic and economic fronts.

Third, Korea began stretching its diplomatic ties to China and the

---

[33] As for the process of nuclear negotiation with North Korea, refer to Yoon Dukmin, *Daebuk Hyupsang eui Junmal* (*Nuclear Negotiation with North Korea: The Course of Events*) (Seoul: Haereu, 1995).

[34] Chongsuh Koo, "Evaluation of the President Roh's Diplomatic Policy," *Foreign Relations* (December 1992), p. 26.

[35] President Kim Young Sam said in 1993, "Korean diplomacy since the division of the country has been preoccupied with the idea of competing with North Korea. Now the competition is over." Young Sam Kim, "The Pacific Era and Korea's New Diplomacy," *Foreign Relations*, vol. 26 (June 1993), p. 19.

Part II: National Visions and Experiences of Cooperation in Europe and Asia

Soviet Union but also to areas where North Korea held a diplomatic edge in the past. East European and Southeast Asian countries were actively approached by Seoul to exploit new possibilities for cooperation. In particular, Korea's advancement in the Asia-Pacific region made meaningful sense in this period.

Finally, it is from this phase that North Korea, out of an increasing sense of diplomatic isolation and economic hardship, adopted provocative tactics like terrorist attacks and clandestine nuclear weapons development. The North Korean question became an international concern, going beyond being solely an inter-Korea issue.

5. Period Four: Korea's Initiative to Build Northeast Asian Community — from the late 1990s to the present —

5.1. Phase One: The Kim Dae Jung Era
The year 1998 was another epoch-making year for Korea's regional strategy construction. In 1997, Korea experienced a financial crisis after ensuing economic crises in Southeast Asian countries. After this crisis, a sense of regional identity emerged. It was thought that regional cooperation was necessary to keep Asian economies from being abruptly destabilized. Also, Kim Dae Jung, long-time dissident and opposition leader in the ROK, was elected president, opening a new era of Korean democracy. Around 1998, North Korea came to be perceived as a nation of hunger and desperation. The military threat from North Korea seemed to be sharply on the decline.

With increased confidence over North Korea, the Kim Dae Jung administration pursued the "Sunshine policy." At the back of the policy initiative was ameliorating the relationship with China and Russia. Those two countries also wanted North Korea to transform itself to accommodate international norms. Based on a principle of asymmetrical, non-simultaneous reciprocity, South Korea launched a series of cooperative

9. The Development of Korea's Regional Strategy in Northeast Asia

projects with North Korea with a view to inducing a long-term transformation of the regime in Pyongyang.[36] This policy line culminated when Kim Dae Jung and North Korean leader Kim Jong Il held a historic summit meeting in June 2000 in the North Korean capital. It paved a road to furthering bilateral cooperation in various fields. South Korea was ready and willing to engage North Korea with an aspiration for building up the bases for unification in the future.[37]

Not only did Korea engage North Korea, but the Kim Dae Jung administration also took an assertive initiative to improve relations with the two regional powers, Japan and China. President Kim and Prime Minister Obuchi of Japan made a historic declaration for opening a new era of cooperation between Korea and Japan. In the declaration, two summits made it clear that Korea and Japan should work on future-oriented cooperative projects, getting beyond the burden of historical animosity. Based on this accord, cultural doors were flung wide open to each other. Talks on establishing an FTA went on. Exchanges between two countries at various levels were promoted. Above all, Korea and Japan successfully co-hosted the FIFA World Cup in 2002. In this way, Korea drastically improved relations with Japan. Kim also gave importance to upgrading ties with China, proposing the idea of constructing a comprehensive Sino-ROK partnership. Areas of cooperation were not confined to economic issue areas. Through these gestures of diplomatic advancement, Korea linked itself to two nations in Northeast Asia systematically. This was, in a sense, a strategic attempt on the part of Korea to induce cooperation from regional neighbors to closely work on North Korea. In this regard, the first ever Japan-DPRK summit meeting was held in September 2002, bringing Prime Minister Junichiro Koizumi of Japan to Pyongyang to visit Kim Jong Il. The summit meeting in particular represented the extended embodiment of Korea's efforts to bring

---

[36] Se Hyun Chung, "Changes in Unification Milieu and Korean Government's Policy toward North Korea," *Foreign Relations*, vol. 48 (January 1999), p. 22.
[37] Ministry of Foreign Affairs and Trade, *Fifty Years of Korean Diplomacy*, p. 113.

in regional powers to realize peace on the Korean peninsula.

Korea began taking another active regional initiative toward Association of Southeast Asian Nations' (ASEAN) countries. The economic crisis that had swept through a number of Asian countries brought up a sense of community among Asians and the need for mutual cooperation. ASEAN invited national leaders from Korea, China, and Japan to its summit meeting in December 1997, and ever since then, ASEAN+3 became an institutionalized forum of regional leaders in Asia. With regard to the ASEAN+3 formula, Korea took a strong initiative to lead the discussion. President Kim proposed a process of composing an East Asia Vision Group (EAVG) and East Asia Study Group (EASG) as a provider of visionary guidance toward regional cooperation. From 1999, national leaders from Korea, China, and Japan launched an informal meeting among the three of them and since then it was regularized as a part of the ASEAN+3 meeting. This meeting set the stage for driving networks of regional cooperation in Northeast Asia.

In a word, the Kim Dae Jung administration took a bold and ambitious initiatives to build a new Northeast Asian order. Two new strategic postures were attempted. One was to incorporate North Korea with a view to inducing internal change in North Korea. Without cooperation from Japan and China, this adventure would be hard to attain. That is one of the reasons why Korea took a strong initiative to reassure friendly ties with these two neighbors. The other initiative was to link ASEAN and three Northeast Asian countries in an integrative way. It was an attempt to strengthen Asian identity, though it was never an anti-Anglo American order.

The Bill Clinton administration in the United States did not hesitate to accept Korea's new initiative to engage North Korea in the hope of drawing the DPRK out of its shell. After George W. Bush was elected President of the United States, he took a very critical, skeptical, hard-line stance toward North Korea, making a drastic U-turn in U.S. policy toward the DPRK. During the Kim Dae Jung administration, the perception gap between Korea and the United States with regard to North Korea did not narrow down. As a result, Kim's diplomatic initiative was pushed at the expense of soundly managing U.S.-Korean relations.

5.2. Phase Two: The Roh Moo Hyun Era

Currently, President Roh Moo Hyun is trying to continue the basic foreign policy line set by the Kim Dae Jung administration. While Kim put emphasis on dismantling the cold-war structure on the Korean peninsula, Roh seems to be focusing on building a regional community founded on the spirit of peace and prosperity. On the one hand, the Roh administration is trying to speed up the process of building a Northeast Asian economic prosperity zone, where countries in the region first establish a free trade zone and utilize a common financial market as a base for furthering economic cooperation. This is part of the long-term vision of building a prosperous regional community. On the other hand, inducing changes in North Korea while reducing tensions and threats from the North is another pillar of the new regional strategy. Establishing a peace process on the Korean peninsula is not an endpoint. Rather, building a nuclear-free Korean peninsula is a way toward constructing a peaceful regional community. Therefore, it is critically important to solve the North Korean nuclear standoff through peaceful means.

Concrete steps to proceed with building a regional community are in progress. Even though not by design, six-party talks have been set up as a mechanism for solving the North Korean nuclear issue. It represents a type of practical multilateralism centered on the single issue of North Korea's nuclear weapons development This issue-specific, contingent coalition of the willing may work as a foundation for building an institutionalized security dialogue among nations in the region. More promising, this institutionalized mechanism of security dialogue may continue regardless of the North Korean question.

Also noteworthy is the Korea-Japan-China summit meeting held in October 2003, something that developed out of ASEAN+3. But the meeting signifies an independent initiation of cooperative framework in various areas of mutual concern. For the moment, this seems to be increasing the level of cooperative initiative in facilitating the community building process.

6. Conclusion

From the above analysis, one can recognize a few characteristics of the Korean approach to Northeast Asian regional order. Korea's regional strategy has been a rational adaptation to the regional context in Northeast Asia.

First of all, it is undeniable that Korea's utmost concern lies in the question of how to deal with North Korea. The North Korean question is a built-in bias of the Korean regional strategy. While the North Korean question is a secondary concern to other countries, how to peacefully coexist with and eventually unify North Korea has always been on Korea's mind. This built-in bias toward the DPRK was both an asset and a liability for Korea. It has been an asset because Korea had an incentive to actively develop a regional strategy whenever regional circumstances change. Koreans could not complacently sit down and watch what was going on outside. At the same time, that bias has been a liability for Korea in that Korean regional strategy is bound up tightly with the North Korean question. Until the two Koreas are united, it is in the interest of Korea to make North Korea a not-so-threatening, reform-oriented nation, which will eventually plug itself into the regional order and stop provoking or burdening countries in the region.

Second, Korea has designed its regional strategy with full consideration of the U.S. stance in this region. Under Korea's situation of division, Korea is in need of assuring a security commitment from the United States to deter a military threat from the North. Also, the United States is one of the largest export markets of Korea. Accordingly, when Korea fashions regional strategy toward Northeast Asia, coming to terms with the U.S. stance has always been a strategic consideration. Living on the only cold-war island in the sea of global and regional integration, Korea's regional strategy contains a strong fixation on security. While its Northeast Asian neighbors are making smooth progress toward economic integration, security concerns posed by the North Korean threat inevitably drags Korea toward its extra-regional security guarantor, the United States.

Despite these characteristics of Korea's strategy toward Northeast

9. The Development of Korea's Regional Strategy in Northeast Asia

Asia, we can identify a few noticeable trends over the last few decades.

First of all, North Korea is no more regarded as a nation that should be defeated or overcome, but rather incorporate into Korea's future. Rather than taking a containment strategy, Korean governments since the early 1990s have adopted policies of engaging North Korea to induce domestic reform within the DPRK, as well as external opening, though the intensity and width of the policies have varied.

Second, in accordance with political and economic progress of Korea, the ROK shifted its focus of regional strategy from a follower's stance to a middleman's posture. Accordingly, Korea's interest areas are gradually widening to encompass a variety of issue areas. Korea now approaches the region from a wider standpoint, which encompasses trade, investment, technology, sports, and cultural domains.

Third, a multilateral approach is gradually emerging in the region. Korean strategy has long been characterized by bilateralism, especially with the United States. However, rapidly evolving international order widely opened Koreans' eyes. The North Korean nuclear issue brought many regional powers into action, which made a multilateral approach a natural course to take. Also, on the economic front, interdependence—or interpenetration—has become a norm rather than an exception. Korean, Japanese, Chinese, and ASEAN markets are closely linked with a combined element of competition and cooperation.

Despite these positive trends gradually emerging in Northeast Asia, countries in the region have challenging tasks ahead in order to attain meaningful regional integration. There is no common security umbrella that connects the regional powers in Northeast Asia. As Akihiko Tanaka points out, three different worlds of international relations coexist in this region: a world of advanced democratic countries in which countries do not fight each other; a world of developing countries where balancing rivals prevails, and a world of nascent states where disorder is widespread.[38] In those complex situations, cooperative security is still a

---

[38] Akihiko Tanaka, *Atarashii Chusei* (*The Age of the New Medievalism*) (Tokyo:

challenge, not a reality. Consequently, countries in the region take dual approaches: bilateral alliance combined with efforts to develop multilateral security setup. Korea is no exception.

Unlike the European economic environment, developmental gap between countries in the region still persists. Some cultural and geographical boundaries remain closed. As a result, countries in the region are opening their economic doors to other nations while cultural doors remain closed or only partially open due to lingering wariness of each other. Under such a situation, it is difficult for regional identity to develop. Unfortunately, Northeast Asian countries have a long way to go until they can fully integrate themselves into a regional order.

The question of who can provide the needed leadership in Northeast Asia is another lingering goblin that haunts the process of regional integration. Japan, though economically affluent and democratically governed, finds it difficult to take the reins because of its historical baggage as colonial occupier. China, though aspiring to be a regional leader, is yet to develop its political system in a democratic way in addition to furthering the market economy principle. Korea is still preoccupied with the North. However, in its favor, Korea does not carry the same historical baggage weighing down Japan, nor does it feature itself as a dominant hegemon in the region. Also, Korea attained democratic political order combined with the principles of a market economy. In this sense, Korea may be in a better position to play a role of middleman-ship or mediator, though not that of a leader.

References

Tanaka, Akihiko. *Atarashii Chusei* (*The Age of the New Medievalism*). Tokyo: Nihon Keizai Press, 1996.
Cha, Victor. *Alignment Despite Antagonism*. Stanford: Stanford University

---

Nihon Keizai Press, 1996).

Press, 1999.
Chung, Se Hyun. "Changes in Unification Milieu and Korean Government's Policy toward North Korea," *Foreign Relations*, vol. 48 (January 1999).
Cumings, Bruce. *Korea's Place in the Sun*. New York: Norton, 1997.
Heo, Man. *Hanbando wa Oegyojungchaekron (Korean Peninsula and Foreign Policy)*. Seoul: Gyoyuk Kwahaksa, 1988.
Kim, Hakjoon. "Essential Diplomatic Tasks of the 6th Republic," *Oegyo (Foreign Relations)*, vol. 24 (December 1992).
Kim, Han Kyo. "South Korea's Unification Policies: A Reassessment," *Asian Perspective*, vol. 10, No. 1 (Spring-Summer 1986), pp. 3-19.
Kim, Jung Won. *Divided Korea: The Politics of Development 1945-1972*. Cambridge: Harvard University Press, 1975.
Kim, Jungwon. *Hanguk Oegyo Baljonron (Development of Korean Diplomacy)*. Seoul: Chipmundang, 1996.
Kim, Sekyun. "Northern Policy and Unification Policy," *The Korean Journal of International Relations*, vol. 29, No. 2 (1989).
Kim, Young Sam. "The Pacific Era and Korea's New Diplomacy," *Foreign Relations*, vol. 26 (June 1993).
Koo, Chongsuh. "Evaluation of the President Roh's Diplomatic Policy," *Foreign Relations* (December 1992).
Koo Youngnok. *Hanguk kwa Kukka Iik (Korea and the National Interest)*. Seoul: Bupmunsa, 1996.
Lee, Chong Sik. *Japan and Korea: The Political Dimension*. Stanford: Hoover Institute Press, 1985.
Lee, Dosung. *Park Chung Hee and Korea-Japan Talks*. Seoul: Hansong, 1995.
Lockwood, Robert. "The Global Soviet Threat and U.S. Security Commitment to South Korea," *Asian Perspective*, vol. 6, No. 2 (Fall/Winter 1982), pp. 1-29.
Ministry of Foreign Affairs and Trade, *Fifty Years of Korean Diplomacy*. Seoul: MOFAT, 1999.
Ministry of Foreign Affairs and Trade, *White Paper on Korean Diplomacy* (Seoul: MOFAT, 2003).
Morley, James. *Japan and Korea: America's Allies in the Pacific*. New York: Walker & Co., 1965.
Office of the Secretary to the President. *The 8th Collection of President Park Chung Hee's Speeches*. Seoul: Office of the President, 1972.
Park, Joon Young. *Korea's Return to Asia: South Korean Foreign Policy 1965-1975*. Seoul: Jin-Heung Press, 1985.
Park, Sil. *Hanguk Oegyo Bisa (Hidden Stories of the Korean Diplomacy)*.

Part II: National Visions and Experiences of Cooperation in Europe and Asia

Seoul: Jungho Press, 1984.
Roh, Tae Woo. *Uidaehan Botongsaramdeul eui sidae* (*The Era of the Great Middle Mass*). Seoul: Ulyou, 1987.
Sejima, Ryuzo. *Sejima Ryuzo Memoir*. Tokyo: Fushosha, 1995.
Woo, Jung En. *Race to the Swift*. New York: Columbia University Press, 1991.
Yoon, Dukmin. *Daebuk Hyupsang eui Junmal* (*Nuclear Negotiation with North Korea: The Course of Events*). Seoul: Haereu, 1995.

CHAPTER *10*

JAPAN IN AN EAST ASIAN COMMUNITY BUILDING

Toshiya HOSHINO

1. Introduction

East Asia, for Japan, is the region of utmost affinity and proximity. Indeed, geographically speaking, Japan is situated in the northern tier of this dynamic region. It is, therefore, natural for the people in Japan to share an East Asian regional identity, particularly that of Northeast Asia. In this sense, there is no doubt that Japan belongs to East Asia. That said, however, it is not so uncommon to hear the Japanese officials and intellectuals refer to their policies toward East Asia, not toward *the rest of* East Asia, as if Japan is located somewhere outside of the region. At the United Nations, for example, Tokyo routinely consults with the members of "West Europe and Others" group as well as with the United States even after the Cold War East-West rivalries have been terminated and when it still officially belongs to "Asia" regional grouping. If one's sense of belongings has a political implication, it would be this duality of Japan's perceptions toward the rest of East Asia that has largely affected its regional performance.

In fact, Japan's diplomacy in East Asian context, due exactly to its closeness, has been an ambivalent one. And this ambivalence was reflected in two distinct visions of an "Eat Asia Community" that Japan put forward. First one was pursued by the Empire of Japan as expressed in the form of territorial ambition to build a "Greater East Asia Co-Prosperity Sphere" in the region in the earlier part of the 20th century. Behind the alluring word of co-prosperity lied an outright desire of domination, creating a world in which East Asia belongs to Japan and not vice versa. Consequently, the questions that are related to these negative historical legacies have remained between Japan and its regional counterparts. But the situation has certainly changed overtime. The relationship has demonstrated a fundamental change during the past sixty-plus years. And one clear manifestation of this transformation, in this author's view, is Prime Minister Junichiro Koizumi's proposal to build an "community that acts together and advances together" in East Asia. The idea was formally expressed in his policy speech in Singapore in January 2002[1]. This can be taken as the second vision of Japan to lead an East Asian Community building effort, which is totally different in scope and philosophy from the previous one. No final picture has yet to be in sight in the time of this writing as to how this regional community would be like. But one important point here to take note is that the political environment in East Asia has changed so much that it would permit Japan to take an initiative of regional community building without much animosities and suspicion of domination or control from its regional counterpart countries.

    This chapter is intended to review Japan's place in contemporary East Asia in the midst of growing web of regional interdependence and interactions. The chapter will be divided into three sections. First, it will revisit the basic principles of Japanese diplomacy which were originally introduced in the spring of 1957 to identify the key changes in its diplomatic priorities. Second, it will review the post-World War II developments of Japan-East Asia relations. Here, by particularly looking back the recent history, it is emphasized that common experiences in tackling various crises in East Asia, from the situation in the Persian Gulf to the vast shocks caused by Asia Economic Crisis and myriad of other

---

[1] Speech by Prime Minister of Japan Junichiro Koizumi "Japan and ASEAN in East Asia: A Sincere and Open Partnership," January 14, 2002, Singapore [http://www.mofa.go.jp/region/asia-paci/pmv0201/speech.html].

regional challenges particularly in the turbulent post-Cold War period, a foundation was forged on which Prime Minister Koizumi's proposal is favorably received in the region. And third, given the fact that any "East Asian Community" conception would *not* include the United States if it sticks to the objective reality of geographic boundaries, it will discuss how it can be done and what the role of Japan would be. It will also discuss the emergence of a strategic picture in East Asia that would reflect a convergence of the "balance of power"-type dynamism and the "community-building"-type of incentive and argue that the Japan-U.S. alliance has rather inadvertently as well as purposely contributed to promote this convergence. Major strategic challenges remain such as China-Taiwan question or the future of Korean Peninsula, any failure to manage their peaceful resolution would invoke grave consequences in and beyond the region. Nonetheless, the chapter will conclude the fundamental importance of seizing the opportunity to build a region-wide community in East Asia, and Japan's commitment to pursue it, as it represents an only viable avenue to avert tragic consequences.

2. Japan's Diplomatic Approaches to East Asia

2.1 Background of "Three Principles of Japanese Diplomacy"
It was spring of 1957 when the government of Japan published its first Diplomatic Bluebook called *Waga Gaiko no Kinkyo* (Recent Developments of Our Diplomacy)[2]. This 100-plus page volume with blue soft cover is best known by its section which described the "three principles of Japanese diplomacy." These three "principles" are (1) *"Kokuren Chushin shugi"* ("the United Nations Centrism"), (2) Cooperation with the Liberal Democracies (Western Bloc), and (3) a Member of Asian Countries.

The first principle of "UN Centrism" has frequently been debated in the Japanese policy circle whether Tokyo has had been so much faithful

---

[2] Gaimusho (Ministry of Foreign Affairs), *Waga Gaiko no Kinkyo* (Recent Developments of our Diplomacy), Vol.1, March 1957.

and putting that level of priorities in its UN diplomacy sufficient to declare that the UN is a center, if not the only center, of the government foreign policy. It was questioned then. And the same queries have been made whenever this principle was mentioned in different time and context to test its intent particularly in comparison with the strategic importance of Japan-United States alliance which is considered as the cornerstone of Tokyo's foreign and security policy making.

It can easily be understood why this UN centrism principle was placed at the top of three if we see the timing of the drafting of the text, which coincided with the long-overdue admission of Japan to the UN in December 1956. For the post-World War II Japan, the membership to the UN was almost a synonym to the return to a full-fledged member of the international community. In a sense, the "passport" was given at the time of the San Francisco Peace Treaty of September 1951, which marked the end of Allied occupation and Japan's political independence. But the passport was valid only among the Western bloc under the severe Cold War confrontation between the United States and the Soviet Union. In fact, Japan's admission to the UN, fulfilled only after more than five years since the request had been submitted immediately after the signing of the San Francisco Peace Treaty in 1951, was a product of political compromise between the two opposing blocs at the UN, which were competing for clout at this international organization.

With the long-held aspiration finally fulfilled, it was no wonder that Japan placed the sentiment of UN centrism on the first of three principles. It should be noted, however, that the Bluebook was realistic enough to stress the primacy of Japan-US security arrangements for Tokyo's foreign and security policies. Given the divided world of Cold War, and having had experienced the diplomatic hardship in achieving the aspired UN admission against that unfavorable current, it was understandable for the post-War political leaders of Japan to opt for the reliance on the alliance with the liberal bloc led by the powerful United States.

In comparison with these two strategic choices that directed Japan's post-World War II diplomacy, the third principle of membership in Asia would sound too mundane, just reflecting the geographic reality. To some degree, it was a recognition of simple matter of fact. But in a more profound sense, it signified an important shift in mindset that would emphasize that Japan is truly a part of Asia and should never be the one that would dominate nor conquer it from outside.

2.2 Scope of Discontinuity in Japan's Diplomatic Priorities

What, then, this quick review of Japan's three diplomatic principles would tell us? One of the useful ways to interpret this would be identifying the elements of discontinuity in the foreign policy orientation of Japan from its militarist past and see how relevant those elements are since the end of World War II up until present post-Cold War juncture. To draw a distinction in Japan's policy choices, I would like to employ the concept of unilateralism, bilateralism, and multilateralism as defined by a leading theorist of international politics, John Gerald Ruggie.

One distinctive contribution of Ruggie's study on multilateralism rests on its qualitative, as opposed to nominal definition. In a nutshell, "what it distinctive about multilateralism," Ruggie says, "is not merely that it coordinates national policies in groups of three or more states, which is something that other organizational forms also do, but that it does so on the basis of certain principles of ordering relations among those states.[3]" Ruggie stresses not so much the nominal number of actors as the role of fundamental principles that would characterize the nature of policy coordination among those actors. The test of multilateralism, in this sense, is to see whether those principles are universally applicable or not. In fact, Ruggie stresses the indivisibility of values, such as peace and free trade. As a result, such mechanisms of collective security and global free trade, in their original recipes, do qualify the test of multilateralism.

According to this qualitative definition of multilateralism, the supposedly "bilateralist" trade agreements can be considered multilateral in substance. It would be interesting to recognize that those tariff reductions negotiated between two countries under the global regimes, for example, can be seen "multilateral" as long as it opens the equal

---

[3] John Gerald Ruggie, *Constructing the World Polity: Essays on International and Institutionalization* (London and New York: Routledge, 1998), p.106. Please see also, Ruggie, *Multilateralism Matters* (New York: Columbia University Press,).

opportunity (of most-favored-nation [MFN] treatment, for example) to the rest of the world. Conversely, an arrangement by three or more members may *not* constitute multilateralism, though it may be multi*national*, if it does not satisfy this qualitative test.

Then, what is bilateralism? The simplest definition of bilateralism is an arrangement between two actors. By limiting the number of actors to two, it is exclusionary at least in form, if not in substance. What makes bilateral arrangement so distinct is the specific nature of reciprocity, or "specific reciprocity," a clear cut give and take relationship between the two. Multilateral arrangement is also reciprocal, but its reciprocal relations are more diffuse in nature, i.e., operated on "diffuse reciprocity."

Looking from these perspectives of reciprocity in international relations, unilateralism is a unique form of diplomacy in the sense that it can deny the existence of reciprocal relations from the very beginning. Unilateral approach is normally reserved for the powerful actors who can live by without depending on the resources provided by reciprocal arrangements from others. In this regard, the most typical of unilateralist actor is an Empire that would expand its sphere of influence.

In retrospect of the history of its diplomacy in early 20th century, Japan had two different sets of future plan. One was to take the path of multilateral internationalism by continuously taking a leadership as a permanent member of the League of Nations. The other was to follow the unilateral imperative and to take the Imperialist positions. It was a fatal choice of Japanese political leaders to take the second path. And this Imperial expansion of Japan took place mostly in East Asia. Japan's withdrawal from the League in the wake of Manchurian Incident of 1931, through which Japan proclaimed the establishment of the puppet state of Manchukuo and obtained a stronghold for its subsequent territorial expansion in Asia. This strategic move from Japan, which triggered a major shift in power balance in East Asia, sparked a turmoil that brought the region into World War II.

The fierce defeat of Japan led its political leaders to completely transform both the foundation and priorities of Japanese foreign policy. Three principles, thus, can be seen as the reflection of this discontinuity in policy priorities.

10. Japan in an East Asian Community Building

First, the emphasis on the "UN centrism" can be interpreted as Japan's renewed commitment to multilateralism. This is a clear departure from the aggressive military expansionism in favor of the spirit of Japanese Peace Constitution as well as a "peace-loving state" status depicted in Article 4(1) of the United Nations Charter. What exactly the "UN centrism" means has continue to be a subject of debate. And it is tested whether Japan has had been so faithful to this principle. Nonetheless, there is a unique tendency in Japanese foreign policy making to value multilateral authorizations (in the form of the Security Council) or requests from international organizations (particularly the UN agencies) in promoting its international peace and economic cooperation[4].

Second is the principle of strengthening ties with the Western Democracies, in which the Japan-U.S. alliance plays the pivotal role. The alliance was a product of mutual interests between Japan's defense needs (for complementing its own limited capabilities under the constraints of the Peace Constitution) and the U.S. strategic needs (for fortifying its forward presence in the Pacific Command region). It marked a discontinuity from the war-time alliance with the totalitarian Axis states. Japan did not stay neutral (nor Non-alliance) option, either. In this regard, Japan's alliance with the United States represents its strong commitment to liberal and democratic values. The alliance was is certainly for strengthening Japan's own defense.

But when it comes to the bilateral Japan-U.S. alliance, it should be noted that the arrangements are expected to play a broader role both in the context of Asia-Pacific region and in a global scale, just as it provide common goods. As to be discussed more fully in the next section, it is important to recognize that the alliance has been "reviewed" and "reaffirmed" its continued relevance as "the cornerstone for achieving common security objectives, and for maintaining a stable and prosperous environment for the Asia-Pacific region" towards the 21st century[5].

---

[4] Toshiya Hoshino, "Nihon no Takokukan-gaiko (Multilateral Diplomacy of Japan)," Yoshihide Soeya and Masayuki Tadokoro (eds.) *Nihon no Higashi-Ajia Koso (Japan's East Asia Conception)*, Keio University Press, 2004.

[5] Japan-U.S. Declaration on Security—Alliance for the 21st Century, 17 April 1996.

Moreover, Japan and the U.S. have launched the Common Agenda for Cooperation in Global Perspective (the Common Agenda) since 1993 to jointly seek "solutions to global problems, such as increasingly pressing environmental degradation, overpopulation, and damage from both natural and man-made disasters[6]." If it can provide common goods for regional and global needs, it may well be said that the alliance has a "multilateral" orientation of Ruggie's sense of the term.

What about, then, the third principle? What discontinuity can we find with regard to this idea of Japan as "a member of Asia Countries"? No doubt that Japan was and continues to be a part of Asia at least geographically. But in view of the past when it pursued territorial ambition in Asia, Japan was certainly *not* a member, but a conqueror of Asia. Japan was engaged in a unilateral and Imperial aggression of the most classic sense. Japan' return to Asia, as its strong desire to be a part of it, therefore, symbolized a distinctive discontinuity of Japan's policy orientation beyond the simple recognition of a geographical reality.

3. Japan's Diplomacy in East Asia

At the end of World War II in 1945, Japan was taken fully responsible for the damages it had inflicted on the world. But the actual terms of these duties and responsibilities have become subject to the development of international affairs surrounding Japan, first, during the occupation period, and, second, in the context of Cold War in East Asia. The settlement of war naturally involved many dimensions. As the Government of Japan would stress that most of the cases have been closed with regard to the legal and technical aspects of this question, save the conclusion of peace treaties with Russia and North Korea. But when it comes to the other aspects, including more moral and emotional sides of the equation have often sparked political turmoil. The repeated controversies over the Japan's language of apology, the description of history in textbook, and the

---

[6] The U.S.-Japan Common Agenda for Cooperation in Global Perspective, April 1999 [http://www.mofa.go.jp/region/n-america/us/agenda/gpers9904.html].

political leaders' visit to the Yasukuni shrine that commemorate those who lost their lives for the country, including Class A war criminals, are representatives of these long-standing issues. But before discussing Japan's present place in East Asia and the prospects for future regional community building, let us quickly review how the post-World War II settlement issues have come about in Japan vis-à-vis East Asia. Roughly said, we can look back the post-War developments in five separate periods.

3.1 Five Periods of Japan's East Asian Diplomacy
First period (1945-51): "By enduring the unendurable and suffering what is unsufferable," the Emperor Hirohito declared that Japan had "resolved to pave the way for a grand peace for all generation to come[7]." With this radio broadcast message, Japan's post-WWII period began. An American historian, John Dower called the text "a polished ideological gem," in spite of the fact that it was drafted in a highly chaotic situation, under which a group of hard-line military officers tried to stop this surrender option[8]. No mention of "surrender" or "defeat" was there in the Rescript, but the reality was clear. What followed the formal surrender came the occupation of Japan under the U.S.-red General Headquarters (GHQ) of Allied Powers. The transformation of Japan, from the military-led, totalitarian state to a democratic, peace-oriented statehood was identified and formally codified in what comes to be known as the Peace Constitution. It is within a common knowledge that the constitution was based on a draft originally prepared under the direction of then-GHQ Supreme Commander, General Douglas MacAurther. In Japan side, Prime Minister Shigeru Yoshida, with his realist and pragmatic impulse, took a strong initiative to conclude a Peace Treaty with the former-Allied Powers, even if it meant a "partial" peace that did not cover the Soviet-block countries. The breakout of new war on the Korean Peninsula (1950-53) certainly helped bring Japan closer to the Western camp. And as discussed above, the successful conclusion of

---

[7] *Imperial Rescript*, August 14, 1945.
[8] John Dower, *Embracing Defeat: Japan in the Wake of World War II* (New York; W.W. Norton, 2000) Chapter 1.

Part II: National Visions and Experiences of Cooperation in Europe and Asia

the San Francisco Peace Treaty and the Security Treaty with the United States have firmly formed Japan's new post-WWII international identity.

Second period (1952-1972): In these two decades, much of Japan's legal settlements of war with former victim countries, as stipulated in Article 14 (a) and (b) of the San Francisco Peace Treaty, were put into effect and Japan's reintegration into international community was advanced. Most of Japan's disrupted diplomatic relations were normalized, including with those who were not the parties to the San Francisco Peace Treaty, with the Soviet Union (1956), with the Republic of Korea (1965), and with the People's Republic of China (1972) among others. As described above, Japan's admission to the United Nations was also achieved in 1956, soon after the Japan-Soviet normalization of diplomatic relations. It is based on these developments that the government of Japan announced the above mentioned three principles of Japanese diplomacy in its first Diplomatic Bluebook (1957). Other important diplomatic deals, such as the reversion of Okinawa from the U.S. administration in 1972, followed. Japan's regaining of sovereignty over these southern most chain of islands with large American military installations was a symbolic one as then-Prime Minister Eisaku Sato considered that "the post-war era would not be put to an end" without the reversion of Okinawa.

With regard to the war reparations issues, the Peace Treaty stipulated that "It is recognized that Japan should pay reparations to the Allied Powers for the damages and suffering caused by it during the war" (Article 14(a)) but agreed that the Allied Powers would "waive all reparations" unless otherwise provided in the Treaty (Article 14 (b)) considering that the resources of Japan at that time was not sufficient to make full reparation payments. As a result, to only four countries Japan paid their reparations—among them, two were treaty parties (the Philippines in 1956 and Vietnam [South] in 1959 as they did not agreed to waive the right) and two non-treaty parties (Burma [present Myanmar] in 1954 and Indonesia in 1958). For the rest of the treaty parties, Japan generally took the policy of extending economic and technical cooperation in place of their commitment of waiving reparation payments. For example, in the wake of normalization of diplomatic relations with South Korea, Japan initiated this "economic cooperation" approach together with its normalization

10. Japan in an East Asian Community Building

treaty of 1965. (With the Democratic People's Republic of Korea, the similar formula is contemplated as described in Pyongyang Declaration of September 2002, concluded when Prime Minister Koizumi visited there to meet with General Secretary Kim Jong-il if the two governments were ever able to reach an agreement in their tough and rocky negotiations[9].) Japan took similar approaches vis-à-vis Cambodia (1959), Laos (1959), Malaysia (1967), Singapore (1967), and others. These options were only possible for Japan as it went hand in hand with the government-led rapid economic reconstruction and rehabilitation in the 1950s and 60s.

A special explanation would be in order with reference to Japan's war settlement with the People's Republic of China. In fact, two delicate issues, among many other complex matters to be discussed with this giant neighbor, took Tokyo government off guard when Japan switched its official diplomatic relations from the Republic of China to the Mainland. One is about the language of apology, that is, the PRC government demonstrated a strong displeasure to the translation of then-Prime Minister Kakuei Tanaka's word of Japan's past deed as too light. And the other was on the very arrangement of renouncing reparation payments. Actually, an arrangement of waiver was already made in the peace treaty that Japan concluded separately with ROC government in 1952. But when Tanaka met PRC Premier Chou En-lai in July 1972 to issue a historic joint communiqué, Chou expressed a sense of "contempt" as he learned that the Japanese Ministry of Foreign Affairs would consider that the case of reparation was already closed with China because of its dealing with Chang Kai-Shek—thus the Beijing government had "no need" to renounce—according to the disclosed diplomatic records[10]. In the final analysis, the term "right (of demanding reparation)" was deleted when, as the language of communiqué indicated, Beijing declared, "in the interest of the friendship between the Chinese and the Japanese peoples," that it

---

[9] Text of Japan-DPRK Pyonyang Declaration of September 17, 2002 (provisional translation by the Japanese Ministry of Foreign Affairs) can be found at [http://www.mofa.go.jp/region/asia-paci/n_korea/pmv0209/pyongyang.html].

[10] "Nicchu Kokko Seijoka Kosho no Kiroku (Records of the Japan-China Normalization Talks)," *Yomiuri Shimbun*, June 23, 2001.

renounced "its demand for war reparation from Japan."

Third period (1973-84): This is a period in which Japan's legendary "high economic growth period" was over but the security ties with the United States have been reinvigorated. The oil crises, which hit the world twice in the 1970s, reminded people of the importance of non-military threats to security. And when it comes to the more traditional type of threat, after a respite of détente period, the advent of the "new-Cold War" shocked the globe in the wake of the Soviet invasion to Afghanistan. These developments were taken place when the U.S. economy was in bad shape. Under these circumstances, Japan took basically two separate actions concurrently to enhance its security interests; one was to devise a strategy of "comprehensive security" under the Ohira Cabinet, and the other was to reinforce Japan's position in the Western-camp under the Suzuki and especially Nakasone Cabinets.

As to the history question, it should be noted that the first round of tough textbook controversy took place in June 1982 when major Japanese newspapers reported a story that the Ministry of Education forces to change the wordings that describe Japan's "aggression" to China into a more euphemistic term of "advancement," in the process of government review. Subsequently, the story was proven to be on a misinformation. Nonetheless, this episode, together with many other instances of high-ranking Japanese government leaders' improper remarks on Japan's past deeds, highlighted how the historical legacies questions were politically delicate.

The next section will discuss the developments of Japan's post-World War II diplomacy during the forth (1985-89) and fifth periods (1990-present) in the context of post-Cold War East Asia.

3.2 Japan's Place in East Asia in the post-Cold War Context

Forth period (1985-89): This period is generally considered as the ending phase of the Cold War. It was marked by the series of reform in the former-Soviet Union which were initiated by Mikhail Gorbachev, and his personal chemistry with the leaders in the Western camp, Presents Ronald Reagan and George H.W. Bush, among others. In contrast, however, the Japan-U.S. relations began to go through a difficult path, tackling one trade friction after another, as the U.S.-side felt the decline of competitiveness vis-à-vis Japan's economic threat. The management of bilateral Japan-U.S. relations was considered urgent as the severe economic rivalries began to adversely affect their mutual public sentiments. It was a time when the peoples were getting difficult to take the favorable bilateral Japan-U.S. relations for granted. Against these backgrounds, one era came to a close in Japan, quietly and solemnly. It was the reign of Emperor Hirohito who passed away in the Imperial Palace on January 7, 1989. It was the end of the turbulent era of "Showa," as well.

Fifth period (1989-present): Japan entered the twenty-first century more with anxiety than hope. The 1990s and the first years of the new century would be remembered as "the lost decade" in Japan because of the repeated failures in managing its economic house in orderly fashion after the bursting of "bubble economy."

Contrary to this negative economic performances, Japan has embarked on new roles and engaged in proactive initiatives in political and security fields in the context of East Asia. The overall end of Cold War confrontation, and the subsequent change in strategic picture in the region, did open the opportunity while the tough challenges remained. The remnants of the Cold War were evident in the region most notably in the form of divided Korean Peninsula, the Cross-Strait China-Taiwan relations, and the division of Southeast Asia between ASEAN (the Association of Southeast Asian Nations) and its Indo-China neighbors. In responding to these and other challenges, Japan has managed to expand the policy tools to deal with them bilaterally with the U.S., regionally with the regional counterparts under the auspices of ASEAN Regional Forum and ASEAN plus Three (Japan, PRC and South Korea), and globally with the United Nations.

The nature of crises was varied. The first major post-Cold War crisis occurred in the Persian Gulf region in 1990-1991, then upon the dispatch of its Self-Defense Forces to the UN Peacekeeping Operations in Cambodia in 1992, then over the North Korean nuclear program in 1993-94, the rape incident by American service members in Okinawa in 1995, across the Taiwan Strait in 1996, and in tackling economic downturn across East Asia in 1997. The nuclear tests that India and Pakistan conducted in 1998 alarmed the fragility of Non-proliferation regime to all of us. DPRK's Teapodong Missile launch in 1998, together with the infiltration of spy ships and the mounting issues of abducted Japanese nations, became the urgent political issues to be tackled including at the highest levels between two states. The atrocities in East Timor in 1999 was a tragedy against which many countries in the region, including Japan, contributed to welcome the first independent state in the 21st century. The came the 9-11 terrorist attacks in the United States in 2001 that opened the "War against Terrorisms" first in Afghanistan and in 2002 and in Iraq in 2003. In East Asia, another crisis was forging again in Pyongyang as it declared the restarting of its nuclear development programs.

It is unnerving to list these heavy weight challenges that we faced over years. All of these have had strong implications and impacts on the developments and international relations in East Asia. But I did this not for the purpose to despair but to recognize that all the positive forces were also consolidated to deal with these difficulties. The reaffirmation of Japan-U.S. alliance, that I discussed earlier, was one of them. And the forging of regional security dialogue, as materialized in the forms of ASEAN Regional Forum (ARF) and ASEAN Plus Three, were other examples. Four major powers in the region, the U.S., Japan, China, and Russia, all began to stabilize their respective bilateral "partnership" relations since the latter half of the 1990s and especially so after the 9-11 in dealing with international terrorism that does not respect national borders. As to the sensitive issues of Japan's dispatch of the Self Defense Forces abroad, neighboring states have now generally been accepted as a necessary activity for peacekeeping and humanitarian cooperation. It was with these common experiences and meetings of minds which enabled to build a strong foundation on which Prime Minister Koizumi proposed a making of "Community that acts together and advances together" in East Asia in January 2002.

4. Converging Balance with Community in East Asia

The stage may be set for forging a community in East Asia. It would be an expression of regionalism in an increasingly globalized world. But it should also be noted that any grouping would not be happening in a vacuum. In this section, let us analyze the dynamism that can be found in the process of community building in East Asia and identify the role of Japan in that process. The underlying question is largely related to the role of the United States, the only superpower after the demise of the former Soviet Union. The reason is obvious because any "East Asian Community" initiative would be something that would *exclude* Washington as long as it sticks to the objective reality of geographic boundaries. If so, how is that possible?

4.1 With the U.S. or Without the U.S.?
Forging a multilateral institutional framework in East Asia was a delicate matter for various reasons. No doubt that it was a welcoming turn of events for the opportunities to be opened in the post-Cold War Asia. Unlike Europe, where institutional efforts were made even from the 1970s across the ideological/political/economic divides under the auspices of the Conference of Security Cooperation in Europe (CSCE, now OSCE), there was no region wide multilateral dialogue mechanisms up until the beginning of 1990s. Some plans were made, most notably from Australia and Canada, to build a community that would embrace the Asia-Pacific region—the area that include East Asia (Northeast and Southeast Asia), North America, and Oceania. In the field of economy, the Asia-Pacific Economic Cooperation (APEC) was already established in 1989. But when it comes to the security affairs are concerned, parties were generally suspicious, particularly Washington, and Tokyo for that matter, about any multilateral form of arrangement as it might undermine the existing rigid "hub-and-spoke" bilateral alliance mechanisms[11].

---

[11] James A. Baker, III, "America in Asia: Emerging Architecture for a Pacific Community," *Foreign Affairs* (Winter 1991/92).

Part II: National Visions and Experiences of Cooperation in Europe and Asia

America's concern was legitimate in a sense that there were several attempts that would exclude or at least reduce the dominant U.S. influence in favor of regional initiatives. China obviously did not hide this intent whenever it stressed its preference of "multipolarity" in international order. Malaysia under Prime Minister Mahatir Mohammad, for example, expressed his displeasure against the U.S. dominance and proposed EAEC (East Asian Economic Caucus) in 1994. Japan adamantly opposed to these set of initiatives to maintain the stable U.S. presence in East Asia and the Pacific and keep the validity of Japan-U.S. alliance. This, however, is an argument based on the premise that the multilateral security frameworks and the bilateral alliance mechanisms are destined to have a trade-offs.

But as the debates progressed, the complementarity between the two were begun to be recognized by looking at the differences in missions in which the alliances had a potential for hard military deterrence and responses while cooperative security arrangements were conceived to enhance confidence-building and dialogue. Japan, after recognizing the utility of strengthening what then-Foreign Minister Taro Nakayama called "mutually reassuring measures" in his speech in July 1991, proposed that ASEAN Post-Ministerial Conference (ASEAN-PMC) to take up subjects that would involve political and security affairs. This proposal was not directly linked to the establishment of ASEAN Regional Forum. But it can be said that the spirit was largely shared with the rest of participants. In fact, during the formative period of ARF, the role of Japan was believed to be more relevant vis-à-vis the United States than with the ASEAN partners. That is, Japan factor can be identified, though it is not the only factor, that helped Washington to change its perceptions against the initiatives to build a regional multilateral framework. In order for the regional security architecture to be effective and credible, the U.S. participation is crucial. But at the same time, there was a need to convince the U.S. that the mechanism, when actually forged, would not adversely affect its own interest. Japan's advocacy of building a multilateral security framework in the Asia-Pacific region, as the ardent ally to the U.S., provided a good reason for Washington to consider positively on the development[12].

Contrary to the region-wide security cooperation mechanism of ARF, the emerging conception of "East Asia Community" is more focused on the affairs in "East Asia." Here, the United States is obviously not a part of it.

4.2 Koizumi Initiative—Pursuing Balance of Power within a Community
Unlike the time when Prime Minister Mahatir of Malaysia proposed EAEC for the explicit purpose of excluding the U.S. from East Asian decision making, the question of U.S. membership, or the lack of it, however delicate it may be, has no longer become a major obstacle in pursuing the East Asia specific regional initiatives in recent years. One important reason is the strengthened alliance relationship between Tokyo and Washington which has made Japan an interlocutor who represent the joint Japan-U.S. interest in East Asian context.

None the less, the active debates, and tug of war, have begun to define its membership and terms of reference. When Prime Minister Koizumi proposed his idea in January 2002, it was labeled as a "community that acts together and advances together" with ASEAN Plus Three (Japan, PRC, ans South Korea), Australia and New Zealand as core members. As Susumu Yamakage said, it is probably the first time that the Japanese Prime Minister proposed the conception of "community" building in a policy speech[13].

According to Prime Minister Koizumi, the idea was based on the (1) best use of the framework of ASEAN Plus Three, (2) the deepening of Japan's cooperation with China and the Republic of Korea, and (3) the strengthening of economic partnership in the region (such as the initiative

---

[12] Please see, Toshiya Hoshino "Ajia-taiheiyo chiki anzenhosho no tenkai—ARF to CSCAP wo chushin to shite (The Developments of Regional Security in the Asia-Pacific region—ARF and CSCAP)," *Kokusai Monda*i, No. 494 (May 2001).

[13] Susumu Yamakage, "Higashi-Ajia Chiikishugi to Nihon-ASEAN Patonashippu (East Asian Regionalism and Japan-ASEAN Partnership," Susumu Yamakage (ed.) *Higashi-Ajia Chiikishugi to Nihon Gaiko* (East Asian Regionalism and Japanese Diplomacy) (Tokyo: Nihon Kokusaimondai Kenkyujo, 2003), p.6.

for Japan-ASEAN Comprehensive Economic Partnership and the ASEAN-China Free Trade Area). Also to be noted is the scope of this community vision which recognizes (1) the "indispensable" role of the United States both for security and economic reasons, (2) the importance of cooperation with Southwest Asia (including India), and (3) the importance of cooperation with the Pacific nations through APEC, and with Europe through ASEM (the Asia-Europe Meeting).

There are certain reluctances on the part of ASEAN countries to see Australia and New Zealand involved in the blueprint, favoring a community composed primarily among ASEAN plus Three members. But the Koizumi initiative was adamant to include these two Oceania states as the important political and economic partners for the future stability and prosperity in the region.

It is too premature to predict in what form this East Asia Community conception would finally be materialized. Moreover, it is not certain to what degree Japan's own preference can be reflected in the eventual picture of this community. Whatever form this community would be taking, the role of the United States, most certainly as the powerful outside power, could not be ignored. And it would be the role of Japan to mediate this situation.

It was John Ikenberry and Jitsuo Tsuchiyama who rightly pointed out that today's Asia-Pacific region, or East Asia for that matter, is somewhere "between balance of power and community.[14]" Indeed, the region is in transition. And the sense of community is being shared by the states and peoples in the region to the level which was rather unimaginable even a decade ago. In this regard, what we are witnessing in East Asia is a convergence of the "balance of power"-type dynamism and the "community-building"-type of incentive in which the Japan-U.S. alliance has rather inadvertently as well as purposely played a contributing role to promote this convergence. Major strategic challenges remain such as China-Taiwan question or the future of Korean Peninsula, and any failure

---

[14] G. John Ikenberry and Jitsuo Tsuchiyama, "Between Balance of Power and Community: the Future of Multilateral Security Co-operation in the Asia-Pacific," *International Relations of the Asia-Pacific,* Vol. 2 (2002), pp. 69-94.

to manage their peaceful resolution would invoke grave consequences in and beyond the region. But, the fact that these strategic challenges remain, together with the growing necessity of collaborating to counter such new threats as terrorism and the proliferation of weapons of mass destruction in the post-9/11 period, have opened a window of opportunity for major powers in East Asia to forge strategic partnerships within the enhanced community consciousness. The role of Japan, backed by the alliance relationship with the U.S., would serve as a strong building block for this purpose.

5. Conclusion

East Asia was a region which was rather inhospitable to regionalist approaches. Obviously, the "Iron Curtain" was there to split the region at the height of the Cold War, and that divisions still remain in some corners, that prevented occasional regionalist initiatives from moving forward. Even among the Western bloc, the regional collective arrangements, such as SEATO (the Southeast Asia Treaty Organization) or a proposed Pacific Charter mechanism of the 1950s, did not work. The bilateral alliances surrounding the U.S. alone survived[15]. These so-called "hub-and-spokes"-type alliances have played a significant deterrence role that provided stability and predictability in the international relations in East Asia and the Pacific region. Amongst them, the Japan-U.S. alliance has served as a key building block for the regional international order. Views are certainly mixed with regard to its effectiveness (or counter-effectiveness) to the stability in the region. But at least in the present historical juncture, had it not for the Japan-U.S. alliance, the region's balance of power would have had to be much more volatile and fluid.

Given the fact that all the alliance mechanisms are inherently limited, thus exclusionary, in membership, and even if the bilateral Japan-U.S.

---

[15] Russell Trood, William Tow, and Toshiya Hoshino (eds.) *Bilateralism in a Multilateral Era: the Future of San Francisco Mechanism* (Brisbane: Centre for the Study of Asia-Australia Relations, 1997).

alliance would claim to provide public goods of regional and global significance, it would not a priori be accepted as such. This is the reason why we need region-wide political frameworks that promote all-inclusive community-mindedness. This chapter has taken up two such mechanisms—ARF in the Asia-Pacific region and ASEAN Plus Three in East Asian regional context—that have developed to provide additional layers to regional security architecture.

Convergence of the logics of balance of power and community-building is going to be the prerequisite for these regional efforts to grow. "To be successful in assuring the stability and prosperity of the Asia-Pacific region" through this type of "convergent security," William Tow argues that "a dual commitment from the United States" are required[16]. One is "the continuation of a significant American strategic presence in the region" and the other is "a simultaneous American willingness to re-orient its security objectives to bring them more into line with the predominant security concerns of its Asian allies." Tow's prescription to Washington is for them to gradually revise "its regional outlook and strategies away from a predominantly defensive posture of checking hegemonic rivals through power balancing, and towards a more positive and active concentration of strengthening Asia-Pacific norms and institutions." If this is the case, Japan, as a strong ally to the U.S., is perfectly situated to navigate Washington, who has demonstrated more unilateralist imperatives after the 9-11 incidents, to be more adaptive to, and not to be more counter-effective to, the internal working of East Asian way of doing business. This is going to be one of the most important, if not the only, tests for the present Japanese government to materialize its initiative to build a community in the region "that acts together and advances together."

---

[16] William T. Tow, *Asia-Pacific Strategic Relations: Seeking Convergent Security* (Cambridge: Cambridge University Press, 2001), p. 10.

References

Chalermpalanupap, Termsak. "Towards an East Asia Community: The Journey has Begun," a paper presented at the Fifth China-ASEAN Research Institute Roundtable on Regionalism and Community Building in East Asia, organized by the University of Hong Kong's Centre of Asian Studies, 17-19 October 2002 [http://www.aseansec.org/13202.htm].

Fukushima, Akiko. *Japanese Foreign Policy: the Emerging Logic of Multilateralism*, New York: St. Martin's Press, 1999.

Hoshino, Toshiya. "Nihon no Takokukan-gaiko (Multilateral Diplomacy of Japan)," Yoshihide Soeya and Masayuki Tadokoro eds. *Nihon no Higashi-Ajia Koso (Japan's East Asia Conception)*, Tokyo: Keio University Press, 2004.

Ikenberry, G. John and Jitsuo Tsuchiyama. "Between Balance of Power and Community: the Future of Multilateral Security Co-operation in the Asia-Pacific," *International Relations of the Asia-Pacific*, vol. 2, 2002.

Tow, William T. *Asia-Pacific Strategic Relations: Seeking Convergent Security*, Cambridge: Cambridge University Press, 2001.

Tow, William T., Ramesh Thakur, and In Taek Hyun, eds. *Asia's Emerging Regional Order: Reconciling Traditional and Human Security*, Tokyo: United Nations University Press, 2000.

Trood, Russell William Tow, and Toshiya Hoshino eds. *Bilateralism in a Multilateral Era: the Future of San Francisco Mechanism*, Brisbane: Centre for the Study of Asia-Australia Relations, 1997.

Wanandi, Jusuf et al. *ASEAN-Japan Cooperation: A Foundation for East Asian Community*, Tokyo: Japan Center for International Exchange, 2003.

Yamakage, Susumu ed. *Higashi-Ajia Chiikishugi to Nihon Gaiko* (East Asian Regionalism and Japanese Diplomacy), Tokyo: Nihon Kokusaimondai Kenkyujo, 2003.

＜編者＞

張　　　勳（JAUNG Hoon）　Preface, Chap. 1
中央大学（韓国）政治学部教授

森 井 裕 一（MORII Yuichi）　Chap. 5
東京大学大学院総合文化研究科助教授

＜執筆者＞

栗 栖 薫 子（KURUSU Kaoru）　Chap. 2
大阪大学大学院国際公共政策研究科助教授

小 川 有 美（OGAWA Ariyoshi）　Chap. 3
立教大学法学部教授

李　　在　勝（LEE Jae-Seung）　Chap. 4
外交安保研究院（韓国）助教授

康　　元　澤（KANG Won-Taek）　Chap. 6
崇實大学（韓国）政治学部助教授

八谷まち子（HACHIYA Machiko）　Chap. 7
九州大学大学院法学研究院専任講師

丁　　　偉（TING Wai）　Chap. 8
香港バプティスト大学副教授

朴　　喆　熙（PARK Cheol-Hee）　Chap. 9
外交安保研究院（韓国）助教授

星 野 俊 也（HOSHINO Toshiya）　Chap.10
大阪大学大学院国際公共政策研究科教授

Cooperation Experiences in Europe and Asia

2004年（平成16年）6月30日　　第1版第1刷発行　3330-0101

編　者　張　　勳・森井裕一
発行者　今　井　　貴
発行所　信山社出版株式会社
〒113-0033 東京都文京区本郷 6-2-9-102
電　話　03（3818）1019
ＦＡＸ　03（3818）0344
Printed in Japan

Ⓒ張勲・森井裕一ほか，2004．印刷・製本／松澤印刷
ISBN4-7972-3330-3 C3331

軍縮国際法	黒澤 満 編
	本体 5,000円
ソ連のアフガン戦争	李 雄賢 著
	本体 7,500円
国際人権・刑事法概論	尾﨑久仁子著
	本体 3,100円
国際社会の組織化と法──内田久司先生 古稀記念論文集──	柳原正治編
	本体 14,000円
ヒギンズ国際法　ロザリン・ヒギンズ著　初川満訳	
	本体 6,000円
不戦条約（上）（下）	柳原正治編著
国際法先例資料	各 本体 43,000円

──────── 信山社 ────────